T0339779

SOCRATES AND JESUS

Socrates and Jesus

The Argument
That Shaped Western Civilization

Michael E. Hattersley

Algora Publishing
New York

Library of Congress Cataloging-in-Publication Data —

Hattersley, Michael E.
    Socrates and Jesus: the argument that shaped western civilization / Michael
Hattersley.
        p. cm.
    Includes bibliographical references and index.
    ISBN 978-0-87586-729-8 (soft cover: alk. paper) — ISBN 978-0-87586-730-4 (hard
cover) 1. Socrates. 2. Philosophy—History. 3. Jesus Christ. 4. Philosophy and religion.
I. Title.
    B317.H38 2009
    909'.09821—dc22
                            2009021822

Front cover: Designed in house, combining elements from The Crucifixion with the
Virgin and St. John the Evangelist Mourning by Rogier van der Weyden, photo © Francis
G. Mayer/CORBIS, and Roman bust of Socrates, photo © Gianni Dagli Orti/CORBIS

Printed in the United States

I would like to thank my family and several dear friends, Robert Kent, Richard Schneider, Sinan Unel, Michael Carl, Michael Petronio, and Dennis Rhodes for their support and suggestions. I would also like to thank my editors at Algora.

TABLE OF CONTENTS

1. Socrates and Jesus

Socrates and Jesus shared many qualities and experiences: their disinterest in material things, their electrifying influence on their immediate followers, their claims of inspiration, their attempts to define the moral life, their martyrdoms. Neither wrote down a single word that has survived and yet in terms of the degree of their influence on the future of Western civilization, they can be compared only to each other. But this essay argues that what was most important about them was their differences: their opposing definitions of the ultimate or the divine, their radically conflicting views of love and reason, their understanding of civil society and the role of laws, their epistemology (how we know), their eschatology (the ultimate purpose of the universe), and their fundamental understanding of how humankind could progress. The yin and yang of these very different approaches to truth has served as the main engine of Western history. It continues to do so today, as Western history and world history become increasingly intertwined.

Western civilization resulted from the confluence of Greek thought and Judeo–Christian religion that took over the Roman Empire, persisted in Western Europe through the Middle Ages, and extended itself to the Americas. It has dominated most of the globe for the last five centuries. The thesis that Western history comprises a compromise between the Greek philosophical tradition and Judeo–Christianity is nothing new. Scholars in every field have analyzed Western history and culture in terms of dualisms — faith and reason, classic and romantic, thesis and antithesis — all of which have their roots in the clash between Greek thought and Judeo–Christian belief. We will argue that exactly this clash explains why, for better or worse, Western civilization has emerged as uniquely contentious, propulsive, and inquisitive.

Although Socrates died almost precisely four centuries before Jesus' birth, we have more reliable historical information on him than we do on the life of Jesus. The two major sources on Socrates, Plato and Xenophon, studied with him and knew him well. While Plato clearly developed and modified Socrates' ideas in the process of constructing his own philosophical system, few scholars doubt that his early dialogues and the *Apology* capture the essence of Socratic thought. Xenophon's biography is the work of a thorough though limited historian. But we don't need to rely entirely on acolytes for our understanding of Socrates' biography and teachings; he is mentioned, described, and satirized in other contemporaneous literature.

Almost the opposite is true of Jesus. Most of what we know of his life comes from the four (or five, or more) *Gospels*, and was passed down orally for generations. By the time it was recorded, Jesus had become the object of a cult — really several cults, each of which had its own agenda. While Plato and Xenophon generally concur on Socrates' biography, his method, and (to a lesser extent) his message, the *Gospel* writers offer dramatically different and often factually conflicting portraits of Jesus, and there are no contemporary records that even confirm his existence. Very little is known of the years before his baptism by John around 30 CE. The reports of his resurrection are so shadowy as to fail any test but that of prior faith.

And yet there was clearly something profoundly inspiring and historically transformational about his work and personality. Many who knew him (and the evidence on this is strong) devoted the rest of their lives to propagating his message that something new had come into the world, as indeed it had. Socrates, of course, had a similar effect on his friends and students: they too became chroniclers, disciples, interpreters, and teachers of his vision. That Jesus did exist, and that we can generally understand his mission from those points on which the *Gospels* concur, is hard to doubt. But a recent conference of *New Testament* scholars could agree unanimously on the authenticity of only one phrase attributed to him: "Our Father." While we can reconstruct Socrates' life and teachings from reasonably reliable historical records, we must define Jesus' original message from what his followers and their immediate successors made of it.

Both these great men had progenitors, and the following chapters will discuss the forces that influenced them, how each transformed what he had inherited, and the crucial ways in which each shaped the future of Western discourse. Equally importantly, we will explore why their dialogue made European civilization uniquely dynamic in comparison to the great but more hierarchical and static empires of Asia and the Americas.

As Joseph Campbell (*The Masks of God*, New York, Viking Press, 1970) and others have convincingly demonstrated, "It was in the marvelous talent of the Sumerians for their extremely demanding divine play that civilization was born of an aristocracy of spirit" (419). This "play" aligned the chief figures of the government with the orderly movement of heavenly bodies, providing a perpetual refraction between the human and the universal. It also, in its early phases, involved literal human sacrifice, often of the whole court, at astrologically determined intervals such as periodically retrograde planets or the dark of the moon. The history of religion is the study of how this sacrificial bargain between humanity and the divine has been translated into metaphor.

Sumerian civilization provided a successful model that spread worldwide, arriving in Egypt about 2800 BCE, the eastern Mediterranean around 2000, China around 1500, and perhaps the Americas slightly before the Christian era, although there is debate about whether the Aztec and Inca systems arose entirely uninfluenced by the Sumerian model. Its system stressed a static, orderly hierarchy stretching from a divine priest–king down to the faithfully toiling mass of agricultural laborers, all working in harmony with the gods' plans. Such a social order didn't necessarily make for a disadvantage; China, for example, led the world technologically from the fall of the Western Roman Empire until about the fifteenth century. But Western Civilization has taken a different, more contentious and individualistic route.

In his recent comprehensive study of why Western civilization has become world-dominant, Jared Diamond (*Guns, Germs, and Steel*, Vintage Press, 2005) finds the explanation in the fact that Eurasia, especially the Fertile Crescent, was blessed in Neolithic times with an extraordinarily high number of cultivatable crops and domesticable animals. Such fecundity plausibly suggests why the state was invented in Sumeria: agriculture requires collective effort, a variety of skill-sets, and a controlling authority. It doesn't explain, however, why of all these stratified and relatively static societies, Europe alone emerged as especially inquisitive, aggressive, individualistic, and democratic. While the Americas, sub-Saharan Africa, and Australia lacked this cornucopia of plants and animals, these resources were rapidly diffused across Eurasia. Diamond is reluctant to assign much historical causality to individual personalities, but I find a major cause in the debate between Socrates and Jesus. Is this true, and, if so, where is it likely to lead?

We will find the crux of the creative disagreement between Socrates and Jesus in their conflicting definitions of love. Socratic Heavenly Eros taught the existence of a continuum from the human to the ultimate, such that a fallible person who loved the good could proceed from the beauties of the perceptible world to the highest ideals. Jesus, in the Hebrew tradition of Agape, believed that irredeemably fallen man could be brought into contact with eternal truths only through the undeserved love of a remote and arbitrary although sometimes forgiving God. We will see also why both these views, while apparently in stark opposition, are uniquely Western and share a common origin in the joint conviction that man is alienated from, and potentially in opposition to, his creator. The alternating dominance of Eros or Agape defines the stages of Western civilization, with the triumph of one always provoking the resurgence of its antithesis.

It would be easy to characterize the immensely creative debate between the Socratic tradition and Judeo–Christianity as a quarrel between science or reason and theology or faith. But Socrates had a spirit that occasionally whispered into his ear, and, granted his premises, Jesus could make a reasoned argument. This essay is undertaken in the spirit of Nobel Prize Winner Charles Townsend who wrote, echoing Einstein: "Understanding the order in the universe and understanding the purpose of the universe are not identical, but they are also not very far apart" ("The Convergence of Science and Religion," 1966, the IBM journal *Think*).

In the opening chapter of his magisterial study *Mimesis: The Presentation of Reality in Western Literature* (Princeton, New Jersey, Princeton University Press, 1976), Eric Auerbach contrasts two key scenes from the foundational documents of Western culture: Odysseus' return to Ithaca after his twenty years of wandering from the *Odyssey*, and Abraham's aborted sacrifice of Isaac from *Genesis*.

In the scene from Homer, Odysseus, who has returned in disguise, is having his feet washed by his old nurse, Euryclea, when she recognizes him by the scar on his thigh. Homer, with his usual amplitude and leisure, describes every detail of the scene: how Euryclea touches the scar, drops his foot into the water bucket, and is about to cry out for joy when Odysseus, who doesn't want his wife Penelope to know yet that he has returned, restrains her with a combination of threats and endearments. Auerbach observes:

> All this is scrupulously narrated ... There is room ... and time for orderly, well-articulated, uniformly illuminated descriptions of implements, ministrations, and gestures; even in the dramatic moment of recognition, Homer does not omit to tell the reader that it is with his right hand that Odysseus takes the woman by the throat to keep her from speaking, at the same time that he draws her closer with his left. Clearly outlined, brightly and uniformly illuminated, men and things stand out in a realm where everything is visible; and not less clear — wholly expressed, orderly even in their ardor — are the feelings and thoughts of the persons involved (*Mimesis*, 3).

But what particularly captures Auerbach's attention is that at the moment of highest suspense — just when the housekeeper recognizes the scar — Homer interrupts the narrative with a seventy-verse description of how the scar originated at a boar hunt during a visit to Odysseus' grandfather Autolycus. Homer takes the opportunity to tell us everything about Autolycus: his house, his degree of kinship, his touching reaction to the birth of his grandson, the details of the visit, the banquet which welcomes Odysseus, the hunt, the wound, the recovery, his return to Ithaca, his parent's anxious questions. Auerbach continues:

> The first thought of the modern reader — that this is a device to increase suspense — is, if not wholly wrong, at least not the essential explanation of this Homeric procedure. For the element of suspense is very slight in the Homeric poems; nothing in their entire style is calculated to keep the reader or hearer breathless. The digressions are not meant to keep the reader in suspense, but rather to relax the tension. The broadly narrated, charming, and subtly fashioned story of the hunt, with all its elegance and self-sufficiency, its wealth of idyllic pictures, seeks to win the reader over wholly to itself as long as he is hearing it, to make him forget what has just taken place during the foot-washing. But an episode that will increase suspense by retarding the action must be so constructed that it will not fill the present entirely, will not put the crisis, whose resolution is being awaited, entirely out of the reader's mind, and thereby destroy the mood of suspense; the crisis and the suspense must continue, must remain vibrant in the background. But Homer ... knows no background (*Mimesis*, 4).

Auerbach shows that this technique holds throughout all of Homer: every object, every character, every thought, every conversation, can be flushed into the light, and there is plenty of time to do it. Homer repeatedly interrupts his narrative to introduce a new character, his ancestry, his attitude towards the current situation, his position in the hierarchy. A crucial battle scene fades entirely from memory as we learn in intricate detail all the scenes depicted on Achilles' shield. Every time a god appears, we discover where she last was, by what route she arrived at the scene, all her thoughts and intentions. Auerbach notes: "[E]ven the Homeric epithet seems to me in the final analysis to be traceable to the same need for an externalization of phenomena in terms perceptible to the senses." Auerbach believes the originals impetus for this tell-all technique "must have *originated* in the basic impulse of the Homeric style: to represent phenomena in a fully externalized form, visible and palpable in all their parts, completely fixed in their special and temporal relations" (*Mimesis*, 6).

Everything in Homer, indeed everything Homer believes exists, occurs in the foreground. He could easily have inserted the story of the scar's origin two lines earlier and treated it as a recollection, but he does not, and for a reason essential to Homer's style, that is, his world view: "[A]ny such subjectivist-perspectivist procedure, creating a foreground and background, resulting in the present lying open to the depths of the past, is entirely foreign to the Homeric style; the Homeric style knows only a foreground, only a uniformly illuminated, uniformly objective present" (*Mimesis*, 7).

Auerbach finds the exact opposite in the *Genesis* account of Abraham and Isaac. In the *King James* version, the story opens: "And it came to pass after these things that God did tempt Abraham, and said to him, Abraham! And he said, Behold, here I am." (*Genesis* 22:1) Here we are told almost nothing but the essential and startling initiation of dramatic action; we don't know where Abraham is, we don't know where God came from; all details of the sensible world are absent. As Auerbach observes: "The concept of God held by the Jews is less a cause than a symptom of their manner of comprehending and representing things ... Abraham says indeed: Here I am — but the Hebrew word means only something like "behold me," and in any case is not meant to indicate the actual place where Abraham is, but a moral position in respect to God, who has called him — Here am I awaiting your command" (*Mimesis*, 8). Abraham's readiness to obey is all that matters; if he is in the foreground, God isn't just in the background; he *is* the background. Auerbach notes:

> After this opening, God gives his command, and the story begins: everyone knows it; it unrolls with no episodes in a few independent sentences whose syntactical connection is of the most rudimentary sort. In this atmosphere it is unthinkable that an implement, a landscape through which the travelers passed, the serving men, or the ass, should be described ... A journey is made because God has designated the place where the sacrifice is to be performed; but we are told nothing about the journey except that it took three days and even that we are told in a mysterious way: Abraham and his followers rose "early in the morning" and "went unto" the place of which God had told him; on the third day he lifted up his eyes and saw the place from afar (*Mimesis*, 10).

The few details we receive here serve not to embellish the story by developing the context — the sensory world — in which these events are happening, but rather to emphasize the dominance of the background — God's presence and command — over the foreground, the punctual obedience of Abraham.

God says, "Take Isaac, thine only son, whom thou lovest." We learn nothing from this about Isaac as a person; as Auerbach suggests, "Only what we need to know about (Isaac), here and now, is illuminated, so that it may become apparent how terrible Abraham's temptation is, and that God is fully aware of it." (*Mimesis*, 11) In Homer, all the foreground is provided at the expense of suspense, but here the suspense is all the more immediate and terrible due to the absence of foreground. Auerbach concludes:

> I said above that the Homeric style was "of the foreground" because despite much going back and forth, it yet causes what is momentarily being narrated to give the impression that it is the only present, pure and without perspective. A consideration of the Elohistic text teaches us that our term is capable of a broader and deeper application. It shows that even the separate personages can be represented as possessing "background"; God is always so represented in the *Bible*, for he is not comprehensible in his presence, as is Zeus; it is always only "something" of him that appears, he always extends into depths. But even the human beings in the biblical stories have greater depths of time, fate, and consciousness than do the human beings in Homer ... Abraham's actions are explained not only by what is happening to him at the moment, nor yet by his character (as Achilles' actions by his courage and pride, and Odysseus' by his versatility and farsightedness), but by his previous history; he remembers, he is

constantly conscious of, what God has promised him and what God has already accomplished for him — his soul is torn between desperate rebellion and hopeful expectation; his silent obedience is multilayered, has background (*Mimesis*, 12).

The Greek tradition sees everything in the foreground, sensible and explicable. The Judeo–Christian tradition sees everything in the foreground as secondary to inruptions from a background that is absolute and ultimately unknowable. In the following essay, we will explore the profound implications that the clash of these two world-views — or styles, as Auerbach would rightly say — contains for the development of Western civilization.

2. The Historical Socrates

The bare facts of Socrates' life are not in dispute. He was born about 468 BCE in the deme Alopeke, just south of Athens, to Sophroniscus, a stonemason, and his wife Phainarete, probably a midwife. The fact that he served as a young man in the Athenian heavy infantry, which was required to supply its own equipment, suggests that his family lived in reasonably comfortable circumstances. He married Xanthippe, rumored to be of vile temper, and had three sons, two of whom were still quite young when he died at about seventy.

Socrates spent some period studying with Archelaus, himself a student of the great pre-Socratic philosopher Anaxagoras. According to the later Roman writer Diogenes Laertes, Archelaus taught that there are two causes of coming into being, hot and cold, and that animals come to be from slime and that the just and the disgraceful exist not by nature but by convention. These words seem consistent with what we know of Anaxagoras, who exerted profound influence on Socrates' great contemporary Pericles. Anaxagoras believed that Mind was distinct from the material and was the source of motion and order in the cosmos.

It is reasonable to suppose, therefore, that Socrates' education emphasized an apparently chaotic world informed by a higher, ideal reality accessible to the true philosopher. As his comments recorded by Plato and Xenophon make clear, Socrates was also aware of his other great predecessors, including Thales, the founder of European natural philosophy; Pythagoras, a brilliant polymath who taught that reason could elucidate the apparent contradictions in the universe, guide ethical conduct, and provide contact with the divine; and Protagoras, who taught a social-contract concept of law in which citizens voluntarily cede some individual rights in return for the protection of the *polis* (city-state). All these great teachers and others, including his muse, the prophetess Diotima, fed into what we can reasonably determine to be Socrates' philosophy and method.

Socrates also inherited the traditions of his culture including its religious practices and the founding documents of Homer, with their illuminated celebration of the warrior, the explorer, the adventurer, and the Olympic pantheon. By Socrates' day, sophisticated circles treated the gods as metaphors, but more important was the Greek view of human–divine relations. The gods were not entirely *other* to the Greeks; certainly they possessed divine powers but, especially as depicted by Homer, they loved, grew angry, squabbled, and deceived; in short, they experienced and identified with the whole range of human behaviors. They lacked a critical capacity of the Judeo–Christian God: omniscience. Even as perceived by the most conventionally pious, the gods existed along the same continuum as human beings, that is, in Auerbach's foreground. As with most polytheistic religions, one's piety in ancient Greece was judged not so much by one's beliefs, which could vary considerably, as by one's participation in traditional religious rituals, which by definition were civic ceremonies as well.

One particular Greek god, not himself an Olympian, captures the Greek relation between man and the gods, and offers a typically Hellenic parallel to the *Old Testament* insistence on original sin. Prometheus, as described in Hesiod's *Theogany* (lines 507–616), was a Titan, an earlier generation of the Greek Gods who had been superceded by the Olympians and, like all his race, made from clay, rather than from Olympian Aither. No doubt resentful at the triumph of the Olympians over his more earthbound incarnation of deity, he decided to take revenge on the King of the Gods, Zeus. At a meeting designed to reconcile differences between the mortals and the immortals, Prometheus challenged Zeus by setting before him two offerings: beef hidden inside an ox's stomach, and bull bones covered in glistening fat.

Zeus, of course, chose the second, more immediately attractive tribute, and this had consequences: henceforth mortals were free to keep the best of the sacrifice, offering up to the Olympians only burned bones. Infuriated by the deception, Zeus took his revenge by hiding fire from mankind, plunging the earth into chaos and darkness, and simultaneously preventing humans from petitioning the Gods with sacrifices.

Prometheus talked his way into Olympus and managed to steal a coal from the Chariot of the Sun. He restored fire to mankind, rekindling civilization. This time, Zeus took twofold revenge. First he send Pandora's Box into the world, that, when opened, spread all manner of evils throughout humanity, such as the schemings of women and the necessity to work in the sweat of one's brow. Second, he chained Prometheus eternally to a rock in the Caucasus, where a vulture ate out his liver (the organ most sensitive to pain) daily.

Note the similarities to the story of Adam and Eve: knowledge or a metaphor for it, fire, that is, mortal independence, can only be achieved by defying the Divine. In both cases, though in separate ways, evil, including toil, enters the world through woman. Mankind receives his autonomy from a half-god, Satan or Prometheus, who, like humans, lusts for power. In the Greek version, tensions between the human and the Divine exist from the beginning, or why would a meeting be necessary to reconcile them?

Provocative as these parallels are, however, unlike the *Genesis* version, the Greek legend leaves room for the human beings and gods to coexist in the same world. Prometheus mediates between the two camps, and eventually, we find, Heracles, in one of his great labors, slays the vulture and liberates Prometheus from his chains. Even Zeus' commands are subject to human intervention and reversal (as opposed to disobedience). Along with, or perhaps one should say, among all the evils released from Pandora's box rises hope. But both parables make the central lesson clear: Mortals and their advocates will have to suffer terribly in wrestling knowledge from the Gods.

But perhaps the most important factor contributing to the historical context of Socrates' life, one of the handful of truly transformative events in world history, was Athens' recent victory in the Persian Wars. Socrates was born about twelve years after Athens had led the small and scatted Greek city–states in a stunning victory over the great Persian Empire. Socrates grew up among then men who had won that ten-year conflict (parallel to the Trojan War) and the woman who had suffered through it, at one point evacuating the whole city of Athens to save it.

He grew up in an atmosphere of triumphant self-confidence, heroic war stories, and a sense of limitless possibilities in a previously obscure town that had only yesterday become one of the known world's greatest powers. The victory over the Persians had been so unlikely and so complete that Athenians could be forgiven for believing that their city had been divinely chosen to unite the Greeks and lead them to greatness. Only an understanding of the Persian Wars can help us explain the astonishing achievements of the Athenians during Socrates' lifetime.

In 500 BCE Athens, the capital of the small state of Attica, was experiencing one of the experiments in democracy that had characterized its politics for the last century or more. In 621, concerned about increasing conflicts between the city dwellers and the population of the countryside, and increasingly vulnerable to attacks along its shores by privateers and other city–states, the broadly based oligarchic governing council chose Dracon to codify and rectify the laws. At this point Athens still had a King, although he had already ceded most of his power to more popular religious and civic bodies. The table of laws which Dracon drew up — one could be executed for stealing a cabbage — was considered so severe than one Athenian wit commented that it had been "written not in ink but in blood" (hence Draconian). Dracon appointed fifty-one judges, probably in association with the religiously based governing council of the Areopagus. On balance, Dracon's legislation favored the wealthier classes, but having the law written down and enforced benefited the poor as well.

Nevertheless, civic unrest grew in Attica. Small landowners were ruined by mortgages they could not pay and even enslaved for debt, larger landholders increased their property, and popular discontent grew to the point of rebellion. But out of this crisis emerged a man who probably more than anyone else was responsible for Athens' eventual greatness. Solon was an aristocrat, but unlike most of the aristocracy, largely composed of country squires concerned only to expand their estates, he was also a merchant, alive to the economic impact of trade and in touch with the concerns of the common people. As J. B. Bury observes (*A History of Greece*, New York, the Modern Library):

> We are fortunate enough to possess portions of poems — political pamphlets — which (Solon) published for the purpose of guiding public opinion; and thus we have a view of his situation in his own words. He did not scruple to speak plainly. The social abuses and the sad state of the masses were clear to everybody, but Solon saw another side of the question; and he had no sympathy with revolutionary agitators who demanded a redistribution of lands. The more moderate of the nobles seem to have seen the danger; and thus it came to pass that Solon was solicited to undertake the work of reform. He ... was elected archon, with extraordinary legislative powers, for the purpose of healing the evils of the state, and conciliating the classes (174).

Several things about the nature of the Athenian polity can be deduced from these observations. Athenians possessed sufficiently literacy to be persuaded and moved by pamphlets. Public opinion could influence the decisions of the nobles. Radical forces were capable of installing a tyranny that would redistribute property.

At this point in Athenian history, Archons, or chief officials, were elected by at least a segment of the population and held more power than the King, whose role by this time had become largely ceremonial; in any case the vestigial monarchy vanished soon after these events. All the essential conditions for the emergence of a democracy obtained, and here, in Athens, it happened for the first time.

Solon served as Archon for a year, probably 594–93 BCE. He cancelled old debts and passed a law that forbade debtors to be enslaved. He limited the amount of land one person could hold to prevent the accumulation of disproportionate power and saved the family farms. He forbade the export of any other product than oil, since corn fetched high prices in foreign markets and the populace was on the verge of starvation. In short, he found a balanced solution that gave no one everything they wanted but was widely regarded as fair. He introduced to Athens for the first time a native coinage, much facilitating the exchange of goods and freeing Athens from dependence on the financial fluctuations of its neighbors. But as Bury continues:

> What Solon did to heal the sores of his country entitled him to the most fervent gratitude, but it was no more than what might have been done by any able and honest statesman who possessed men's confidence. His title to fame as one of the greatest statesmen in Europe rests upon his reform of the constitution. He discovered a secret of democracy, and he used his discovery to build up the constitution on democratic foundations. The Athenian commonwealth did not actually become a democracy till many years later; but Solon not only laid the foundations, he shaped the framework. He retained the old graduation of the people in classes according to property. But he added the Thetes (the land-owning peasantry) as a fourth class and gave it certain political rights (*A History of Greece*, 175–76).

While the Thetes at this point could hold no office, they were admitted to attend the Ecclesia, or Assembly. The secret of democracy that Solon had discovered was to give all citizens a share in choosing the judiciary, encouraging just rule of law.

After accomplishing these world-shaking reforms, Solon did something extraordinary: he left Athens for ten years. Since none of his laws could be changed without his approval, Athens was forced to live with his system, and discovered that it worked. Over the next century, Athens experienced an alternation among oligarchies, periods of democracy, and a tyranny, but the basic principles of Solon's constitution held. The Pisistratid family, with the support of the lower classes, held a popular tyranny for most of the period between 561 and 510 BCE, but until near the end, they preserved most of the forms, as well as the spirit, of Solon's constitution. They were responsible for beginning the great works of architecture that made Athens a model for the world, and initiating trading expeditions, including to the Black Sea, which assured Athens' grain supply.

At the time the Persian Wars broke out, Athens possessed a stable if limited democracy commanding the full loyalty of its citizenry despite squabbling among political factions. Even at its height sometime later, the population of Athens including metics (resident foreigners) and slaves amounted to probably no more than a quarter of a million people. By contrast the Persian Empire, a semi-divine autocracy, ruled most the known world from certain Greek islands to India. Along the coast of Asia Minor, called Ionia, in what is now Turkey, the population, largely Greek, grew increasingly restless under Persian rule, and periodic rebellions began to erupt. In 494 BCE the Persian Emperor Darius send an expedition under his general Mardonius who subdued the Ionic states, crossed the Hellespont, and conquered much of northern Greece including Macedonia and Thrace. Athens, to Darius' annoyance, had sent military support to aid the Asian Greeks, and the city only avoided attack due to a terrible storm that destroyed much of the Persian fleet.

Most Greek cities had submitted to Darius' forces, sending a symbolic tribute of earth and water to the Persian Emperor, but Athens and Sparta had not. Darius vowed revenge. The exiled Pisistratid tyrant Hippias resided at Darius' court, and constantly urged an expedition that would return him to power. This time, Darius resolved to strike directly across the Aegean. The Persian fleet, 600 strong by some accounts, set sail from Samos and attacked Euboea, an independent island immediately off the Attic coast. The Persian force burned its capital Eretria to the ground, enslaving all its citizens, and the fleet now drew up within sight of Attic soil.

Bury describes the situation of Athens on the eve of the battle of Marathon:

> Athens had changed much since (the tyrant) Hippias had been cast out (in 510 BCE), though a generation had not passed. Athenian character had been developed under free democratic institutions. It has been said that if the Athenians had not been radically different from their former selves, Hippias would easily have recovered Athens.... The Persian invasion was brought about by the same political causes which enabled Athens to withstand it. The Ionian Greeks would not have risen in revolt but for the growth of a strong sentiment against tyrannies, the same cause which overthrew the Pisistratids and created Marathonian Athens (*A History of Greece*, 237).

In a wonderful example of emerging Athenian democracy, it was left to the citizens to decide whether to confront the Persians at their landing, or wait to defend the city of Athens itself. At the Assembly, the great general Miltiades argued that the Athens should meet the enemy at Marathon. His proposal carried, and the Athenian army of about 9,000, led by Miltiades and Callimachus, and accompanied by 1,000 of their Plataean allies, marched forth. It deployed in a strong position, protected by surrounding hills, and looking down on the enormous Persian army camped on the beach with their fleet at anchor behind them. So things stood for several days, which suited the Greeks perfectly, because they were hoping for reinforcements from Sparta (they arrived two days late).

Eventually, growing impatient, the Persian generals ordered an advance. Callimachus very cleverly deployed his army with a thin center line and most of the forces concentrated in his two wings. When the Persians attacked, the center gave way, but the stronger wings routed their foes, and then turned to destroy the main body of the Persian forces. About 192 Athenians and 6,400 Persians were slain. Leaving some troops to guard the dead on the field, the Greek army promptly marched back to Athens and positioned itself in defensive positions about the city. The Persian Admiral Datis still had huge forces at his disposal; he boarded his ships, swung the fleet around Cape Sunium, and drew up before Athens. But finding it defended, he withdrew. Athens would not face another threat from Persia for ten years. Bury observes:

> The history of the world does not depend on proximate causes. The clash of Greece and Persia, the efforts of Persia to expand at the expense of Greece, were inevitable. From the higher point of view it was not a question of vengeance; where Darius stopped, the successors of Darius would go on. The success of Marathon inspirited Greece to withstand the later and greater invasion; but the chief consequence was the effect which it wrought upon the spirit of Athens itself. The enormous prestige which she won by the single-handed victory over the host of the Great King gave her new self-confidence and ambition; history seemed to have set a splendid seal on her democracy; she felt she could trust her constitution and that she could lift her head as high as any state in Hellas. The Athenians always looked back to Marathon as marking an epoch. It was as if on that day the gods had said to them, Go on and prosper (*The History of Greece*, 244).

The Persians under Darius' son Xerxes did indeed return in 480 BCE with an even more massive force, but now, convinced they could win, many of the Greek states united and coordinated their defense. Three hundred Spartans, led by Leonidis and supported by allies some of whom who left during the battle, held back a land force of hundreds of thousands of Persians in the narrow northern pass of Thermopylae for long enough to give Greece more time to prepare for the main onslaught. In a final charge against the Persian Immortals, all the Spartans as well as several thousand allies perished, but they had done their job and shaken the morale of the Persian forces. The words reported of one soldier captured the spirit of the Greeks at this time; when told the Persian host was so enormous that their arrows hid the sun, he replied, "So much the better; we shall fight in the shade." Meanwhile, under the canny leadership of Themistocles, Athens was evacuated. The Persians all but burned it to the ground, but by a series of brilliant naval maneuvers Themistocles was able to defeat and cripple the Persian fleet at Salamis just off Athens.

The Persians spent some time licking their wounds; the battle of Salamis had delivered a decisive blow to the Persian navy, but the Great King still had hundreds of thousands of troops in Greece. A winter respite allowed a now united Greece to assemble its full forces. Led by the Spartan Pausanius, the Greeks engaged the vastly superior Persian forces commanded by Mardonius near the town of Plataea. The Greeks attacked with more flexibility than the Persian army was organized to handle, going straight for the center, and when Mardonius fled, the Persians troops deserted and the battle of Plataea turned into a rout. The combined Greek forces drove the Persians out of Greece.

Athens and Sparta now received universal recognition as the co-leaders of Greece. But while the Spartans returned to their customary insularity, the Athenians immediately began to reap the rewards of victory. Their fleet, now virtually unchallenged, cajoled or subdued most of the Aegean island states into joining a confederation that soon took on all the trappings of a mercantile empire. Athens became the effective capital of Greece, grew extremely wealthy, launched massive construction programs that gave us, among other supreme works of genius, the Parthenon, and began to receive admiring visitors from all over the known world.

This was the Athens into which Socrates was born. He spent his early years following his father into a position as a stonecutter, absorbing what he could from the now cosmopolitan atmosphere of Athens, and conversing with his growing circle of sophisticated friends. We learn little more of his activities until he reached middle age.

At the outbreak of the Peloponnesian War (432 BCE) between Athens and Sparta, Socrates served in the Athenian army that besieged Potidea, and apparently saved the life of Pericles' nephew Alcibiades. All evidence suggests that his courage and indifference to the harsh winter weather became legendary during this period; according to several sources he favored ostentatiously simple clothing and went barefoot even in blizzards. It's clear that he had begun teaching by the 420s, for he is mocked (affectionately, one hopes) in the comedies of the period, especially in Aristophanes' *The Clouds*.

Aristophanes portrays Socrates as an atheistic natural philosopher in the tradition of Anaxagorus, as a Sophist, who teaches how to make a good case out of a bad one, and as an ascetic completely indifferent to the pleasures of this world. Every point in this caricature is demonstrably false: Socrates was no Sophist teaching politicians and lawyers to lie effectively; his concern was the opposite: to elicit truth through reason. He was no atheist, since he regularly received promptings from his inner "daimon," or god, as to the correct course of action. And though he lived simply, Socrates was no extreme ascetic like Diogenes: he did not beg, he kept a home and raised a family, and he was welcome at sumptuous symposia hosted by many of the wealthiest and best-educated people in Athens. The historical importance of this satire, therefore, is that it demonstrates that by his forties, Socrates was seen by the comic writers, and the general public, as the most prominent and paradigmatic philosopher in Athens, and that what prejudices were general against philosophy attached to him.

However good-natured Aristophanes' ribbing of Socrates, it clearly contributed to his death. *The Clouds* falsely portrays Socrates as rejecting the traditional gods in favor of "Air, Aither, Clouds, Chaos, Tongue, and Heavenly Swirl." In fact, all the hard evidence suggests that Socrates observed the conventional religious practices of his city and time. But in the end this would not save him from the charge of being a natural philosopher who used reason to probe the mysteries of the universe and offended conventional sensibilities.

Socrates devoted his remaining years to teaching (as amply recorded in Plato and Xenophon) and military service. He famously refused any payment for offering instruction, instead seeing himself as a student of truth who argued and questioned, challenging his interlocuters' pretensions and fixed beliefs (behavior which certainly, over time, accumulated enemies). As a soldier, he fought at

Delium in Boeotia in 424, where his leadership in a disastrous retreat seems to have won him wide respect, and at Amphipolis in 422. C. C. W. Taylor in *Socrates* (Oxford University Press, 1998) says of the mature Socrates:

> [E]xceptional physical courage was an element in the accepted picture of Socrates, along with indifference to physical hardship, a remarkable capacity to hold his liquor, and ... a strongly passionate temperament in which anger and sexual desire were kept under restraint by reason.... We are given a detailed picture of his physical appearance in middle age in Xenephon's *Symposium*, where he describes himself as snub-nosed, with wide nostrils, protruding eyes, thick lips, and a paunch, which exactly fits Alcibiades' description of him in Plato's *Symposium*.

As to what Socrates actually taught during these years, Taylor provides a convincing if minimalist summary. Relying on a scholarly consensus that Xenophon's writings are infused with a determination to defend Socrates as a pious citizen against the charges for which he was ultimately executed, and that Plato's early dialogues best reflect Socrates' personal views, Taylor concludes:

> i. Characterization of Socrates. Socrates is predominantly characterized not as a teacher but as an inquirer. He disclaims wisdom and seeks, normally in vain, elucidation of problematic questions from his interlocutors, by the method of elenchus, that is, by critically examining their beliefs. In some dialogues, notably *Protagoras* and *Gorgias*, the questioning stance gives way to a more authoritative tone.

> ii. Definition. Many of the dialogues are concerned with the attempt to define a virtue or other ethically significant concept. *Euthyphro* asks "What is holiness or piety," *Charmides*, "What is temperance," *Laches*, "What is courage," *Hippias Major* "What is fineness or beauty." Both *Meno*, explicitly, and *Protagoras*, implicitly, consider the general question, "What is virtue or excellence?" In all these dialogues the discussion ends in ostensible failure, with Socrates and his interlocutor(s) acknowledging that they have failed to find the answer to the central question; in some cases there are textual indications of what the correct answer is.

> iii. Ethics. All these dialogues are concerned with ethics in the broad sense of how one should live. Beside those dialogues that seek definitions, *Crito* deals with a practical ethical problem: should Socrates try to escape from prison after his sentence; and both *Gorgias* and *Euthedemos* examine what the aims of life should be....

> iv. Sophists. In several of these dialogues ... the topic is pursued via the portrayal of a confrontation between Socrates on the one hand and various sophists and/or their pupils and associates on the other. These dialogues thereby develop the explanatory project enunciated in the *Apology* (*Socrates*, 45–46).

This provides as good a short summary as we're likely to get of what and how Socrates taught. He constantly posed radical questions, operating on the premise that any person could approach the truth through logic if he set aside ingrained prejudice and received knowledge. As he said, "(F)or this reason I go about to this very day in accordance with the wishes of the god seeking out any citizen or foreigner I think to be wise; and when he seems to me to be not so, I help the god by showing him he is not wise." (*Apology*) "Wise" to Socrates meant commanding the facts, logic, and intuition to support your argument. He essentially invented human reason. Great predecessors, such as Thales, Anaxagorus, and Pythagorus had grounded their philosophies largely in mysticism or speculation. Socrates believed his method could approach eternal and immutable truths about the purpose and right conduct of human life. He focused especially on the definition of ethical conduct. He insisted that when it comes to the vital intangibles — courage, goodness, virtue, excellence — the critical step is *defining* the principle you are trying to practice and teach.

Socrates' philosophy can be called hedonist in the most rigorous sense since he repeatedly states that every person seeks out what his good for him or herself, that is, a life that achieves the best balance of pleasure over misery. He teaches that the most pleasurable life is the life most consonant with the highest ethical precepts, and that knowledge of these can be achieved through reason and argument. No one would intentionally act against his own well being and therefore bad behavior is due not to a natural propensity towards evil (as in *Genesis*) but to a mistaken definition of what is really in one's self-interest. Aristotle, a rigorous observer if there ever was one, wrote in *Nichomachean Ethics* that Socrates argued, "no one acts contrary to what is best in the belief that he is doing so, but through error." The teaching of "what is best," therefore, consists in rooting out error and this almost entirely explains Socrates' pedagogy.

The methodology Aristotle describes implies a number of corollaries that can reasonably be attributed to the historical Socrates. He concluded with Thales and Anaxagoras that the sensible world has arisen through the conflict and combination of elements and energies. He believed with Pythagoras that this world was directly connected with an ideal world of immutable values, and that we can get from here to there primarily through the use of reason as represented by argument, philosophy, mathematics, and music. He believed with Protagoras that the citizen of a polis that had created the conditions for the good life should obey the laws of that polis even if they sometimes produced an unjust result — as he explains so powerfully in the *Apology*. In short, he conceived the universe as a continuum stretching from slime to the highest values, and believed that these values could best be approached — even if imperfectly — in a well-governed community.

The most contemporary, evolutionist, rational humanist, could hardly improve upon these concepts. They constitute a complete and coherent philosophy of life. But three other elements contribute to making Socratic philosophy one of the two crucial engines of Western civilization. First, Socrates insists that while ideal reason could hypothetically penetrate the ultimate mysteries of the universe, no human being, including Socrates, possesses such capacity. Hence his occasional reliance on his "daimon," his instinct or divine inspiration, which repeatedly directed him towards the right course of action. Many philosophic descendants of Socrates have interpreted his daimon's interventions as messages from the vast fund of common sense available to a moral genius. Recent research into brain function suggests that while we usually solve a problem logically, weighing the pros and cons, occasionally (especially under conditions of relaxation or distraction) the solution pops full-blown from a sudden collaboration among normally disparate parts of the conscious and unconscious mental processes. Einstein and others have reported similar experiences, and this may be the best modern explanation of Socrates' divine whisperings. Second, Socrates committed himself to the succinct sentence posted over the entrance to the Delphic oracle: "Know thyself." Only rigorous self-knowledge — in his words, "knowing what we don't know" — could set one on the path from the slime to the ideal. For Socrates, the unexamined life was not worth living. Although he mostly put his codification of both inductive and deductive argument in the service of identifying the ideal, it was equally useful for this purpose (Plato) and for the purpose of scientific inquiry (Aristotle). Third, Socrates believed that the highest flights of human achievement in philosophy, art, science, morality, and religion originate in the outward reaching of sensual desire, what we would call today sexual sublimation.

In 406 BCE, by lot, Socrates happened to be the presiding official of the Athenian Assembly investigating the city's disastrous defeat in the naval battle at Aegospotami that prefigured final defeat in the Peloponnesian War with Sparta. A citizen proposed that the Assembly try the ten naval captains collectively for failing to rescue survivors from the water (a task that, given the wind conditions, Socrates probably knew had been impossible). An outraged population was crying for blood, but according to Xenophon Socrates "did not allow them to pass the motion," because collective trials were unconstitutional. Although the details are hazy, the operation of the Assembly during this period suggests that the motion was finally approved only after another moderator had succeeded Socrates. Here we find the single recorded example of Socrates' personal values going into political action.

Unless, that is, we count the famous trial for impiety which cost him his life. Xenophon's account of this world-historical event so obviously aims to defend Socrates by demonstrating that he was conventionally pious — which was true in the outward forms, but not in his deepest beliefs — that we must prefer Plato's. In 399 BCE, an otherwise unknown young man, supported by currently powerful but ephemeral politicians, brought the following charge against Socrates: "Meletus son of Meletus of Pitthos has brought and sworn this charge against Socrates son of Sophroniscus of Alopeke: Socrates is a wrongdoer in not recognizing the gods which the city recognizes, and introducing other new divinities. Further, he is a wrongdoer in corrupting the young. Penalty: death."

We must understand the political context of Meletus' charge to comprehend the trial's result. Following Athens' final defeat in the Peloponnesian War, Sparta had installed a brief and tyrannous oligarchy led by Critias, formerly one of Socrates' students. Once the yoke of Sparta had been lifted, Athens restored its democracy whose greatest hero had been Alcibiades, a brilliant, extravagant, and mercurial statesman and another of Socrates' pupils, who had recently been murdered in exile. Thus the leaders of both the most reactionary and the most radical factions in Athenian politics — factions that many blamed for bringing the state to catastrophe — were both Socratic students. In this poisonous atmosphere of defeat and recrimination, therefore, Socrates became a natural target. Aristophanes' old parody of Socrates as a crazy purveyor of new ideas, no doubt firmly fixed in the public's mind, had returned to haunt him.

Critias had governed through brutal purges, and conventional wisdom held that Alcibiades had been an occasional traitor and regular traducer of the gods. Others of Socrates' students had been involved in the celebrated 415 BCE scandal in which Alcibiades had allegedly led a drunken mob of privileged youth to destroy the god Herms' statues, which protected many Athenian households, on the eve of the crucial — and disastrous — Athenian expedition to conquer Syracuse in Sicily. (Since Alcibiades was wild but no fool, it's possible that conservative Athenians who opposed his leadership of the Syracuse campaign instigated the destruction of the herms.) By the standards of the times, in other words, at least the "corrupter of youth" charge could be construed as true. But as Socrates himself realized, the substance of the charge was true as well: he had taught the questioning of received authority. Some tradition of persecuting freethinkers existed in Athens (though perhaps less so than anywhere else in the world at the time or in most periods since). Socrates' teacher's teacher, Anaxagoras, had reportedly been driven out of Athens for declaring that the sun was "a red hot stone."

Surviving descriptions of the trials of Jesus and Socrates share curious similarities, suggesting that the iconography Plato developed around Socrates' trial may have influenced at least the Greek physician Luke if not other evangelists. In both cases, according to their proponents, they are unjustly charged, refuse to provide a convincing defense, and willingly die to exemplify their beliefs. While the writers of the *Gospels* differ sharply on the details of Jesus' trial(s), the general outlines of what happened to Socrates are pretty clear from contemporary sources, although no actual transcript exists. He was tried before an assembly of 500 Athenian citizens in the spring of 399 BCE. Both sides produced witnesses and Socrates was allowed to make his extended apology — perhaps best translated as "explanation."

Xenophon and Plato disagree on exactly what Socrates said. Xenophon portrays him as insisting on his conventional piety and asserting that his occasional reliance on divine voices and oracles was a commonplace of contemporary religious practice. Plato's version claims to be the texts of three separate speeches, one given in Socrates' defense against the charges, one delivered after his conviction, and a final one responding to his sentence of death. Plato offers us a Socrates who proudly defends his divinely inspired mission to seek out the truth through constant questioning. Most scholars prefer Plato's account and it seems the more likely on two grounds: first, Socrates' profound impact on all who knew him could not have been generated by a conventionally pious Athenian, and, second, such radical claims of a higher wisdom were precisely the sort of comments that would provoke the jury into convicting him.

In Plato's version, Socrates explains the source of his mission. He tells us that a friend of his, Chaerephon, once visited the Delphic oracle, asked whether anyone was wiser that Socrates, and was told no. When this was reported to him, the oracle's response puzzled Socrates; he claimed to feel he had no expertise of any sort. So he sought out every self-proclaimed expert he could find and discovered to his surprise that they were no more knowledgeable than he. He therefore came to the conclusion that true wisdom consisted in knowing what you didn't know. This embroidered story reflects a message that can safely be attributed to the historical Socrates. Plato says much more about Socrates in his *Apology*, but since considerable debate has raged about how much of this is Socrates and how much Plato, we'll leave examination of that topic to the next chapter, which examines Socrates' legend. Here is Plato's version of Socrates' defense:

> Do you suppose that I should have lived as long as I have if I had moved in the sphere of public life, and conducting myself in that sphere like an honorable man, had always upheld the cause of right, and conscientiously set this end above all other things? No by a very long way, gentlemen; neither would any other man. You will find that throughout my life I have been consistent in any public duties that I have performed, and the same so in my personal dealings: I have never countenanced any action that was incompatible with justice on the part of any person, including those who some people maliciously call my pupils. I have never set up as any man's teacher; but if anyone, young or old, is eager to hear me conversing and carrying out my private mission, I never grudge him the opportunity; nor do I charge a fee for talking to him...

> But how is it that some people enjoy spending a great deal of time in my company? You have heard the reason, gentlemen; I told you quite frankly. It is because they enjoy hearing me examine those who think they are wise when they are not; an experience which has its amusing side. This duty I have accepted, as I said, in obedience to God's commands, given in oracles and dreams and in any other way that divine dispensation has ever impressed a duty upon man (Plato, *The Last Days of Socrates*, New York, Penguin Books, 1954, 65–66).

We know the trial's outcome. Socrates was convicted of the charges against him by a fairly narrow vote of about 280–220. Invited to recommend an appropriate penalty, he at first facetiously suggested that the city award him free meals for life as a public benefactor. Ultimately, friends offered to pay the considerable fine of half a talent. But the damage had been done, and in the sentencing phase the jury voted for death by a wide margin of about 360–140. Plato has Socrates as much as admitting that he has engineered his sentence, saying that his inner daimon had suggested it would spare him the senility of old age.

Because Socrates' trial took place at the beginning of a sacred Athenian embassy to the island of Delos, the judicial process postponed his execution for a month, during which he was allowed to receive his friends and converse freely. It's very likely even the authorities that had conspired in his conviction urged him to flee into exile; the execution of such a prominent citizen, it rapidly became clear, would constitute a tremendous embarrassment to the free city of Athens, already known as the "light of Greece." But Socrates refused; he was determined to teach his polis a lesson in just governance. Accordingly, on the day the ship from Delos returned, Socrates drank his hemlock and passed away in what modern medical knowledge suggests was probably more agony than appears in Plato's account. And so, as Frank J. Frost points out in *Greek Society* (Lexington, Massachusetts, D. C. Heath and Company, 1992), "Scholars and philosophers ever since have discussed the irony of the first great moral philosopher being executed by the first great democracy" (110).

This represents a lot to know, and know pretty reliably, about an annoying Athenian citizen of modest means who lived twenty-five hundred years ago. When one considers the effort brilliant men over the next two and a half millennia took to record, interpret, and apply the teachings of Socrates, it's clear that he was one of the two most influential figures in Western history. And his influence was due to the fact that he had synthesized a rigorous new method of rational thinking and moral inquiry that is still pervasive and productive today. How pervasive becomes clear as we explore what his successors made of him.

3. The Socrates Legend

Plato, a young Athenian aristocrat, Olympic boxer, and aspiring playwright fell under the spell of Socrates' teaching in his teens and decided to devote his life to codifying the great teacher's philosophy. While we can rely on Xenophon for some factual information about Socrates, the Socrates who went into action in Western history is the Socrates of Plato's *Dialogues*. Socrates' life, while decorated and systematized by his biographers and interpreters, was not mythologized like Jesus' because although he was a pious man, he did not lead a religious movement; in fact, puncturing myth and received wisdom was one of Socrates' main points. Plato did not ahistorically claim divine parentage for Socrates or surround his birth with miraculous events, as the evangelists did for Jesus. His audience knew Socrates too well for that.

Nevertheless, it's clear that as Plato developed his own philosophical system over decades of teaching and writing, he often put words in Socrates' mouth. One rough rule of thumb to identify this trend: notice when Socrates pronounces conclusions. Sometimes — increasing so in the later dialogues — "Socrates" makes authoritative statements. In the early dialogues, however, he often suggests that his thesis hasn't been proven or the required definition of a given virtue hasn't been achieved — even when it's pretty clear to the reader what he (or Plato) think the right answer is. This is the historical Socrates, insisting on knowing what he doesn't know, and thereby defining what is worth knowing. The eccentric, highly individualized Socrates of Plato's early works gradually recedes in the middle and late dialogues before a Socrates who personifies the archetypical "philosopher" — that is, Plato himself. Indeed, Socrates does not appear in late works of Plato such as the *Laws*.

Once Plato had immortalized Socrates he was stuck with him. The later dialogues increasingly systematize, applying the Socratic method of inquiry to achieve a definition of values, right governance, the Laws, proper human relations, and the ultimate meaning of the universe. Taken as a whole, Plato's work constitutes the single most ambitious and influential effort in the entire history of philosophy, which in his time included as well the whole domain of science. While it's fair to say that Plato had his idealized character take positions on subjects Socrates probably never addressed, it would be unjust to suggest that, in developing Socrates' philosophy, Plato ever fundamentally violated it. Taylor summarizes Socrates' central belief:

> The Socratic picture is that there is a single integrated knowledge of what is best for the agent, which is applied in various areas of life, and to which the different names are applied with reference to those different areas (for example, his definitions of courage, piety, goodness, self-control, and so forth). Thus, courage is the virtue which reliably produces appropriate conduct in situations of danger, piety the virtue which reliably produces appropriate conduct in relation to the gods, etc., and the virtue in question is the same in every case, namely, the agent's grasp of his or her own good (*Socrates*, 67).

We can doubt whether Socrates would fully have approved some of the grand constructions Plato created later in life: his prescription for the perfect Republic, for example, governed by an oligarchy of philosophers and exiling poets to protect against precisely the sort of mob rule that had led to Socrates' execution. Socrates famously refused to involve himself in politics unless required by civic duty, a lesson Plato failed to learn to his own detriment. In mid-career, he accepted an appointment as tutor to the future tyrant of Syracuse with the aim of creating the ideal philosophical state. The upshot appears to be that he was sold into slavery and sent back to Athens in chains, though friends rapidly rescued him. His experience of practical governance appears not to have affected his political philosophy or his view that philosophers should govern. Plato strayed from Socrates' teaching only when he applied it.

While scholars dispute whether Socrates himself fully developed the idea of Forms, that is, ideal incarnations of which the perceivable manifestation — object or virtues — are merely imperfect copies, the essential concept is clearly present in the teachings of the historical Socrates. The importance of the Forms in later Platonic writing — best manifested in the famous parable of the Cave — extends Socrates' teaching, rather than departing from it. According to this view we live in a world in which we can perceive only shadows or imperfect replicas of the ideal reality because our senses are limited, but the right application of reason and inquiry can help us turn to the light and approach that permanence infusing the physical and ethical universe. Plato immortalized Socrates, in short, by putting his prose into poetry. Surely St. Paul had passages such as Plato's description of the Cave in mind when he wrote, "Now we see but through a glass darkly, but then we shall see face to face." But while Socrates thought the royal road to eternal truths lay through reasoned inquiry, Paul believed it could be achieved only by faith in revealed truth. This, in miniature, is the debate between Socrates and Jesus that would shape the future of Western civilization.

Plato not only revolutionized philosophy; he revolutionized how information was organized, sequenced, and communicated. Unlike Socrates, he wrote. In *Understanding Media* (New York, McGraw-Hill, 1964), Marshall McLuhan observes:

> [A]ny technology gradually creates a totally new human environment. Environments are not passive wrappings but active processes. In his splendid work, *Preface to Plato* (Harvard University Press, 1963), Eric Havelock contrasts the oral and written cultures of the Greeks. By Plato's time the written word had created a new environment that had begun to detribalize man. Previously the Greeks had grown up by benefit of the process of the *tribal encyclopedia*. They had memorized the poets. The poets provided specific operational wisdom for all the contingencies of life — Ann Landers in verse. With the advent of individual detribalized man, a new education was needed. Plato devised such a new program for literate men. It was based upon the Ideas. With the phonetic alphabet, classified wisdom took over from the operational wisdom of Homer and Hesiod and the tribal encyclopedia. Education by classified data has been the Western program ever since (Preface, viii).

Socrates' influence on subsequent classical philosophy was universal; virtually every major school in Greece and Rome claimed descent from him by hook or crook:

The School of Aristotle. If, as Alfred North Whitehead wrote, all philosophy is a series of footnotes to Plato, then Plato's pupil Aristotle's work comprises the biggest footnote. Plato emphasized Socrates' teaching that all knowledge gained through the senses is partial or compromised, but in his later dialogues, it's likely he exaggerated Socrates' skepticism about the capacity of the available sensory data to guide us to a comprehensive synthesis of the material world and ethical value. Aristotle (384–322 BCE), Plato's student, turned this Platonic bias on its head. For Plato, the soul alone can have knowledge of the Forms. For Aristotle, cataloguing and organizing the sensory manifestations of the Forms constituted the best approach to understanding them. Here he paid more tribute than Plato himself to Socrates' trust in observation, logic and reason.

Aristotle applied Socrates' method of inquiry to a vast array of topics including natural history, physics, logic, ethics, politics, language, and metaphysics. In contrast to Plato's idealism, he was an empiricist who catalogued every example he could find on a given subject, whether it be plants, ethical strategies, or rhetorical devices, before drawing general conclusions. Frank J. Frost writes in *Greek Society*: "Aristotle forced his students to collect evidence about a certain subject until they could honestly say they possessed all the available data. Only then did he start to sort out his information and attempt to generalize…. Aristotle was perhaps the most learned man of antiquity, and his method of organizing and disseminating knowledge — if not the content — has been little changed to the current day" (12–13). Aristotle's most notable pupil, of course, was Alexander the Great.

While Plato developed the deductive implications of Socrates' logical method ("If honorable pleasure is the highest human good, we can obtain it in the following ways"), Aristotle developed the inductive ("By examining a wide range of successful polises we can discover they all share these common characteristics"). These were opposite ways of arriving at Socrates' apprehension of the ideal ethics or the ideal plant, but both developed from his method of rational inquiry. It's not much of a stretch to say that Aristotle laid the foundation for modern Western science. He didn't quite arrive at the vital principle of the repeatable experiment, but under his influence Archimedes did decades later.

The golden century from Socrates' emergence as a serious teacher (420s) to Aristotle's death (320s) saw Greek learning diversify into a number of specialized disciplines: ethics, aesthetics, rhetoric, astronomy, music, mathematics, botany, geology, medicine, history, physics, and many more. Before Socrates all these were contained within the word "philosophy," but the difference in the approaches between Plato and Aristotle resulted in a profusion of disciplines that can best be grouped under "philosophy" and "science," the first following Plato's predominately ethical concerns, pursued primarily from deduction, and the second following Aristotle's investigative and categorizing methods, pursued primarily by induction.

PHILOSOPHY

Cynicism. Socrates' pupil Antisthesnes, generally credited as the founder of Cynicism, maintained a number of doctrines common to Socrates' opponents, the Sophists. But he largely adhered to Socrates' ethical doctrines and emulated his austere life-style. Socrates' emphasis that only a simple life could protect judgment against the inevitable welter of conflicting desires became the central tenet of the Cynics. A century later, Cynicism's ultimate apotheosis, Diogenes, sometimes lived in a barrel outside Athens and begged for his living. Encountering him on his way to conquering Asia, Alexander the Great reportedly said, "If I were not Alexander, I would be Diogenes." The asceticism of the Cynics profoundly influenced early forms of Christian monasticism. In its extreme form, however, it led to a conclusion that Socrates would never have endorsed: that material things were ephemera, false gods, idolatrous distractions from eternal truth. Imperfect, Socrates might have said, but not unreal, and often not unattractive. In short, both the stimulus to desire and evidence for an argument.

Skepticism. Skepticism descended from Socrates' associate Aristippus, a north African native attracted to Athens by Socrates' reputation, who founded the

Cyrenaic School. Its principle ethical doctrine held that sensory pleasure is the supreme good, for we can know nothing for certain about either the past or the future. It derives from Socrates' view that the rational agent always acts on his grasp of his own good, but its "live for today" implication defies a central principle of Socratic philosophy: that learning leads to personal growth. Early skeptics, such as Aristippus, apparently shored-up this potentially self-indulgent premise by emphasizing, like Socrates, that one's supreme good could not be achieved without reliance on education, self-knowledge, study, and self-control. Stripped of these controls, however, skepticism could easily slip into hedonism, and often did in the hands of later writers.

Stoicism. Founded by the Hellenized Phoenician Zeno, and claiming its derivation from Socratic Cynics like Diogenes, Stoicism maintained that the purpose of life was to living according to nature and that since humans are naturally rational, life should be lived according to the precepts of reason. The Stoics thus accepted Socrates' central premise that virtue is knowledge. Stoics taught that the brotherhood of man transcended national and social barriers and that a rational life in this context meant practicing justice, compassion, self-restraint, and a serene submission to fate.

In *Hellenistic Civilization* (Meridian Books, Cleveland and New York, 1968), W. W. Tarn writes:

> Zeno, in his Ideal State, exhibited a resplendent hope which has never quite left man since; he dreamt of a world which should no longer be separate states, but one great city under one divine law, where all were citizens and members of one another, bound together, not by human laws, but by their own willing consent or, as he phrased it, Love. This is sometimes called cosmopolitanism, a word coined by the Cynics to signify that they belonged to no state and it has acquired such unpleasant associations that it is well to avoid it, for it does not at all express what the Stoics meant; it implied a shirking of national duties which no Stoic would have tolerated, for the wise man (they said) would do his duty to his country, and they seem to have realized that if their brotherhood were ever realized it must be through the national state and not by its denial. Even the practical world was influenced, in spite of itself, by Zeno's dream, through the insistence of Zeno's school on certain notions of equality and brotherhood and by the fact that the "inhabited world" or *oecumene* now began to be treated as a whole; the stranger could no longer be *ipso facto* treated as an enemy, and Homonoia received perhaps more tributes than any other Hellenistic concept (79–80).

Stoicism eventually became the dominant philosophical strain in the Roman world. Canonized in the *Meditations* of the second-century Emperor Marcus Aurelius, Stoicism, with its emphasis on subordinating individual desire to the collective good, became the most popular philosophy among Empire intellectuals. Its stress on nobility of soul, human brotherhood, and the transience of purely sensual pleasure created fertile ground for spreading Christian doctrines of universal fellowship.

SCIENCE

Epicureanism. Epicurus, born in Samos in 341 BCE, established his school in Athens in 307. He defined philosophy as "the art of making life happy," and thus would seem to have much in common with Aristippus and the Skeptics. He differed with the Cyrenaics, however, in considering their concept of sensual pleasure silly; he wrote "We cannot live life pleasurably without living prudently, gracefully, and justly; and we cannot live prudently, gracefully, and justly without living pleasurably." Certainly Epicurus saw himself as a philosopher and taught extensively about how to live the ethical life. But what made him exceptional in his time was his materialism. Epicurus' identification of the gods as subject to material forces like the rest of nature led him to develop — or more properly, synthesize — a view of the natural world that would have profound implications for the future of science. Tarn writes:

> The world (Epicurus taught) was only a machine. No gods, good or evil, affected it; it was not made or guided by design; it came into being through certain mechanical principles. He revived Democritus' atomic theory: atoms (he meant molecules) fell in a ceaseless rain through the void, and their clashing formed the world. But at once he had two difficulties. Atoms falling in a straight line through the void could not, as he understood it, clash. Also, he cared nothing for atoms, and very much for free will. He solved his two problems together: the atoms had the power of deliberately swerving a little, in order to meet; that is, he gave them free will.... The rest was easy, and Empedocles' idea that many less adapted animal forms had been tried and died out helped him; the result can be seen in the wonderful description of life on earth in the supreme moment of this school, Lucretius' poem *On the Nature of Things*. Epicurus' aim was, by constructing a world on scientific principles, to free men from fear of the gods and the evils of superstition; man's soul at death dissolved again into the atoms that made it (*Hellenistic Civilization*, 328–29).

Thus did Epicurus' effort to solve moral problems lead to an analysis of the universe's workings startlingly consonant with the discoveries of modern science.

History. Herodotus, "the Father of History," who wrote *The Persian Wars* slightly before the period of Socrates' greatest influence, while invaluable and generally accurate, included much mythological and fabulous material. Since many of these legends contain a grain of truth and make for fabulous reading, we would be poorer without them: they enable us to understand world history as the classical Greeks understood it. What Herodotus had experienced personally or from reliable sources he reported faithfully; our account of the battle of Marathon and its aftermath depends upon him almost entirely. But for Herodotus, we would know relatively little about the greater region in which the Greek genius incubated — the Persians, the Middle East, the Egyptians and Phoenicians, the creative intercourse with the Greek city-states and other cultures they had learned from and influenced in Asia Minor.

Thucydides, who wrote *The Peloponnesian Wars* during and after Socrates' dominance of Athenian intellectual life, established rigorous standards of research and accuracy unsurpassed to this day. He lapsed, by modern standards, only in his tendency to compose speeches appropriate to historical figures in crucial military or political situations, a forgivable compromise in an era when transcripts were rarely available. We can trust, however, that in the great speech where Pericles explains Athenian exceptionalism, Thucydides expresses the true sentiments of the great statesman:

> Our constitution does not copy the laws of its neighboring states; we are a pattern to others rather than imitators ourselves. Its administration favors the many rather than the few; this is why it is called a democracy. If we look to the laws, they afford equal justice to all in their private differences; if to social standing, advancement in public life falls to reputation for capacity, class considerations not being allowed to interfere with merit; nor again does poverty bar the way, if a man is able to serve the state he is not hindered by the obscurity of his condition. The freedom which we enjoy in our government extends also to our ordinary life. There, far from exercising a jealous surveillance over each other, we do not feel called upon to be angry for our neighbor for doing what he likes, or even to indulge in those injurious looks which cannot fail to be offensive, although they inflict no positive penalty. But all this ease in our private relations does not make us lawless as citizens. Against this fear is our chief safeguard, teaching us to obey the magistrates and the laws, particularly such as regard the protection of the injured, whether they are actually on the statute book, or belong to that code which, although unwritten, yet cannot be broken without acknowledging disgrace.
>
> Further, we provide plenty of means for the mind to refresh itself from business. We celebrate games and sacrifices all the year round, and the elegance of our private establishments forms a daily source of pleasure and helps banish the spleen; while the magnitude of our city draws the produce of the world into our harbour, so that to the Athenian the fruits of other countries are as familiar a luxury as those of his own (*The Peloponnesian War*, New York, the Modern Library, 1951).

This noble moment in Western culture, from Pericles' Funeral Oration after the first serious losses in the Peloponnesian Wars, demonstrates that all citizens of free Athens were guided by sentiments similar to those expressed by Jesus: take care of the least among you. Pericles vindicates the faith in just law, free from class bias, originally instituted by Solon. But the Greek version depends, in the end, on a shame culture, in which the unwritten laws are enforced by the contempt of the populous, rather than on the guilt imposed by Judeo-Christian disobedience of a divine command. What's most remarkable here is Pericles' brilliant insistence that a healthy democracy should provide its citizens opportunities for leisure, play, joy, and not intrude into different but socially harmless variations in others' private lives. Finally, Pericles celebrates Athens openness to the ideas, and the luxuries, of the world. A healthy state, in other words, provides for both the physical and spiritual nurture of its citizens.

Thucydides offers us as well the beginnings of a philosophy of history; he dissects every practical possibility and theory of government to be worked out over the following two and a half millennia of European history in his analysis of the feuding Greek states: monarchy, oligarchy, tyranny, democracy, socialism, and communism. He brings to bear the full moral authority of tragedy in his analysis of Athens' overreaching and ultimate defeat.

Hellenism produced any number of fine historians but their work, including that of the greatest of them, Hieronymus of Cardia, is mostly lost. Writing in the third century BCE, he wrote a history in the manner of Thucydides that ran from the death of Alexander to about 280 BCE. We know of him only because he was a primary source for later historians including Diodorus, Arrian, and Plutarch. Tarn comments that Hieronymus "exercised a steadying force on the whole of our broken tradition of the period; the more that period is studied, the stronger the conviction grows of the presence of a great lost writer behind it" (*Hellenistic Civilization*, 284).

Astronomy. Applying the Socratic method to the cornucopia of information that Alexander had acquired by conquering Babylonia, Hellenistic astronomers made startling advances unimproved upon until Copernicus. The traditional Greek view held that the sun, moon, and planets revolved around a fixed earth, but Heracleides (c. 320 BCE) insisted that the earth turned on its axis and that Mercury and Venus revolved around the sun. Aristarchus of Samos (310–230) thought that the sun was 300 times the mass of the earth. This led him to conclude that the geocentric model was impossible, and he decided that while the earth and the planets revolved around the sun in circles, the sun and the fixed stars were stationary. Here, however, things went off track: "Unfortunately this did not lead to the discovery of elliptical orbits" (*Hellenistic Civilization*, 297). In the second century BCE, Seleuces provided a valiant defense of the heliotropic system, but Hipparchos of Nicea, by adding in epicycles and eccentric circles, made the geocentric system work again and this version, adopted by Ptolemy, survived until the discoveries by Copernicus almost two millennia later.

Geography. Alexander's discoveries greatly stimulated interest in the shape and extent of the earth. His own surveyors returned with a treasure trove of detailed observations and measurements. Eratosthenes of Cyrene (275–200), by measuring the arc of the meridian (the curve of the earth) between Alexandria and Syene, calculated the circumference of the world and appears to have come within a couple of hundred miles, the best estimate until very recent times. Noticing the similarity of the tides between the Atlantic and Indian Oceans, he determined that all oceans were one, and that a man could sail east from Spain to

India, although the voyage was not actually accomplished until Vasco da Gama. More remarkably, he accurately concluded that one could sail *west* from Spain to India. In short, the average citizen of Hellas was well aware that the world was round. Pytheas and Seleuces recognized that the orbiting of the moon caused tides. Poseidonius accepted Erathosthenes' geography of the globe but he got the size too small. His misinformation, passed down for sixteen hundred years, led directly to the voyage of Columbus.

Mathematics. Greek interest in mathematics goes back at least as far as Pythagoras in the 6th century BCE and over the next centuries, many mathematicians pursued his brilliant but rather mystical suggestions, increasingly in the spirit of Socratic logic. The Greeks never invented numerical notation, but in one way this worked to their advantage: it spurred them to perfect their geometry. In about 300 BCE, Euclid gathered their work into his *Geometry*, an achievement so great that it was used as a standard textbook into the last century. Greek geometry included many elements of what we would now call algebra.

Archimedes. Archimedes of Syracuse (d. 212) excelled in so many areas that he deserves a category of his own here. Tarn writes:

> The greatest name of all is Archimedes. He wrote monographs on many subjects, and the mere list of his technical achievements is a long one; among other things he calculated limits for the value of pi; ... invented a terminology for expressing numbers up to any magnitude; laid the foundations of the calculus of the infinite; and founded the whole science of hydrostatics.... He was also the greatest theoretical mechanician of the ancient world; and though he held with Plato that a philosopher should not put his knowledge to practical use, it was in fact the practical use of his knowledge which caught the world's imagination (*Hellenistic Civilization*, 300).

Archimedes invented a moving planetarium driven by hydraulic power, a windlass for shifting heavy weights, and the endless screw, useful equally for bailing out a boat or draining the fields after the Nile floods.

Tarn continues:

> Everyone knows the stories about him: how he was too absent-minded to remember to eat; how one day he discovered specific gravity by noticing the water he displaced in his bath, and jumped out and ran naked home shouting *Eureka*, "I have found it'; how when difficulties arose over the launching of Hireo's great Syracosia he launched the ship by himself, and told the king, "Give me where to stand and I will move the earth"; and how during the siege of Syracuse the solitary geometrician kept the whole strength of Rome at bay for three years with his grapnels and catapults. He is the only mathematician who ever became legend (*Hellenistic Civilization*, 300–301).

Perhaps Newton and Einstein might be added to Tarn's list of legendary mathematicians. Other inventors in this period discovered the powers of compressed air and steam, which raises the question: why wasn't there an industrial revolution in the Hellenic or Roman world? Cheap slave and paid labor throughout the period provides an important part of the explanation. But another factor was cultural and deeply rooted, embodied in Archimedes' failed allegiance to Plato's dictum: philosophers should be above mechanical work. This class prejudice, reflected in literary style, would set a limit to the technical achievements of the ancient world.

The Greek philosophical schools and their offshoots, all claiming descent from Socrates, dominated Western thinking and teaching from the time of his death until the middle period of the Roman Empire some six hundred years later. Each school emphasized a different aspect of Socrates' teaching: his insistence on reasoned inquiry; his belief that phenomena could lead one to the ideal; his conviction that acting in one's rational self interest would lead to goodness; his assertion that pleasure was the ultimate purpose in life; his essentially evolutionary natural philosophy; his ascetic insistence on simplicity, justice, and self-control; his conviction that all men were capable of reason and therefore potentially equal; his belief that the individual must cede some autonomy in return for living in a healthy state. The dynamic development and interplay of the ideas he unleashed permeated and transformed social history, human relations, ethics, logic, science, religion, and politics.

Moreover, Socrates, like Jesus, had that most crucial requirement for turning a collection of ideas or principles into an enduring and dynamic cultural force: a compelling narrative. The fact that he had willingly — even happily — sacrificed his life for his principles reified them and made them immortal. Since over the past two millennia the struggle for rational knowledge, defensible ethical standards, and right governance of the self and the state has consisted largely in the effort to recover, preserve, and interpret the teaching of Socrates and his successors, it's safe to conclude that he is one of the two most influential figures in shaping the future course of Western history.

4. The Historical Jesus

Most objective researchers — those not obliged by faith to take the *Gospels* as God's literal truth — would undoubtedly conclude that all the material we have on Jesus' first thirty years is mythology, except perhaps for the likelihoods that he was the child of Mary and Joseph, had several siblings, and came from Nazareth. Probably literate, he must have had some rabbinical teaching and had studied deeply in the Old Testament. Much of the course and purpose of his three-year mission remains obscure, beyond the probability that he was a heterodox Jewish rabbi, believed he heralded the imminent end of the world, taught total submission to God, encouraged a radical compassion for the poor and disenfranchised, and was crucified.

Still, we can make some reasonable deductions about Jesus' early life and character by comparing the times he lived in to the man he became. He was born into a people burdened by an ancient history both heroic and tragic. Certainly a Jewish state existed by about 1000 BCE. It's likely that this people shared distant ancestors who spent time in servitude in Egypt and had accepted the laws of a prophet named Moses. These distant ancestors might in turn have been able to claim some relation, in inherited cultural tradition, if not in blood, from one Abraham, who could well have led his clan from Mesopotamia to Palestine somewhere around 1800 BCE. This might represent the first direct cultural incursion from Sumerian civilization into the near Middle East.

Time after time, stories that persist in an intact culture for scores of generations, dismissed by scholars as legend, prove to have a basis in historical fact. Schliemann found Troy in the late nineteenth century, two thousand years after it had been branded as myth, simply by following the directions provided by Homer. The 16th century BCE culture revealed by the excavations at Knossos in

Crete closely resembles the Minoan civilization portrayed in ancient Greek legends of Theseus. We should approach the undoubtedly embroidered history in the *Old Testament* with these examples in mind.

So it is overwhelming likely that the *Old Testament* contains much historical fact intermixed with centuries of mythological accretion. The lists of Kings, the essential teachings of the prophets, the major conquests and subjugations, the evolution of Jewish theology, are all the sorts of things that a tight culture with an ancient tradition of erudite scholarship would likely preserve. There's no doubt that parts of *Genesis* contain material dating back to the Sumerian mythology of around 2000 BCE, and that the early Hebrew laws preserve both residues of, and intentional departures from, old Babylonian practice. God's covenant with Abraham and the founding of the Jewish faith in a supreme (though not sole) God, turns on Yahweh's rejecting the Mesopotamian practice of Isaac's human sacrifice.

The history and faith Jesus inherited proclaimed a clear central theme: God had chosen his people, they had refused to live up to the Laws he had bestowed upon them, and in retribution he had repeatedly handed them over to their enemies for punishment. The primal scene here is Adam and Eve in the garden. The opening chapters of *Genesis* offer an interesting exception to Auerbach's rule that the *Old Testament* is all background: in the first chapter, as God moves upon the face of the water, divides day and night, makes heaven and earth, strings the sky with the moon, the sun, and the stars, and populates his creation, the early verses of *Genesis* teem with grass, herbs, trees, fish, birds, cattle, snakes.

> So God created man in his own image, in the image of God created he him; male and female created he them:
>
> And God blessed them and God said unto them, Be fruitful and multiply, and replenish the earth and subdue it; and have dominion over the fish of the sea and over the fowl of the air, and over every living thing that moveth upon the earth....
>
> And the Lord God took the man, and put him in the garden of Eden to dress it and keep it.
>
> And the Lord God commanded the man, saying, Of every tree of the garden thou mayest freely eat:
>
> But of the tree of the knowledge of good and evil, thou shalt not eat of it: for in the day that thou eatest thereof thou shalt surely die.
>
> And the Lord God said, It is not good that the man should be alone; I will make him an help meet for him.
>
> And out of the ground the Lord God formed every beast of the field, and every fowl of the air; and brought *them* unto Adam to see what he would

call them; and whatsoever Adam called every living creature, that *was* the name thereof.

And Adam gave names to all the cattle and to the fowl of the air, and to every beast of the field; but for Adam there was not a help meet for him.

And the Lord God caused a deep sleep to fall upon Adam, and he slept: and he took one of his ribs, and closed up the flesh instead thereof.

And the rib, which the Lord God had taken from man, made he a woman, and brought her unto the man.

And Adam said, This *is* now bone of my bone and flesh of my flesh: she shall be named Woman, because she was taken out of Man.

Therefore shall a man leave his father and his mother, and shall cleave unto his wife: and they shall be one flesh.

And they were both naked, the man and his wife, and were not ashamed (*Bible*, King James version, Chapter One, verses 27–28, Chapter Two, verses 15–25).

Much can be observed about this passage, but, read in full, the first thing likely to strike the careful reader is that everything is said twice, and in slightly but importantly different ways. Scholars of the *Bible* are unanimous on the cause of this: two traditions developed during a time when Israel was divided into two kingdoms, Judah and Israel, in the ninth century BCE. The Judah tradition names God Yahweh, and the Israeli tradition, written a little later, names God Elohim. When the two Kingdoms united some time later, the two texts were intermingled, preserving the language sacred to both parties.

Several points emphasized in this passage are crucial for the future of Western history, literature, and theology. Adam is given permission to name things, which in almost every religious tradition conveys a mystical power of possession and control. Adam and Eve are "not ashamed" of their nakedness because the notion that the body could be evil had not yet entered creation. The passage, in Auerbach's terms is all foreground because God and man still exist in the same, unitary world.

The passage continues:

Now the serpent was more subtil than any beast of the field which the Lord God had made. And he said to the woman, Ye shall not eat of every tree in the garden?

And the woman said unto the serpent, We may eat of the fruit of the trees in the garden:

But of the fruit of the tree which *is* in the midst of the garden, God hath said, Ye shall not eat of it, neither shall you touch it, lest ye die.

And the serpent said unto the woman, Ye shall not surely die:

For God doth know that in the day ye eat thereof, then your eyes shall be opened, and ye shall be as gods, knowing good and evil.

And when the woman saw that the tree *was* good for food, and that it *was* pleasant to the eyes, and a tree to be desired to make *one* wise, she took the fruit thereof and did eat, and gave also unto her husband with her; and he did eat.

And the eyes of both of them were opened, and they knew they were naked; and they sewed fig leaves together, and made themselves aprons (*Genesis*, Chapter Three, verses 1–7).

The serpent equates knowing good and evil with being as gods and the temptation has remained with man ever since. Here we learn how different God is from Zeus; he is absolute in his power to give or withhold; while the Greeks knew it was risky, Hellenic culture thought it noble to aspire to godhood. Knowledge and evil enter the world through woman. The first consequence of knowledge is self-consciousness and the first product of self-consciousness is shame. The human and the Divine world crack apart, opening a vast abyss. When God appears next, he speaks from a very deep background, a background of judgment:

And they heard the voice of God walking in the garden in the cool of the day: and Adam and Eve hid themselves from the presence of the Lord God amongst the trees of the garden.

And the Lord God called unto Adam, and said unto him, Where *art* thou?

And he said, I heard thy voice in the garden, and I was afraid, because I *was* naked; and I hid myself.

And he said, Who told thee that thou *wast* naked? Hast thou eaten of the tree, whereof I commanded thee that thou shouldest not eat?

And the man said, The woman whom thou gavest to be with, she gave me of the tree, and I did eat.

And the Lord God said unto the woman, What is this *that* you have done? And the woman said, The serpent beguiled me, and I did eat.

And the Lord God said unto the serpent, Because thou hast done this, thou are cursed above all cattle, and above every beast in the field; upon thy belly shalt thou go, and dust shall thou eat all the days of thy life:

And I will put enmity between you and the woman, and between thy seed and her seed: it shall bruise thy head, and thou shall bruise his heel.

Unto the woman he said, I will greatly multiply thy sorrow and thy conception: in sorrow thou shall bring forth children; and thy desire *shall* be to thy husband, and he shall rule over thee.

And unto Adam he said, Because thou hast hearkened to thy wife, and hast eaten of the tree, of which I commanded thee, saying, Thou shall not eat of it: cursed is the ground for thy sake: in sorrow shalt thou eat of it all the days of your life:

Thorns also and thistles shalt it bring forth to thee; and thou shalt eat of the herb of the field.

In the sweat of thy face shalt thou eat bread, till thou return unto the ground; for out of it wast thou taken: for dust thou *art*, and unto dust shalt thou return.

And Adam called his wife's name Eve; because she was the mother of all living.

Unto Adam also and to his wife did the Lord God make coats of skins, and clothed them.

And the Lord God said, Behold, the man has become as one of us, to know good and evil, and now, lest he put forth his hand, and take also of the tree of life, and eat, and live forever:

Therefore the Lord God sent him forth from the garden of Eden, to till the ground from whence he was taken.

So he drove out the man; and he placed at the east of the garden of Eden Cherubims, and a flaming sword which turned every way, to keep the way of the tree of life (*King James* Chapter Three, verses 8–24).

The second consequence of self-consciousness is fear. The third is blame: Adam blames Eve and God in the same sentence. This is deeper than shame; it is guilt, and with guilt is born the interior self or unconscious; man becomes doubled and partly hidden from himself. The fourth is punishment, injury, and suffering, especially in childbirth. The fifth is lust. The sixth is war with nature. The seventh is labor. The eighth is mortality. The ninth is domination over Eve, the beginning of human hierarchy, power, and government. At the end, God makes a compassionate gesture, as if not entirely abandoning his creation. But from now on God will fear man, perhaps as much as man will fear God. A battle of wills has been engaged.

Judeo–Christian man is doubly trapped, alienated from his God and from himself. Later the fall would be interpreted in many ways: as evidence of man's utter worthlessness before an angry God, as a permanent breach between man and nature, as evidence of the necessity for man to find God's word in the Law, as the occasion that required Jesus' suffering to heal the gap between man and God, even as a fortunate event that made possible God's overflowing grace. The fall gave birth to the need for a literature that could interpret a now alienated and inscrutable world of phenomena, and also became a central subject of that interpretation.

Hence the tragic structure of *Old Testament* history reenacts a cycle of falls or exiles: Abraham driven out of Ur of the Chaldees before he could practice monotheism, the enslavement by Egypt, the Babylonian captivity, the Roman conquest. Less than forty years after Jesus' death, Romans under Vespasian would invade to repress a vigorous independence movement (led by another Messiah-claimant, Bar Kochba), brutally scattering the Jewish people once again and creating the chiliastic climate (for both Jews and Christians) in which the synoptic *Gospels* would be written.

Conquest and dispersion represents the likely pattern for any small people surrounded by great contending Empires. Ancient Israel was the Poland of its era. The genius of the Jewish people reveals itself in the fact that of dozens of petty states contested among Babylonians, Egyptians, Hittites, Assyrians, Persians, Greeks, and Romans, Israel alone survived with its laws, culture, great literature, and religious practices essentially intact. As each wave of conquest receded, a Jewish state would be reestablished on its native ground accompanied by prophetic warnings to return to the purity of the original Covenant.

But by Jesus' time, another factor had shaped the environment in which he learned and taught: unlike the periods which had inspired most of the *Old Testament* writings, Israel no longer consisted solely of a collection of tribes or a temple–state; it had joined an international community. Christianity can perhaps best be seen as the ultimate flower of Hellenism, that underrated three centuries between the death of Alexander the Great (323 BCE) and the founding of the Roman Empire by Octavian Augustus, who reigned at the time of Jesus' birth. Alexander's conquests, consciously modeled on the policies of Cyrus the Great, had created the world's first true international system whose influence stretched from Italy and North Africa through Greater Greece, the Mid-East, and much of central Asia to India. Alexander had quadrupled the size of the known world. A student equally of his crude but brilliant father Phillip II, who unified Greece, and Aristotle, who schooled him thoroughly in Socrates and Plato, Alexander offered the profound vision of a world comprised of many different but equal peoples, perhaps his greatest contribution to Western history.

Tarn writes:

> Man as a political animal, a fraction of the *polis* or self-governing city state, had ended with Aristotle; with Alexander begins man as the individual. The individual needed to consider both the regulation of his own life and also his relations with the other individuals who with him composed the "inhabited world"; to meet the former need there arose the philosophies of conduct, to meet the latter certain new ideas of human brotherhood. These originated on the day — one of the critical moments in history — when, at a banquet at Opis, Alexander prayed for a union of hearts

(*homonoia*) among all peoples and a joint commonwealth of Macedonians and Persians; he was the first to transcend national boundaries and to envisage, however imperfectly, a brotherhood of man in which there should be neither Greek nor barbarian (*Hellenism*, 79).

It was on this point that Aristotle broke with his friend and former pupil; unable to accept race equality, he proved himself more parochial than Alexander. Some contemporary historians suggest that several of Aristotle's allies in the field with the army began conspiracies against Alexander. This treachery seems particularly ungrateful, since Alexander had been sending Aristotle samples of newly discovered phenomena that, according to Tarn, increased "knowledge on many lines, botany, zoology, geography, ethnography, hydrography...." But in contributing to the growth of science, Tarn adds, "it was probably of greater importance that he brought Babylon into the Greek sphere. The result was that for a few generations after his death there was such a true growth of science as the world was never to see again for very many centuries; the supremacy of the period, till quite modern times, is unquestionable." (*Hellenistic Civilization*, 295) Cloaked with mythology and heavily dependent upon astrology, the Babylonian materials nevertheless contained two millennia of accurate observation of natural phenomena that the Hellenistic world, under the influence of Socrates' methods, could unpack, test, and verify.

The consequences of the Hellenistic transformation were enormous:

1. Alexander's vast Empire broke up after his death into several kingdoms founded by his successor generals — the Seleucid in Asia, the Ptolemaic in Egypt, and the Antigonid in greater Greece, as well as many transient states. But henceforth all were in constant communication, their rulers were generally related by blood, and a vigorous international commerce ensued in goods, arts, science, philosophies, religions, and cultures.

2. For all their border squabbles which resulted in constantly shifting boundaries, the Hellenistic states generally (on Alexander's model) provided stable, efficient government, encouraged education, down-pedaled race-prejudice, constructed workable judicial systems, tolerated or encouraged many local democracies, and (to the greatest extent yet seen in the world) empowered their middle and upper classes — although, of course, millions of peasants, especially in Egypt and Asia, saw little change in their daily lives. The status of middle and upper class women generally improved. Slavery, though not abolished, was mitigated except for some agricultural work and the dreadful galleys and mines. Many a prominent citizen of Hellas rose to high station from servitude. Fairly humane rules of war and diplomacy developed and were often observed. Macedonians and Greeks remained the dominant ethnic groups everywhere, but, increasingly, one could become a citizen of Hellas simply by adopting the Greek language and culture. Merchants, scholars, soldiers, scientists, doctors, philosophers, spiritual teachers, politicians, and ordinary tourists canvassed the known world using

demotic Greek, spoken everywhere. Populations and economies, on average, boomed.

3. The major Hellenistic dynasties founded hundreds of cities on the Greek model with their civic governments, gymnasia, schools, theaters, and places of worship. The syncretic Alexandrine spirit easily absorbed regional gods and ideas alike. All this resulted in the world's first international culture. Social mobility was probably the greatest it had been or would be until modern times and this trend continued into the first centuries of the increasingly Hellenized Roman Empire.

The rise of a large mass of autonomous individuals who were no longer merely cogs in the machine of their particular state or economy created, in some sense, many citizens of the world. They needed systems of belief that transcended loyalty to particular local governments, cultures, or gods. For the first time, the educated — and they were numerous even among working people under the influence of the Greco–Macedonian tradition — could choose what to believe among a bewildering variety of Greek philosophies, Eastern mystery religions, and popular superstitions. Before Alexander, one believed in one's local rulers and deities. After Alexander, philosophies and religions could claim a universal validity that overrode local interests. Of the philosophies, Stoicism came closest to achieving universality, at least among the intellectual classes, by stressing the brotherhood of all mankind. But it was Christianity that ultimately achieved a near-universal following that trumped locality or nationality. Thus the schools descended from Socrates had prepared the ground for Jesus.

Two other important religious sources must be identified as having been in the air during Jesus' lifetime:

Zoroastrianism. Zoroaster founded the Persian national religion. His very existence is somewhat uncertain, unlike that of Jesus, hovering as he does at the ancient border between history and legend. Although the Persian orthodoxy in ancient times placed him as an historical figure flourishing around 600 BCE, linguistic and geographical evidence suggests he probably carried out his mission somewhere in Eastern Iran or Afghanistan as early as 1000 BCE. But we can date his influence on Median–Persian culture back to at least the seventh century BCE. An enormous body of sacred text was attributed to Zoroaster, as testified to by various citations of the content of the Library of Alexandria. Although most of this has been lost in the fire kindled by Egypt's struggle with Rome, we still have fragments of the *Gathes* and the *Avestas*, no doubt containing the core of Zoroastrian teachings and the interpretive and mythological accretions of the religion's early centuries.

Zoroaster's earliest legends variously describe him as a receiver of revelations from the Divine who taught, gained a number of disciples (perhaps twelve), struggled with the ruling classes and an entrenched priesthood, was initially unwelcome in his mother's home town, defeated devils, and was tempted by an evil spirit to renounce his faith.

We can be more certain of Zoroaster's message, which was recorded in historical times. He believed that the universe was the stage for a perpetual struggle between *asa*, or Truth, and *druj*, or the Lie. Human beings could live the most happy and successful life by allying with the Truth and eschewing the Lie. Importantly, Zoroaster taught that individuals had the choice to side with either *asa* and *druj* and that the struggle between the two would be eternal. A consequence of this situation was that individuals had sovereign and eternal Free Will, perhaps Zoroaster's greatest contribution to theology.

This dualistic vision would have profound consequences for the history of Western religion from antiquity to this day. The Greeks were aware of Zoroaster, and many philosophers flirted with absolute dualism, although the majority tradition retained Socrates' unitary continuum from the slime to the sublime. The Jewish tradition, with its enormous gap between God and fallen man, was inherently dualistic from the start, but with a difference: Eventually God would return as the Messiah to redeem his true believers. Christianity would extend this promised salvation to the whole world, but from the beginning, in its orthodox form, it would struggle with Gnostic (dualistic) versions of Jesus' message from the composition of *The New Testament* on.

Egyptian Religion. Egyptian religion developed over millennia. Gods appeared, rose and fell in the hierarchy, vanished, and transformed themselves. Pharaoh's divinity provided the one constant, and as dynasties replaced each other, the new Pharaoh would naturally elevate the gods of his own region over those of the dynasty he'd deposed. Figures from Egyptian mythology permeated into the antique world and contributed to the general religious climate. Three Egyptian gods became major figures in the Hellenic pantheon, probably because they bore clear resemblances to gods in other systems:

Osiris and Isis. Osiris originated as a nature god, and his wife Isis represented nature's fecundity. His Kingship aroused the envy of his brother Set, who developed a complex conspiracy to dispatch him. Set designed a coffin that exactly corresponded to Osiris' measurements, and then held a ceremony in which the coffin would be the prize for whoever fit it best. Osiris, of course, fit perfectly, and as soon as he had settled in comfortably, Set snapped down the lid, sealed the coffin in lead, and dropped it into the Nile. Osiris' wife Isis, bereft, searched the world for him, and finally found the coffin embedded in a trunk of cedar that had been incorporated into the structure of a palace in Lebanon. Isis escorted the coffin back to Egypt and buried it.

Set, however, found the coffin, opened it, cut Osiris into parts, and distributed these remains throughout Egypt. Isis faithfully searched until she had assembled twelve of the thirteen parts but the thirteenth was a crucial one, the penis, which she cast out of gold. Then she sang to Osiris, he returned to life and, presumably because of his familiarity with the subject, he became Lord of the Dead. With the aid of Osiris' new member, he and Isis conceived Horus.

Osiris therefore became the most prominent of the many resurrected gods populating early antiquity. Although other polytheistic systems offer numerous parallels, the most striking comes from Greece. Demeter, the goddess of nature and fertility married Hades, the Lord of the underworld. Since she had reservations about spending the rest of her life among the dead, she and Hades worked out an arrangement. For six months of the year she would reside with him in Hell, but in the spring, she would return to the earth to restore fertility. Reenactment of this return seems to have provided the central material for the Eleusinian mystery ceremonies in Athens.

Horus. As the Sky God, Horus had analogues in every other mature polytheistic religion from Babylon to Italy. Early versions of the legend claimed that his right eye was the sun and his left the moon. This imagery may have originated from the fact that Horus was popular in Upper (northern) Egypt, while Set held sway in the south, and that the two were united around 3000 BCE in what amounted to a conquest of Lower Egypt by the north. Associated with the falcon, with or as which he is often depicted, he evolved from the god of hunting to the god of war.

Isis became the focus of one of the largest cults in the Greco–Roman world, and Osiris and Horus were worshipped alongside her. Early Christians were constantly competing with the Egyptian trinity for proselytites. During this process, Horus became so associated with Jesus that it is difficult to tell what Christ-like features attributed to him were truly ancient, and which were the product of Hellenic–Roman syncretization. One website (*Ontario Religious Tolerance*) lists the following parallels: Horus and Jesus were both born of a virgin, announced by an angel, threatened with death by powerful figures in their infancy, baptized at 30, taken from the desert onto a high mountain by their enemy, resisted temptation, raised a man from the dead, were transfigured on a mountain, descended into Hell and were resurrected after three days, claimed to be the saviors of humanity, had twelve disciples, and were referred to as the good shepherd, lamb of god, bread of life, son of man, the Word, the fisher, and the winnower. At least some of these characteristics were likely associated with Horus in the original Egyptian mythology, but the larger point is that all this imagery was available from multiple sources in the period immediately following Jesus' crucifixion.

The intersection of Judaism with these trends in world history clearly shaped Jesus' understanding of his mission. Jesus' radical originality — and if we don't know this about him we don't know anything — is that he saw himself not merely as a prophet calling his people back to their God's Laws, but as the fulfillment of God's Covenant with Abraham: the culmination of the *Old Testament* narrative, the end of history. As the sacrificial lamb he, unlike Isaac, would not be spared at the last moment, though there is some evidence he hoped to be.

Much of what Jesus is reported to have said — many of the Beatitudes, the entire Lord's Prayer, and other of his teachings consist of quotes and paraphrases, mostly from the Prophets. Jesus, a rabbinical Jew, sought out the more mystical and messianic passages of the *Old Testament* and fused them into a compassionate apocalyptic vision. God did not want his people to suffer such oppression and misery and Jesus would serve as the instrument to transfigure the wretched and the temporal into a joyous and eternal fellowship with God.

What Hellenism contributed to Jesus' message aside from the necessary mythological decoration — and this is implicit, though perhaps half-conscious in many of the statements and actions attributed to Jesus — is the implication, later developed by Paul, that his message held not only for the Jews, but for all humankind. If not to him, then to his followers, his Father was the first universal God.

Unlike the case of Socrates, absolutely no contemporary record of Jesus' life exists. We lack any objective evidence to weigh against the later testimony of true believers. Moreover, our primary sources, the letters of Paul and the *Gospels*, agree on precious little about Jesus' life or message during the three years he preached. Each abounds with contradictions, unlikelihoods, impossibilities, and blatant borrowings from other religious and philosophical traditions. But they do coincide on his central message. Max I. Dimont writes in *Appointment in Jerusalem* (New York, St. Martin's Press, 1991):

> All four evangelists concur that, after stating that he must go to Jerusalem, there to fulfill his destiny, Jesus three times made the following four predictions: that he would be arrested by the Jewish priests; that he would be tried by the Romans; that he would be crucified by the Romans; and that he would be resurrected ("rise again" as he expressed it) in three days (6).

Combined with Jesus' clear intention to consummate the Jews' Covenant with God, this summary gives us the essential message the historical Jesus transmitted to his immediate followers and what eventually became the Christian Church. He intended to take on the sins of his generation, fulfill the *Old Testament* prophecies about the Messiah, suffer death at the hands of his persecutors, and rise again to inaugurate a transfigured relationship between God and man. We can safely attribute to Jesus a concept essential to the future success of the Christian church: against the majority tradition of the *Old Testament*, he promised all his followers a better afterlife following the misery of this one. For contemporary analogies or sources for this idea, we must turn to Egyptian religion, emerging Eastern cults, or to the Essenes, the contemporary Jewish fringe group with whom John the Baptist was associated.

If our quest is for the historical Jesus, we must start by stripping away every element of the *New Testament* redolent of syncretic imports from other contemporary cults or from the *Old Testament* itself. Images of a virgin or equinox birth attended by Kings, wise men, and angels; miracles; twelve disciples; a last communion — all are too common to other contemporary religions to be taken as history. The Jewish tradition of Messiahship required a miraculous Bethlehem birth, a Davidic lineage, residency in Nazareth, an exile in Egypt, youthful genius before learned rabbis, a sudden calling, betrayal into martyrdom, giving the dying messiah vinegar rather than water, and a resurrection. Adoptions of miraculous events from other cults and parallels to previous role models were intrinsic to the natural process of turning a man into a God at the time. Some may be true but we can never know factually. Obviously the evangelists and their successors, dedicated to spreading the "good news" of eternal life, shaped their messages to the existing philosophical and religious traditions of those they wanted to convert. In Greece, Paul made much use of language derived from Plato, and this tendency finds it apotheosis in the distinctly Greek *Gospel of John*. Different evangelists lay the blame for Jesus' crucifixion on the Jews or the Romans, depending on whom they were trying to convert.

If we strip away all these impossibilities, improbabilities, and special pleadings, what do we have left? Certainly more than the humane teacher later portrayed by many Renaissance Christian Humanists, Enlightenment Deists, and some modern Christians. We have a core message from an historical figure that within a century of his death was transforming the Roman world. What we can characterize as historically likely about Jesus' three-year mission are the following facts and events:

1. He emerges as an unknown man from Nazareth and is baptized by John. Either John recognized him as his successor, or that legend was spread by Jesus' immediate circle when John was beheaded soon afterward. As mentioned above, John was associated with a fringe Jewish cult, the Essenes, which expected an imminent Messiah and had heterodox views on topics like the individual afterlife. After the baptism, Jesus was known as the Christ, or "Joshua the anointed one."

2. He leaves his career as a carpenter for full-time missionary preaching and faith healing. He and/or his followers claim he performed miracles.

3. He returns to Nazareth to proclaim himself the Messiah. What evidence exists suggests that he was rejected as a blasphemer, even by his parents, and nearly executed.

4. He preaches for a period in Galilee. According to Dimont and others who have tried to construct Jesus' biography, during this period he struggled to convince even his disciples of his divine mission. Nevertheless, it was during this period that he seems most fully to have articulated the compassionate values with which his immediate followers constantly associated him: concern for the poor,

the centrality of forgiveness, the importance of seeking a life in eternity rather than the present. In short, he suggested that one could live daily life in a universal drama with its resolution in sight. It was the Christ who had returned to end history that inspired the martyrs and transformed the future of Western civilization. During this mission he made the first four-point prophecy of his arrest, trials, crucifixion, and resurrection.

5. He rides into Jerusalem and immediately provokes all the powers that be. By now Jesus must have known that his reputation for healing, for proclamations of the Messiahship, for being John the Baptist's heir, for telling his followers to turn from the temporal to the eternal, would go before him. For good measure he apparently attacks the moneychangers in the Temple — in effect, the Roman province's banking system. He denounces major Jewish sects, the Pharisees and the Sadducees, as well as the elders and the scribes. His followers, if not Jesus himself, proclaim him as King of the Jews. These actions were more than enough to make him a wanted man by every faction with any power in Jerusalem, Jews and Romans alike. Absent any contemporary evidence about his crucifixion, it appears he amounted to a minor public nuisance, disposed of expeditiously by the conventional methods. Clearly, it was within Jesus' power to fulfill the first three points of his four-point prophecy merely by showing up in Jerusalem with a throng of believers and making a ruckus.

6. He is arrested. The Gospels differ on exactly how this occurred, for reasons we'll discuss later. But the most plausible explanation, provided by Haim Cohn in *The Trial and Death of Jesus* (New York, Harper and Row, 1959), is that the Romans ordered the Jewish authorities to seize him, and that he was brought to trial before Pilate on the charge of treason to the Roman state.

7. He is crucified. All crucifixions were horrible, and most dragged on two or three days, rather than the agonizing six hours that Jesus apparently endured. Indeed there are some suggestions — such as the Roman soldier piercing his side, perhaps to hasten his death — that he was killed relatively mercifully (although only *John*, the latest *Gospel*, mentions the spear wound; the reference in *Matthew* was clearly interpolated later). The *Gospels* hint that he may have survived his crucifixion and been spirited away for medical attention. His last words on the cross — "Eli, Eli lama sabacthani" — seem authentic, because otherwise there would have been no motive for believers in his divinity decades later to include them in the canon. "My God, my God, why have you forsaken me?" suggests that he had really believed up to that point that God would intervene to prevent his death and by doing so transfigure the world, not in the future, but immediately. Earlier, according to Mark, Jesus had promised "Truly I say to you there are some standing here who will not taste death before they see the Kingdom of God come with power." Why God didn't save Jesus at or soon after the crucifixion is perhaps the essential issue of Christian theology. People fifty and more years later,

at the time the *Gospels* were being written, still clung to the prophecy that Christ "would return before the last among you are dead."

After Jesus' death, his disciples were simultaneously stunned that so much of his prophecy had been fulfilled and in despair about the conclusion of their mission. The descriptions of his resurrection in the *Gospels* themselves seem strangely vague. The original text of *Mark*, the earliest *Gospel*, offers no eyewitness testimony to the risen Christ (the last verses of Mark in orthodox editions are, again, clearly later interpolations), while each subsequently written *Gospel* rallies more and more disciples and angels testifying to the resurrection. Such post-facto accumulating of evidence sounds very like Joseph Smith's quest to round up more and more followers willing to swear they had seen the golden tablets from which he transcribed *The Book of Mormon* before he "destroyed" them according to instructions from the angel Moroni.

Based on the historically verified behavior of many other cults in the face of the death or failed prophecy of its leader, objective analysis would have to lean towards the conclusion that Jesus' immediate followers, convinced by the fulfillment of the first three points of his prophecy, and facing the death of the man they had loved and believed in, either kidnapped his body from the tomb or chose to believe rumors he had briefly returned in the flesh. Given the fact that they had left all that they had to follow him, and the obviously adhesive and charismatic nature of his genius, it would be historically surprising if many of them didn't continue to believe that the entire prophecy had been fulfilled. The view that the disciples kidnapped Jesus' body was common among even believing Christians in the century or two after his death. The early Church Father Tertullian (AD 160–230) wrote, "This is he whom his disciples have stolen away secretly, that it may be said he is risen."

If, on the other hand, Jesus did survive his crucifixion for a short period of time, his immediate disciples would have been aware that the purpose of this pious fraud was to fulfill his prophecy that he would be resurrected. The mysterious Joseph of Aramathia, identified in the *Gospels* as a wealthy Jew, apparently persuaded Pilate to let him take Jesus down from the cross after only six hours; normally crucified corpses were left hanging to rot until the vultures picked at them.

So much we can reasonably posit about the historical Jesus. Historians, however, have a right, in fact a responsibility, to interpret the facts as they see them. Several major schools of thought have evolved on what Jesus intended, all of which can find some support in the historical evidence:

1. Jesus as a political revolutionary. This school portrays Jesus as the leader of a rebellion against Roman rule. Such a movement existed at the time, the Zealots, and the *Gospels* clearly indicate that there were Zealots among Jesus' disciples and other followers. Jesus' "cleansing of the Temple" after he entered Jerusalem

can easily be interpreted as a political act, although if he had actually tried to incite an insurrection, the numerous Roman troops on the site — not to say the Jewish authorities — would no doubt have cracked down hard on him at once. In fact he was allowed to preach in the Temple (which was a huge complex including as well as the sanctuary, the central institutions of Jewish politics, religion, and finance) for several days after the "cleansing" — if this incident had in fact happened at all as the *Gospels* describe. Jesus appears to have entered Jerusalem as a relatively unknown figure, and it may have taken several days for him to catch the authorities' attention.

While it's probable that Zealots briefly flocked to Jesus' cause in his last days and may have seen him as a potential revolutionary leader, there's little evidence that Jesus saw himself that way. *Old Testament* prophecies do sometimes refer to the coming Messiah as a warrior, and Jesus occasionally draws on this imagery ("I come to bring not peace but a sword") but the Gospels offer absolutely no evidence that Jesus had come to Jerusalem to stage a military coup. Quite the reverse; he had come to Jerusalem specifically to be crucified, and had been promising he would for years. The large preponderance of evidence suggests that Jesus did say, or at least mean, "My Kingdom is not of this world."

2. Jesus as a social revolutionary. In this view, Jesus was essentially a pacifist humanist who wanted to uplift the poor and the downtrodden. Many of his comments reported or embroidered in the *Gospels* support this view, and he clearly called his followers to a more compassionate standard of human conduct — indeed, this may be his greatest legacy. While almost all his exhortations to right conduct have easily identifiable sources in the *Old Testament*, collectively it's inarguable that they introduced a "transvaluation of values." In Western civilization, we find similarly noble ethical injunctions on man's responsibility to his fellow man only in the highest reaches of Greek philosophy — that is, in Plato's Socrates and Pericles' great speech. On the other hand, it's clear that Jesus saw this morality as only a consequence of his central message: that he was the long-promised Messiah, come to inaugurate a new era between God and man. He exhorted his followers to respect the existing political realities ("Render unto Caesar...") in the expectation that God's intervention was imminent.

3. Jesus as an Essene. The view that Jesus was an Essene had strong support as demonstrated in Joseph Ernest Renan's mid-nineteenth-century *Life of Jesus* even before the discovery of the Dead Sea Scrolls decisively confirmed Essene influence on the origins and evolution of Christianity. The Essenes, a fellowship of Jewish monks and their followers, lived in a desert commune near the Jordan and rejected the Temple teachings and hierarchy. Established about 150 BCE, their great prophet was known as the Teacher of Righteousness (flourished c. 100 BCE). He portrayed himself — or was portrayed by his followers — as the suffering servant of God who was of the House of David, a "Nazarene," God's

instrument to achieve the salvation of man, and fated to die at the hands of evil priests. His titles included "the Son of Man" and his mission was to restore the true Covenant. The Essenes believed in the immortality of the soul and the imminence of the Messiah. They practiced a "Sacred Supper" in which a priest blessed the bread and the wine.

All of these facts are confirmed about as firmly as anything can be in ancient history. They are contained in documents written over the century before Jesus' birth, and verified by trustworthy Jewish and Roman historians. Moreover, we know the method by which these teachings were transmitted to Jesus. John the Baptist was an Essene or close associate of the group. In the Dead Sea Scrolls we find many passages like the following echo from the Old Testament:

> I was beset with hunger, and the Lord nourished me.
> I was alone, and the Lord comforted me.
> I was sick, and the Lord visited me.

This could hardly be closer to Matthew 25:35–36:

> For I was hungry and you gave me food.
> I was a stranger and you welcomed me.
> I was sick and you visited me.

Jesus clearly got his message and his concept of Messiahship from the Essenes. Where did he get his method?

4. Jesus as impresario. Followers of this school believe Jesus consciously choreographed his passion, and this view has enormous support from the *Gospels*, even though it cuts against the evangelists' central message: that all these events were brought about by God. Jesus himself repeatedly states that he is taking certain actions "so that Scripture can be fulfilled." In other words, he is enacting the role of Messiah laid out in the *Old Testament* as interpreted by the Essenes: claiming descent from the House of David and a Bethlehem birth, coming from Nazareth, arranging to be anointed by a prophet (John the Baptist), comforting the oppressed, entering Jerusalem on an ass, being persecuted by a high priest, maintaining silence before his accusers, suffering betrayal by his most trusted associate (Judas), being sacrificed as a "lamb of God," receiving vinegar rather than water during his agony, and rising on the third day.

Certainly Jesus knew these criteria for Messiahship, and most of them were not difficult to arrange. Claims to Davidic lineage were widespread during the period; David had lived a thousand years before and the Jews were a close-knit, intermarried people. In all likelihood Jesus came from Nazareth; that might have provided the germ of his conviction that he was, or could become, the Messiah. All he had to do was show up and John would baptize, or "anoint," him. Comforting the poor and the sick seems to have been deeply rooted in his nature and was a traditional responsibility of rabbis. It would have been easy to acquire an ass and the *Gospels* make clear that Jesus planned ahead for it. Any disruption of the Temple would almost inevitably bring down the wrath of the High Priest. Keeping silent during his trial — or, to be accurate, refusing to respond directly to questions or offer a defense — lay entirely within his personal control. Certainly, it was also within Jesus' power to ensure the Romans crucified him; once he allowed himself to be hailed as King of the Jews, he was guilty of treason and crucifixion was the ordained punishment in the Roman Empire. If the sponge of vinegar was in fact served to Jesus while he was on the cross, that could also easily have been arranged. And we've already seen that even many early Christians believed that either Jesus' followers removed his body from the tomb, or that he briefly survived the crucifixion. It's very suggestive that Jesus was crucified on a Friday, since a Jewish–Roman agreement specified that convicts would not be crucified during the Sabbath, which began Friday evening. The agreement required that the crucified be taken down from the cross by late afternoon, which is indeed what the evidence suggests happened to Jesus, and could explain the permission Pilate gave to Joseph of Arimathea.

Of these acts the toughest to contrive would seem to be the Bethlehem birth, the youthful exile in Egypt, and betrayal by a close friend. The story of the birth and the flight to Egypt are the most likely of these stations toward Messiahship to be concocted. The *Gospels* claim Joseph and Mary went to Bethlehem to be taxed, but Roman tax records were pretty thorough and there is no record of any such event. As to Judas, the *Gospels* directly state that Jesus commanded Judas to betray him.

In 2006, scholars published a *Gospel of Judas* ("New York Review of Books," nybooks.com/articles/19013), written around 140 CE and unearthed in Egypt several decades ago. It portrays Judas as the favored disciple, the only one who fully understood Jesus' true divinity, and describes a universe filled with both divine and malevolent intermediaries between humankind and the highest truths. His betrayal of Christ appears as an act of fidelity and Christ confides to him the ultimate secret: that Judas alone among the disciples may join the higher — and already extant — "race" of the saved. While the editors of the gospel interpret it as falling on the Gnostic side of a divide between heretical and canonical views of Christ, the NYROB reviewer offers the proper perspective: "[I]t is more productive to view all these early Christian texts as differing positions in the same debate about Christ's meaning and message." Clearly, what made it into the canon had more to do with emerging church politics than with what Jesus had or hadn't actually said. By the late second century CE many sects claimed Jesus for themselves, just as many philosophies had claimed Socrates. But acceptance into what emerged as the orthodox canon cannot be evidence for the objective historian. Given his subsequent vilification over two thousand years of Christian history, Judas could well be considered the most martyred player in the passion drama.

No evidence suggests that Jesus was a fake; in fact it's difficult to imagine that he would subject himself to such a terrible fate unless he truly believed in his mission. We could conclude, however, that he thought he could force God's hand. If we accept this interpretation of Jesus' mission it makes his final words on the cross "My God, my God, why have you forsaken me," all the more poignant.

We're unlikely to get any closer to the historical Jesus. More important is what his followers made of him.

5. The Jesus Legend

We'll define the Jesus legend here as the transformation of the historical Jesus of Nazareth into Christ, the co-equal of God, which took place during the century after his death. While the Christ who became a major figure in the second century Roman Empire would undergo challenges from multiple "heretical" interpretations during the following centuries before being canonized by Augustine during the dying days of the Western Empire, all his essential "orthodox" features were present by the mid-second century. Two major traditions contributed to the second century theological Christ:

The Christ of St. Paul. Paul's *Epistles* represent the earliest surviving Christian writings. Composed over the thirty years following Jesus' death and entirely polemical, they are designed to convert pagans and buck up the resulting churches. Paul was astonishingly successful; by the time of his death in Rome in the mid-60s, he had established congregations in Asia Minor, Greece, Italy, and possibly as far away as Spain. It's easy to agree with the majority of historians who credit Paul with the invention of orthodox Christianity (although he had a major partner). Even Luther based his Reformation more than a millennium after Augustine in a summons to return to the Christ of Paul.

Paul, of course, had never met Jesus. A Jewish Roman citizen of Tarsus in Asia Minor, he actively persecuted the Jerusalem Christians in the years immediately following Jesus' crucifixion. The turning point in his life seems to have been his participation in the stoning to death of the first Christian martyr, Stephen. During this period Jesus' apostles had founded what came to be called the Apostolic Church of Jerusalem, headed by Peter. Its members bore little resemblance to the vast majority of Christians who would emerge over the next century. Orthodox Jews, they worshiped regularly at the Temple, observed Mosaic Law, and met at first in a modest room to share their memories of Jesus. What we know of them strongly suggests that they did not worship a "resurrected Christ." They only differed with their fellow Temple Jews in believing that Jesus was the rightful King of Israel who would return one day to liberate his people from Rome. Over the decade after Jesus' death, they grew from about 120 to 8,000 congregants.

Stephen, however, rapidly emerged as a revolutionary figure, the first Christian theologian, and arguably the co-inventor, with Paul, of Christianity. When he proclaimed that Temple attendance was idolatry, that Jesus was the true Son of God, and that Christ's teachings had replaced the Mosaic Law, fellow Jews put him to death. Here, for the first time, what would become the essential Christian message emerges into history. Paul served as lead prosecution witness in the perfectly legal trial that led to Stephen's execution for blasphemy, and may well have cast the first stone. For several years afterward he led a fanatic attack on the "Nazarenes."

Paul's subsequent writings suggest that he suffered a terrible crisis of guilt over these events that haunted him for the rest of his life. It's probable that the sublime faith of those he persecuted first caused him to doubt the righteousness of his cause, and finally moved him to accept the divinity of Jesus. In his "road to Damascus" moment, on the way to root out another community of Jesus-believers, he experienced a blinding revelation which caused him to adopt Stephen's view of Jesus as the Christ, that is, the Messiah and the Son of God, who had overthrown and superseded Mosaic Law.

Paul vanishes from history for several years after his conversion, but reemerges a decade later as the partner of Barnabus on an extended Christian mission to Asia Minor and Greece. His *Epistles* make clear that during his reflective period (c. AD 36–46) he had reached several conclusions:

> 1. Jesus and the God of the *Old Testament* were essentially one — the Christ — and would return to save the world.

> 2. The meaning of Jesus was contained in his resurrection, which was clearly regarded as either untrue or unimportant by the Jewish Apostolic Church in Jerusalem.

> 3. A similar resurrection was available to every believing Christian.

> 4. As a divinity — or, rather, THE divinity — Christ was not flesh but "the Word," a term derived from the Torah but in its translated form, "Logos," very familiar from Socratic philosophy to the Greek-speakers Paul was trying to convert. Translation from one language to another can of course have profound theological implications: in Greek philosophy "Logos" carried the sense of a divine generative impulse, the initial unity "spoken" as the infinite variety of creation.

Paul's conversion of the Greeks represents an important historical reversal. For three centuries, the Jewish state had been, in effect, a cultural colony of Greece.

More and more Jews had become Hellenized; many Jewish students studied at Greek universities in Israel, Athens, and Alexandria; Paul himself, although Jewish, was a cosmopolitan citizen of the world before his conversion and undoubtedly spoke demotic Greek fluently. The Jews knew a great deal about Greece, but Greece knew very little about Israel. Now the tide had turned, and the Greeks would learn a great deal about the Jewish tradition in its Christian form. Cross-pollination of the two crucial founding Western cultures had begun, although it was soon curtailed by the Roman destruction of the Jewish state in 70 CE. Agape had penetrated to the heart of Erotic Hellas, although Greek Christians would manage to integrate many Socratic elements into their version of Christianity.

Accepting Stephen's version of Jesus, Paul abandoned the Jewish rite of circumcision and the Mosaic dietary laws. From this point on, his challenge was not to convert pagans into practicing Jews, but rather into the newly defined "Christians" — a much easier task. Paul insisted repeatedly that Jesus' return as the Christ was imminent, which probably explains his obvious distaste for sex and human reproduction. There would be no need for future generations, and the flesh distracted from the divine, as many pagan cults demonstrated.

When he returned from his enormously successful mission to the pagans in AD 50, Paul went directly to Jerusalem for a showdown with the Jewish Apostolic Church. Peter had recently been replaced as its leader by Jesus' brother James, a recent convert, Orthodox Jew, and regular temple-goer. The meeting was reportedly contentious, probably because James was not prepared to accept Paul's overthrow of the Mosaic Laws. Nevertheless, the two reached a compromise: as Dimont says, "Paul got the Gentiles and James got the Jews." It appears, however, that the Apostle Peter at least partially accepted Paul's view almost immediately, because he is reported the same year dining with Gentiles in Antioch, a serious violation of Temple Law. Perhaps his sympathy for Paul's version of Christ caused his replacement by James as head of the Apostolic Church.

Paul spent the remaining fifteen years of his life preaching to the pagans and nurturing the Christian churches he had established, largely by means of the letters that have been gathered into his *Epistles*, which along with the Gospels form the core of the *New Testament*. Since the Apostolic Church refused to recognize him as an Apostle, he eventually awarded the title to himself, saying he had received it directly from Jesus. By the time of his death in the mid-sixties, after a trial held at the Emperor's court in Rome, Paul had established a corresponding community of believers that provided the foundation for the Christian Church.

Paul's vision of Jesus as the Messiah and co-equal of God reached its apotheosis in *The Gospel of John*, probably written on the Aegean island of Patmos somewhat after 100 CE. If John the disciple was actually its author he lived to an amazing age, but it likely reflects the traditions of his teachings, which suggests the disciple of Jesus had in turn become the disciple of Paul. John's Pauline premise is that "God sent his son into the world to save the world." Jesus was the Word, the Logos, and "In the beginning was the Word; the Word was with God, and the Word was God." John also first fully develops the third element of the orthodox Christian trinity, the Holy Spirit, which descends to identify Jesus as the Messiah during his initiation by John the Baptist.

Of the four canonical Gospels, John most frankly reflects the Essene influence on Jesus. Like the Essene documents found at Qumran, John adopts a dualistic language reminiscent of Eastern mysticism, especially the teachings of Zoroaster. Light and dark, truth and lies, angels and devils, all suggest a Zoroastrian/Essene battle between equal forces of good and evil.

This dualistic vision foreshadows later Gnosticism, a version of Christianity that broke out to challenge the established church time after time in the following two millennia. Gnostic dualists held that only certain enlightened souls could be in full communion with the Godhead and that lesser beings could achieve contact with the divine solely through them. This cuts against the message of the synoptic *Gospels* and Paul's own teachings, which held more democratically that any believer could be saved by accepting Christ. Had mainstream Roman Christianity adopted a Gnostic view of Jesus, it would probably have remained an esoteric cult without orthodox Christianity's mass appeal. *John* made it into the *New Testament* when it was assembled around 200 CE, but it must have been a close call. So too with the apocalyptic *Revelations*, also attributed to John, which takes the destruction of the Jewish state by Rome in 70 as the beginning of the "last things." To this day, *Revelations* has provided fertile imagery for Christians who long to believe that the end is near and they will be among the raptured generation.

The Christ of the Synoptic Gospels. Mark (c. 70) may have been written by the disciple himself in his old age and provides the most straightforward account of Jesus' mission. *Matthew* (c. 80) was probably assembled by followers of the Apostle who combined his emphasis on Jesus' fulfillment of the *Old Testament* prophecies with material from *Mark. Luke* (c. 90–95), which is aware of both *Mark* and *Matthew*, was written by a Greek physician, convert, and missionary concerned to make his new faith comprehensible within the context of the existing pagan religions, which were very familiar with dying and resurrected Gods. Considered chronologically, each *Gospel* shifts the blame for Jesus death more away from the Romans and towards the Jews. The reason for this is clear: the vast majority of Jews had decisively rejected Jesus as the Messiah. In their mission of converting pagans, the evangelists saw no point in offending the power of Rome. The *Gospel* authors also knew of Paul's vision: Christ resurrected and imminently to return increasing permeates them.

To identify the contribution of the *Gospels* to the Jesus legend, we merely need to add back the syncretic imports from other contemporary cults or the *Old Testa-*

ment itself that we stripped away in our discussion of the historical Jesus: a virgin, Bethlehem, or equinox birth attended by the star of the East; angels; Magi and/or Kings; an exile in Egypt; youthful genius before learned rabbis; a sudden calling; miracles; a resurrection, and so forth.

Surely if Jesus' birth had been attended by such universal celebration, he would not have spent the next thirty years in total obscurity. According to *Gospel* evidence, his own mother, who would have witnessed these events, didn't believe in his mission for many years after he died, if she ever did. Still, it's easy to see why the evangelists added successively more portents to Jesus' advent; numerous classical heroes from Achilles and Alexander to Augustus Caesar, who was ruling when Jesus was born, retroactively acquired divine parentage and miraculous births. Attributing a similar mythology to Jesus made converting the pagans a much easier task.

Another *Gospel* that didn't make it into the New Testament should be mentioned here: *The Gospel According to St. Thomas*, called by some current scholars the fifth *Gospel*. A text of this document, verified by references in the early years of the church, was discovered in Egypt in 1945. Written in the late first century CE and consisting largely of Jesus' sayings, *Thomas* corroborates or paraphrases many of Jesus' quotations from the canonical *Gospels*. It was rejected from the canon because, taken as a whole, it offers a considerably different though equally plausible interpretation of Jesus. Thomas's Jesus is even more frankly Gnostic than John's. He teaches a deeply interior struggle between light and dark, good and evil: "If you bring forth what is within you, what you bring forth will save you. If you do not bring forth what is within you, what you do not bring forth will destroy you." This prefigures Freud and coheres perfectly well with sayings of Jesus in the accepted *Gospels*; Luke himself wrote, "The Kingdom of God is within you." But it clearly took too Gnostic a slant for the editors of the *New Testament*.

Thomas also suggests more directly than John a Socratic influence on Jesus, or at least on his immediate interpreters. It repeatedly cites Socrates' maxim, "Know thyself." As summarized by Elaine H. Pagels, Princeton Professor of Religion:

> What does it mean really to know oneself? To know oneself is to have insight into one's ultimate divine identity. You can go back to understand this to the Greek models, which certainly exist. "Know yourself" is a very old Greek maxim ... that is, you have to know that your own soul is divine, and then you know that you are immortal, whereas the body is the mortal part of human existence. Now this is radicalized in the Gospel of Thomas into saying that everything that is experienced physically and through sense perception, everything that you can perceive in this way is nothing. It is, at best chaos and, at worst, it doesn't even exist in reality. The only thing that really exists is your divine spirit or your divine soul, which is identical in its quality with God himself. (For more of Pagels' analysis, see the website "from jesus to christ: the story of the storytellers: the Gospel of Thomas.")

This idea of a "divine spark" in man waiting to be called back to its heavenly home dramatically contradicts Paul's portrait of humankind as totally fallen, though it coheres well with many passages in Plato. But Thomas's rejection of the sensible world goes far beyond anything Socrates would have endorsed, and borders on some forms of Buddhism. While it seems unlikely — although not impossible — that Jesus quoted Socrates, it's certain that Paul, John, and the author of Thomas were aware of Socrates' teachings.

The evangelical embroiderings in the canonical Gospels contributed something crucial to the Jesus legend. One factor beyond Jesus' teachings or his incarnation as the resurrected Christ must be weighed heavily in determining why the initially obscure writings of Paul, Mark, Matthew, Luke, and John transformed the Roman world and the future of Western history. These five comprised perhaps the greatest single collection of poets who ever shared a cause and worked in the same period. All apparently ordinary men before they encountered Jesus, they were not afterwards. And nothing contributed more to the advance of the Christian faith than the sheer beauty of their narrative, language, imagery, and style.

6. The Argument Between Socrates and Jesus

The legends of Socrates and Jesus, rather than the historical characters themselves, went on to shape the central debate in Western Civilization. While the legends amplified, exaggerated, and even falsified elements of these two historical figures, they also preserved the radical originality of each.

Philosophers and theologians have made much over the last two millennia of the striking similarities between Socrates and Jesus. Both called their respective cultures to a higher ethical vision. Both refused to make distinctions among people on the basis of wealth, class, or ethnicity. Both believed they were acting under divine compulsion, lived extremely simple lives, taught for free, and accepted martyrdom as the final confirmation of their message. In his *Reflections on Jesus and Socrates* (New Haven, Yale University Press, 1996), Paul W. Gooch makes the case for important analogies between these two seminal geniuses:

> [W]hen we have learned something of their stories, we find ourselves intrigued with parallels, as we might be struck by resemblances between two members of a family tree. Their fathers worked with their hands, the one a sculptor, the other a carpenter. They themselves spent their time among the tradespeople and common folk, but were known more for talk than manual work. Neither had any visible means of income; both seemed to hold money of little importance. Their teaching challenged received wisdom and upset religious authorities. Both argued against doing harm to one's enemies and emphasized the value of the soul above the body. Their manner of teaching, in paradoxes and aphorisms and parables, was similarly memorable. Disciples followed them but they also made determined enemies who set about to bring them down. Though innocent, they were both convicted and died a death of witness to the truth (13–14).

Advocates for both men have repeatedly tried to enlist the other in their causes. We have seen that as early as Paul and John, Christian apologists regularly borrowed Plato's imagery and eschatology to explain and justify Christ's message. Many of the Roman Church Fathers, most notably Augustine, attempted a grand reconciliation of Christian revelation and the pagan philosophy epitomized by Socrates. Thomas Aquinas' great compendium of Christian belief, the medieval *Summa Theologica*, depended heavily on Aristotle for its logical method and its proofs of the existence of God.

On the other hand, humanists have regularly tried to cast Jesus as a sort of peasant Jewish classical philosopher. By emphasizing his charity, his concern for the unfortunate, his forgiveness of sinners, his indifference to the social, material, and political distinctions of the world, philosophers from Roman times through the Renaissance, the Enlightenment and to the liberal churches and theologians of our own day have portrayed Jesus as essentially a Socratic teacher of ethics.

But on close examination, these resemblances, though important, turn out to be merely superficial and biographical. The similarities between their narratives and many shared values explain why each man has held an enduring grip on the imagination of the Western world. But in fact they disagreed fundamentally on almost everything: the nature of the divine, the proper practice of reason, the definition of love, the well-spring of ethics, the role of the law, the origin and end of the world, and the proper relation of the individual to the larger political and social community. What is most remarkable, then, in comparing Socrates and Jesus, is how they arrived at similarly humane and world-transforming conclusions by means of radically different premises and methodologies.

Matthew Arnold, in "Hebraism and Hellenism" (*Culture and Anarchy*, Chapter IV, 1868) identified the Greeks and the Jews as the inventors of the two great Western ways of seeing the world rather than emphasizing their similarities. He credits each with creating a distinct vocabulary for understanding the forces that shape our world and calls them:

> the two races of men who have supplied the most signal and splendid manifestations of [strategies to interpret reality], we may call them respectively the forces of Hebraism and Hellenism. Hebraism and Hellenism — between these two points of influence moves our world. At one time it feels more powerfully the attraction of one of them, at another time of the other; and it ought to be, though it never is, evenly and happily balanced between them.

Arnold from the outset sees Hebraism and Hellenism as different but of equal validity. He recognizes that at various times in Western culture, one or the other has predominated. He identifies them as the two poles of Western culture. And he clearly believes that Western culture is at its healthiest and strongest when their influence is equally balanced. He goes on:

> The final aim of both Hellenism and Hebraism, as of all great spiritual disciplines, is no doubt the same: man's perfection or salvation. The very language which they both of them use in schooling us to reach this aim is often identical. Even when their language indicates by variation — sometimes a broad variation, often a but slight and subtle variation, — different courses of thought which are uppermost in each discipline, even then the unity of the final end and aim is still apparent.

We can quarrel with Arnold on this point: Greek perfection and Judeo-Christian salvation are very different things, as we will find in the following discussion. He wrote at a time when to equate Greek Eros and Christian Agape as pursuing equally valid ends was still a controversial position to take in a formally Christian country, and so he is concerned at some level to make their eschatological purposes ultimately identical. But he is very acute on the differences between their methods or approaches to the ultimate good:

> Still, they pursue this aim by very different courses. The uppermost idea with Hellenism is to see things as they really are; the uppermost idea with Hebraism is conduct and obedience. Nothing can do away with this ineffaceable difference. The Greek quarrel with the body and its desires is, that they hinder right thinking; the Hebrew quarrel with them is, that they hinder right acting.

> At the bottom of both the Greek and the Hebrew notion is the desire, native in man, for reason and the will of God, the feeling after the universal order — in a word, the love of God. But, while Hebraism seizes upon certain plain, capital intimations of the universal order, and rivets himself, one might say, with unequalled grandeur of earnestness and intensity on the study and observance of them, the bent of Hellenism is to follow, with flexible activity, the whole play of the universal order, to be apprehensive of missing any part of it, of sacrificing one part to another, to slip away from resting in this or that intimation of it, however capital. An unclouded clearness of mind, an unimpeded play of thought, is what this bent drives at. The governing idea of Hellenism is *spontaneity of consciousness*; that of Hebraism, *strictness of conscience*.

> Self-conquest, self-devotion, the following of not of our own individual will, but the will of God, *obedience*, is the fundamental idea of this form, also, of the discipline to which we have attached the general name of Hebraism.

Arnold is right to emphasize the wide gulf between the Hebraic focus on "capital imitations of universal order" and the Hellenic focus on "the whole play of the universal order." For the Hebrew, God is all, and his various manifestations in the universe are often distractions or worse, occasions for sin. For the Hellene, the play of the universal order in all its manifestations is the point, evidence, increasingly pleasurable steps on the quest towards the Divine. Arnold takes refuge here in an important ambiguity that furthers his goal of equating the two systems as equally valid: the "love of God" can mean either man's love for God or God's love for man, a fundamental difference between the two systems that Arnold fudges. He goes on:

> Both Hellenism and Hebraism arise out of the wants of human nature, and address themselves to satisfy those wants. But their methods are so different they lay stress on such different points, and call into being by their respective disciplines such different activities, that the face which human nature presents when it passes from the hands of one of them to the other, is no longer the same. To get rid of one's ignorance, to see things as they are, and by seeing them as they are to see in them their beauty, is the simple and attractive ideal which Hellenism holds out before human nature; and from the simplicity and charm of this ideal, Hellenism, and human life in the hands of Hellenism, is invested with a kind of aerial ease, clearness, and radiancy; they are full of what we call sweetness and light. Difficulties are kept out of view, and the beauty and rationalness of the ideal have all our thoughts.
>
> It is all very well to talk of getting rid of one's ignorance of seeing things in their reality, seeing them in their beauty, but how is this to be done when there is something which thwarts and spoils all our efforts?
>
> This something is *sin*; and the space which sin fills in Hebraism, as com-pared to Hellenism, is indeed prodigious. This obstacle to perfection fills the whole scene, and perfection appears remote and rising away from earth, in the background. Under the name of sin, the difficulties of know-ing oneself and conquering oneself which impede man's path to perfection, become, for Hebraism, a positive, active entity hostile to man, a mysterious power which I heard Dr. Pusey the other day, in one of his most impres-sive sermons, compare to a hideous hunchback sitting on our shoulders, and which it is the main business of our lives to abhor and oppose. The discipline of the Old Testament may be summed up as a discipline teach-ing us to abhor and flee from sin; the discipline of the New Testament, as a discipline teaching us to die to it. As Hellenism speaks of thinking clearly, seeing things in their essence and beauty, as a grand and precious feat for man to achieve, so Hebraism speaks of becoming conscious of sin, of wak-ening to sin, as a feat of this kind.

Socrates would say, of course, that what the Hebrews define as sin is in fact ignorance or error, acts against our own self-interest, and a profound chasm lies between these two perspectives. One invites us into the joys of the sensual world, the other warns us against them in horror. Arnold does not resolve these contra-dictions. He is determined to assign equal value to both systems and in any case the only possible solution is not to assert a false equivalence (though he does in the end), but rather accept a dialectical interaction. Still, he does great service to the effort to understand how Hebraism and Hellenism have served as the alpha and omega of Western culture, the two poles between which it finds itself oscil-lating, constantly suspended.

To get to the crux of the fundamental disagreement between Socrates and Jesus which has been so fruitful for the subsequent development of Western civilization, we must start with each teachers' view of the essential nature of the universe, that is, the relation between humanity and the eternal as facilitated by Love. For Socrates, coming from the Greek pantheistic tradition, the ideal was immanent in the material world, intermittently approachable through reason, and mediated by Eros: love defined as the connective attraction that binds everything from the slime to the divine. The divine or ideal was accessible through methods of inquiry available to human beings, and Eros, or attraction, was the glue that bound this unitary world together. For Jesus, coming from the Jewish tradition of God's radical Otherness, so absolute a divide existed between the material and the divine that humankind could not feel or reason its way to ultimate things. As fallen (rather than fallible) creatures, people were utterly cut off from any knowledge of God other than his Agape: an unconditional love bestowed for miraculous reasons on a totally unworthy object. For Socrates, wisdom comes largely from the application of reason and inquiry — though he allows for moments of inspiration such as the words whispered in his ear by his daimon. For Jesus, wisdom consists in submitting oneself entirely to an inruption of revelation from the divine. In the Socratic system, man finds his way towards God. In Christianity (and the Judeo–Christian tradition in general) God finds his way towards man.

Since both Socrates and Jesus saw the adhesive force of the universe in what we call "love," nothing can be more instructive in exploring their differences than to compare Eros and Agape, and we depend heavily here on the magisterial work of the Swedish scholar Anders Nygren, *Agape and Eros* (New York, Harper and Row, 1969).

Eros

The doctrine of Eros originated in the ancient mystery religions and achieved its definitive formulation in the dialogues of Plato, especially in the *Symposium*. For the Greeks, the Orpheus cycle explicated the beauty and danger of Eros. Zeus had decided to give his son Dionysus, god of wine, sensuality, and frenzy, rulership of the world. But while Dionysus was a child the Titans, the primitive gods overthrown by the Olympians, lured him into their power, killed him, and devoured him. In revenge, Zeus destroyed the Titans with a thunderbolt and constructed the race of men from their ashes. Henceforth, humankind was double natured: of the earth because of its Titanic component, but with a spark of divinity from the god the Titans had consumed. Dionysiac cults with their attendant orgies and drug-induced ecstasies proliferated in pre-classical Greece, often against opposition from more conservative and decorous religious traditions.

Orpheus came to embody the Dionysus legend because he at first opposed the cult and in consequence was torn to pieces in a Dionysiac outburst by the women of Thrace. His dismembered head, still singing, washed out to sea and landed on the island of Lesbos, giving birth to music and poetry. Subsequent Orphic cults, somewhat domesticated, found homes in the classical Greek polises, especially

Athens, and presided over many major religious and cultural events. Greek tragedy evolved directly from the responsive chanting that was the centerpiece of
Athenian Orphic festivals. Nygren writes:

> The circle of ideas in which we now find ourselves is by no means con-
> fined to Orphism, but appears with insignificant variations wherever we
> turn in the world of ancient Mystery religions. There is in man a Divine es-
> sence which is held captive contrary to its nature in the fetters of sense ...
> It is this immortal, divine, essential being of man that the Mysteries [such
> as the annual initiations at Eleusis near Athens] seek to redeem ... Man is
> the offspring of God; the rational part of his nature is a fragment of the Di-
> vine cosmic reason. What he needs, therefore, is to be made aware of the
> degradation of his present state, put off the earthly trappings that prevent
> his true nature from coming to light, and being thus purified ascend to his
> heavenly home ... Even though ancient Mystery-piety is vividly conscious
> of the human soul's ... need of help, its cardinal assumption is none the
> less always the original Divine dignity of the soul. This is the presupposi-
> tion which alone makes possible man's ascent to the divine sphere; there
> is no insuperable barrier between the human and the Divine, because the
> human soul is fundamentally a Divine being (*Agape and Eros*, 165).

Significantly, Plato does not attribute his definition of Eros directly to Socrates, but rather has Socrates report what he has heard from Diotima, the
prophetess of Mantinea, thus maintaining the link back to the original Orphic
cults. Plato's innovation in the *Symposium*, crucial to the whole future of Western
thought, consists in his assertion that the path from corrupt matter to divinity is
a continuum within each individual, and that it can be followed largely by means
of reason, that is, philosophy. Here he creates a bridge between the ecstatic revelation of the Mystery religions and rational observation of the sensual world.
Plato describes his key parable, the story of the Cave, in the seventh Book of the
Republic. Although Nygren's argument is building towards the climactic resurgence of Agape in the Protestant Reformation, he does justice to Plato:

> Our position in the sense-world is there compared to that of men sitting
> in an underground cave, able to see only the shadows on the cave wall.
> Those who have never seen anything else but these shadows believe them
> to be the true reality. But the philosopher, who has got rid of his chains,
> climbed out of the dark cave, and ascended from the gloom of the sense-
> world to the brightness of the Ideas, knows that true reality is only to be
> found in this upper world and that the sense world shows us only the
> shadow of real being (*Agape and Eros*, 171).

Thus, for Plato, Eros can be considered a rational doctrine of salvation. If we
direct our love to its appropriate object, the real things, the Forms or Ideas, we
move out of the shadows and into the light. But, and this is crucial, we can become aware of the light at first only by paying careful, rational attention to the
shadows. Plato achieves his most mature definition of Eros in the *Symposium*:

> The right way of Eros ... whether one goes along or is led by another, is
> to begin with the beautiful things that are here and ascend ever upwards

aiming at the beauty that is above, climbing, as it were on a ladder from one beautiful body to two, and from two to all the others, and from beautiful bodies to beautiful actions and from beauty of actions to beautiful forms of knowledge, till at length from these one reaches that knowledge which is the knowledge of nothing other than Beauty itself (*Symposium*, 211).

Plato could not make it clearer that Eros stirs first in sensual attraction. This premise distinguishes Eros decisively from Judeo–Christian tradition, rooted in *Genesis*, which sees sensuality as punishment for the original sin of disobeying God. It also explains the erotic in Eros: because each individual consists of a continuum from dust to divinity, all sensory — and sensual — experiences and attractions (the adhesive nature of love) can foreshadow — and point the way toward — the Ideal. The love of beauty, sexual desire, the aesthetic perfection of an athlete, art object, or idea, all, experienced sensually and rationally examined, can lead us to the divine. Here we find the essence of Erotic love.

Norman O. Brown, in his bravura attempt to psychoanalyze history (*Life Against Death*, Wesleyan University Press, Middletown, Connecticut, 1985) traces sublimation — the redirection of sexual energy to external objects of increasingly spiritual value — to the shamans of ancient mystery cults, and claims that Socratic philosophy owes much to them:

Sublimation thus rests on a mind-body dualism, not as a philosophical doctrine, but as a psychic fact implicit in the behavior of sublimators, no matter what their conscious philosophy may be. Hence Plato remains the truest philosopher, since he defined philosophy as sublimation and correctly articulated as its goal the elevation of Spirit above Matter. But, as Frazer showed, the doctrine of the external or separable soul is as old as humanity itself.

The original sublimator, the historical ancestor of philosopher and prophet and poet, is the primitive shaman, with his techniques for ecstatic departure from the body, soul-levitation, soul-transmigration, and celestial navigation. The history of sublimation has yet to be written but ... it is evident that Platonism, and hence all Western philosophy, is civilized shamanism — a continuation of the shamanistic quest for a high mode of being — by new methods adapted to the urban life. The intermediate links are Pythagoras, with his soul-transmigrations, and Parmenides, the great rationalist whose rationalistic vision was vouchsafed to him by the goddess after a ride through the sky to the Palace of Night (157–8).

How could modern Western reason have been born from a Mystery cult? This question obsessed Nietzsche, and he offers an appropriately paradoxical and poetic hint in the opening paragraph of *The Birth of Tragedy from the Spirit of Music* (New York, Random House, 1956, trans. Francis Golffing):

Much will have been gained for esthetics once we have succeeded in apprehending directly — rather than by merely ascertaining — that art owes its continuous evolution to the Apollonian–Dionysiac duality, even as the propagation of the species depends on the duality of the sexes, their constant conflicts and periodic acts of reconciliation. I have borrowed my adjectives from the Greeks, who developed their mystical doctrines of art through plausible embodiments, not through purely conceptual means. It is by those two art-sponsoring deities, Apollo and Dionysus, that we are made to recognize the tremendous split, as regards both origins and objectives, between the plastic, Apollonian arts and the non-visual art of music inspired by Dionysus. The two creative tendencies developed alongside one another, usually in fierce opposition, each by its taunts forcing the other to more energetic production, both perpetuating in a discordant concord that agon which the term art but feebly denominates: until at last, by the thaumaturgy of an Hellenic act of will, the pair accepted the yoke of marriage and, in this condition, begot Attic tragedy, which exhibits the salient features of both parents.

Nietzsche makes his devotion to Eros clear from the start. He approvingly quotes Plato via Schopenhauer: "Men of philosophical disposition are known for their constant premonition that our everyday reality, too, is an illusion, hiding another, totally different kind of reality. It was Schopenhauer who considered the ability to view at certain times all men and things as mere phantoms or dream images to be the true mark of philosophic talent" (*Birth*, 20) — a perception that couldn't be more Platonic.

Nietzsche believed that the Apollonian structure of reason, symmetry, and classical beauty presented to us by Greek culture was erected upon a foundation of grave dread; he quotes Dionysus' companion Silenus, who when trapped by King Midas and asked what he considered man's greatest gift, laughed shrilly and said: "Ephemeral wretch, begotten by accident and toil, why do you force me to tell you what it would be your greatest good not to hear? What would be best for you is quite beyond your reach: never to have been born, not to be, to be nothing. But the second best is to die soon" (*Birth*, 29). Here Nietzsche — and the shadow of Dionysus — warns that all the trappings of rational culture and esthetics are a beautiful illusion erected over a seething swamp of chaos, horror, and death: random nature. Apollo personifies the *principium individuationis* — the integrity of the individual personality. Dionysus personifies the periodic need to escape the chains of individuation and sink back into the primal One (what Freud called the "oceanic" feeling). Eros is the Greek's answer to this conundrum: by yoking Apollo and Dionysus they preserve in dynamic tension the two poles of human life — transience and a connection to the eternal. The result is a compelling, livable, progressive narrative.

Nietzsche argues that the strain of maintaining the Apollonian illusion (Plato's "Ideal") tries individuality beyond endurance, and that only periodic submersion of the self in the sensual Dionysiac chaos offered by Orphism can "tear asunder the veil of Maya, to sink back into the original oneness of nature...." (27) As Nietzsche famously asked, "How else could life have been borne by a race so hypersensitive, so emotionally intense, so equipped for suffering?" (30) Nietzsche concludes that the prodigious contributions of the ancient Greeks to the arts and science were possible precisely because they had built into their society, through their religious ceremonies and tragedies, periodic release valves in the form of exposure to raw Dionysiac despair, pansexuality, and redemption by Orphic ecstasy. Eros provides an ultimately spiritual connection between the slime and the ideal, and a way for fallible human beings to negotiate the journey both ways.

Analyzing Nietzsche via Freud, Norman O. Brown observes:

> Apollo is the god of form — of plastic form in art, of rational form in thought, of civilized form in life. But the Apollonian form is form as the negation of instinct. "Nothing too much," says the Delphic wisdom; "Observe the limit, fear authority, bow before the divine." Hence Apollonian form is form negating matter, immortal form, that is to say, by the irony that overtakes all flight from death, deathly form... (He) is also the god who sustains "displacement from below upward," who gave man a head divine and told him to look upward at the stars ... As Nietzsche divined, the stuff of which the Apollonian world is made is the dream. Apollo rules over the fair world of appearance as a projection of the inner world of fantasy; and the limit which he must observe "that delicate boundary which the dream-picture must not overstep," is the boundary of repression separating the dream from instinctual reality.

> But the Greeks who gave us Apollo also gave us the alternative, Nietzsche's Dionysius. Dionysius is not dream but drunkenness; not life kept at a distance and seen through a veil but life complete and immediate ... The Dionysian "is no longer an artist, he has become a work of art" (*Life Against Death*, 174).

Artists who create poems, paintings, sculptures, or great architecture are by these terms not works of art because they are sublimating their fantasies into things of beauty, an Apollonian projection. Human beings become works of art when they dance, act, make love, or otherwise overflow with a life force that breaks free of the Apollonian ego. Individuals open to the Dionysian, as Rilke tells us, do not "die with unlived lines in their bodies." But individuals who give in to the Dionysiac impulses unreservedly, and without the protection of a proven ritual that guarantees a return to the Apollonian ego, become monsters, or are torn apart like Orpheus.

Nietzsche's insistence on the antiquity and centrality of Orphism frightened and repelled most classical scholars of the nineteenth and twentieth centuries, who were determined to see Greek culture as unique, original, and entirely Apollonian. This was all of a piece with the same scholars' attempts to suppress the central role of homoeroticism in Greek philosophy. But a recent study by Walter Burkert, *Babylon, Memphis, Persepolis: Eastern Contexts of Greek Culture* (Cambridge, Harvard University Press, 2005) decisively demonstrates that Herodotus and Nietzsche were right: Orphism had its origins in Persia and especially in Egypt and supplied a dominant component of Greek culture from its origins. In any event, the idea that classical Greece sprang full-blown from the head of Zeus underrates its real achievement: the transformation of its Eastern and Egyptian sources into something wonderful and new, Western civilization, by the yoking of Dionysius and Apollo.

Plato's mature summary of Eros, predominantly in the *Phaedrus*, gathers together all these strands of Eros into a doctrine that could as well be called religious as philosophical, although the distinction was fluid in his time. Adopting the Orphic assumption that each soul has a divine spark that exists in eternity, Plato extrapolates that in a pre-existent state the soul must have been exposed to the pure ideals of beauty, truth, and good. This explains Socrates' interrogatory method: every individual has within his or her self the memory of these divine things and needs only to examine her conventional prejudices and false assumptions for this inner light to become clear. Plato also believes that the "divine spark" of the soul survives into other individuals or states, although his version of the afterlife is much vaguer than Jesus'. As Nygren says, "Just as the stone in virtue of its nature is attracted downward, so the soul in virtue of its divine nature is attracted upward.... This upward attraction of the soul is Eros" (*Agape and Eros*, 172).

Eros can be kindled by esthetic beauty or sensual attraction because they are the shadows of Heavenly Eros or union with the divine. This characteristic of Eros tells us something important about the gods, for one can desire only what one doesn't have. Since the gods have everything, their function is to be the object of Eros, not subject to it. They dwell in a state of ideal bliss that every wise man aspires to acquire through love of the good.

AGAPE

If Eros is all about man's love for the gods, Agape is all about God's love for man. As fallen creatures, the Jews of the *Old Testament* were separated from God not by gradations of reality that might be ascended through disciplined wisdom, but rather by a vast gulf, an utter difference in the nature of being. This gulf could not be crossed from man's side but only by a gift of revelation from God. For the Jews of Jesus' day, God's love, Agape, had been granted in the form of the Law, which allowed its observers to live in consonance with God's wishes.

Jesus adopted this cosmology but at the same time transformed it. Because the Law was God's Word to man, Judaism had become extremely legalistic: the righteous obeyed God's law and those who did not were sinners. The *Old Testament*'s essential plot is the story of the Jews being specially chosen as God's people, departing from His Law, suffering terrible retribution for doing so, and returning to it with fear and trembling. Jesus did not overthrow the God of the *Old Testament*; his revolution consisted in saying, "I came not to call the righteous, but sinners." Jesus implied strongly that one could obey the Law perfectly and still be a sinner. All humankind was equally fallen and unworthy in God's eyes; the radical gap between God and man could be overcome only by a spontaneous outpouring of love from God that included all people equally. He "fulfilled the Law," in other words, by saying that God's love, and the salvation it promised, applied equally to all men. Agape fuels many of the most beautiful passages in the *Old Testament*, especially the *Psalms*. Jesus — or at least, in his name, Paul — makes Agape absolute and apocalyptic.

God had invited all humankind into a fellowship with him and Jesus was the messenger of that good news. This vision opened the way for Paul's mission to the Gentiles and made Christianity, unlike Judaism, a serious candidate to become a universal religion. Paul seized this opportunity and indeed created the foundation for a catholic — or all-inclusive — church. And no formulation of God's Agape is more rigorous or anti-Erotic than Paul's. Man's role in this drama, then, was simply to accept God's love and join in fellowship with Him.

Nygren stresses the essential features of Agape:

> "Agape is spontaneous and unmotivated." God's love is not a response to man's worthiness but despite his unworthiness. In this sense, it is the exact inverse of Eros both in its direction (God to man rather than man to God), and in its miraculous lack of self-interest (since while man has much to gain in approaching God, God has nothing to gain in saving man). In Nygren's phrase, "Agape is indifferent to value."

> "Agape is creative ... The man who is loved by God has no value in himself; what gives him value is precisely that God loves him. Agape is a value-creating principle."

> "Agape is the initiator of a fellowship with God." Since there is no way from man to God, Agape is God's way to create a community with humankind (*Agape and Eros*, 77–81).

As Agape is "spontaneous and unmotivated, uncalculating, unlimited, and unconditional," so must the individual who has received this divine gift love God and love his neighbors — including his enemies. As Jesus said to his disciples, "Freely you have received, freely give." God's Agape creates adhesion among mankind and between man and God, the new thing, the spontaneous forgiveness and fellowship, the community of the forlorn and oppressed, that came into the world in Jesus' teachings and helps explain the extraordinary success of primitive Christianity.

EROS AND AGAPE

We can now fully identify the fundamental contrasts between the teachings of Socrates and the teachings of Jesus:

1. Socratics taught that the universe was of one substance, a continuum from the material to the divine. Primitive Christians taught that there was a radical disjunction between the material and the spiritual, man and God.

2. Consequently, Socratics professed a higher pantheism: that the divine is inherent in the material, and that the gods, or Ideas, are knowable, if only im-

perfectly. Christians taught the world was worthless except insofar as it could — and would — be redeemed by the arbitrary act of an inscrutable God.

3. Socratic philosophy implied that history was perdurable, perhaps cyclical, and that its end could not be known. Christianity taught that history had a beginning (the Creation), a middle (the advent of Jesus), and an end (the Last Judgment).

4. While Socrates' philosophy included the prospect that an individual could receive inspiration from a higher source, his primary tool for interpreting reality was reason. While Jesus could use techniques of logical argument, his sole method for interpreting ultimate things was faith.

5. Socratic ethics derived from the natural acquisitive instinct to better the self by seeking out the good. Christian ethics derived from faith that God had spontaneously summoned mankind to a higher order of behavior in the person of Jesus.

6. Eros, based on attraction to material things insofar as they were reflections of ultimate things, valued sexual energy in many forms. It could create an erotic bond between student and teacher that stimulated education and tenderness — even if it was not acted upon physically; the chief evidence of Socrates' remarkable self-control was that he did not sleep with the willing and beautiful Alcibiades. Desire for a lover could train the soul in how to seek out a higher good, and in fact could light up the beauty of the world, providing evidence of an even higher ideal Eros-object. There is no credible evidence that Jesus ever had sex, and much suggesting he did not, although there is an erotic tinge to the descriptions of his relationship with the "beloved" disciple John. In any event, his immediate disciples, prominently Paul, saw sexual love as a curse inflicted by man's fallen state.

7. Because he did not expect an abrupt and imminent end to this world, Socrates took great interest in politics, that is, the proper relation of the individual to the state. Because he believed his Second Coming in glory was imminent, Jesus displayed little interest in social or political relations beyond the interpersonal love and fellowship of believers that God had commanded.

8. Socrates and Jesus profoundly and importantly disagreed on the source of evil in the world. Socrates simply and elegantly equates evil and wrongdoing with ignorance because he believed a fully informed person who "knew himself" would naturally pursue the good out of enlightened self-interest. Jesus and his interpreters, by contrast, believed that evil came naturally to fallen man and that only the unmerited Agape of a fathomlessly generous God could redeem humankind into his fellowship. Since explaining the existence of evil and suffering lies at the core of every philosophical and theological system, these radically opposed teleologies defined the agenda for the future of Western thought in ethics, politics, literature, religion, and popular culture.

9. Socrates and Jesus held antithetical views of how human beings could be encouraged to live ethical lives: shame versus guilt. Classical morality was enforced largely by shame: standards of right behavior had been illustrated in Homer's great epics and elaborated by the philosophers; every educated Greek knew them by heart, and failure to abide by them would be punished by public humiliation (Pericles defines this process exactly in his great Funeral Oration cited earlier). In theory, therefore, one could live a perfectly ethical life, and most of his successors believed Socrates had done so. By contrast, according to the Judeo–Christian tradition, all humankind had been born guilty, so the struggle to live a moral life occurred within the individual, rather than between the self and its social context. What mattered was not what others thought of you; it was what God thought of you. Hence Christ had died to redeem the otherwise unforgivable guilt of all humankind.

Capturing something essential about Eros, Camille Paglia in *Sexual Personae* (New York, Random House, 1991) writes, "Paganism is eye-intense." She goes further:

> [T]he eye is the avenue of Eros.... Judeo–Christianity has failed to control the pagan Western eye. Our thought processes were formed in Greece and inherited by Rome ... Intellectual inquiry and logic are pagan. Every inquiry is preceded by a roving eye, and once the eye begins to rove, it cannot be morally controlled. Judaism, due to its fear of the eye, put a taboo on visual representation. Judaism is based on word rather than image. Christianity followed suit, until it drifted into pictorialism in order to appeal to the pagan masses (32–33).

Paglia distills the debate between Socrates and Jesus: the first believed we could approach the purpose of the universe through analysis of the visible world; the second believed we must turn away from it to apprehend ultimate truths.

To summarize:

EROS	AGAPE
Material–divine continuum	Material–divine divide
Pantheism	Monotheism
Man seeks God	God seeks man
Humankind partly divine	Humankind entirely fallen
History ongoing	History about to end
Reason	Faith
Sensual	Anti-Sensual
Secular government	Theocracy
Evil equals ignorance	Evil man's natural state
Shame	Guilt

Eye	Ear
Immanence	Transcendence
Classic	Romantic
Right thinking	Right acting
Foreground	Background

The struggle between these two systems of ultimate value has generated the history of the Western World. Virtually everything progressive and reactionary, creative or destructive that has characterized European, and later, American, history, has resulted from the struggle between them. Eras of Western history over the last twenty-five hundred years have been characterized by periods of Socratic dominance — Hellenism, the early Roman Empire, the Renaissance, the Enlightenment — periods of Christ's dominance — the late Roman Empire, the early Middle Ages, the Reformation — and the intervening eras in which some synthesis of the two defined prevailing values and behavior.

The debate between Socrates and Jesus explains why Western culture has, with the intermission of the Middle Ages, consistently run ahead of other great civilizations scientifically, economically, politically, and socially in terms of including the largest proportion of its people in governance and in giving them the widest scope to explore their individuality. One can argue whether this is a good thing: Marx and many others have; but the fact is indisputable. Other great cultures had their yins and yangs (feminine and masculine principles); China for example alternated between the influences of Confucius and Lao-tze, and South Asian civilizations between Hinduism and Buddhism. But these pairings were on the same continuum, matters of emphasis, rather than being mortal enemies at their cores.

What made the interaction between Socrates and Jesus unique? All meaning beyond raw fact must be contained in metaphor, and Joseph Campbell offers a suggestive clue in his examination of primitive mythologies. After exploring how all cultures share a bedrock of myth based upon the human life cycle combined with variations adapted to local circumstances, he writes: "We observe, for example, that whereas in the Greek and Hebrew versions man is split in two by a God, in the Chinese, Hindu, and Australian it is the God who divides and multiplies" (*The Masks of God*, 109).

Socratic and Judeo–Christian tradition agree that god(s) created man from the slime. In the Greek tradition, man arises from the Titans of the earth who have consumed the divine Dionysus. According to Plato's development of the myth, based on ancient sources, the gods originally created humans doubled: man joined to man, man joined to woman, and woman to woman. Realizing the great power of these new creatures, the gods split them so that ever after each mutilated being must go through life seeking out its other half. In the Hebrew version, God creates an androgynous Adam out of earth also, and then splits him into the sexes by molding Eve out of his rib. Both Western traditions show divine forces shaping humankind from muck and then fragmenting it into contending parts.

By comparison, in the Hindu creation myth:

> The universal self becomes divided immediately after conceiving and uttering the pronoun "I" (Sanskrit *aham* or Om). This illustrates the fundamental Indian conviction that a sense of ego is the root of world illusion. Ego generates fear and desire, and these are the passions that animate all life and even all being; for it is only after the concept of "I" has been established that fear of one's own destruction can develop or any desire for personal enjoyment (Campbell, 109).

Most great civilizations have been based on attempts to flee the ego, while Western civilization has uniquely fled towards it, which may be why the great religious figures of the East are usually portrayed as wise, serene, and joyous, while those of the West often appear angry and judgmental. It is another signifier of problematical Western dynamism.

A vast gulf lies between the eastern conceptions of man as fragments of a broken God that can at least theoretically recover its original unity and the Western formulation in both Greek and Jewish thought that man's nature is essentially different from, and potentially opposed to, God. In eastern cultures divinity is attempting to reassemble itself, while in Western civilization man is striving with divinity for dominance, and flirts as often with the concept that man created God as with the belief that God created man. This dualism, and the further dualism between Socrates' and Jesus' versions of how the God–man battle is ultimately to be settled, has provided the energy driving Western civilization.

7. Socrates and Jesus Fight for the Roman Empire

The followers of Socrates and the followers of Jesus struggled for spiritual — and ultimately political — control of the Roman world. Many other movements contended, of course — other mystery religions, the official Roman political, legal, cultic, and military systems, foreign Empires and barbarian tribes, Christian heresies — but only these two systems offered a comprehensive positive explanation for the purpose of human life. Only one other entry — the "wisdom of Silenus," that life was ultimately meaningless — offered similar coherence and universality. But since it held out no theory of conduct except a sort of hopeless hedonism, nihilism was never likely to develop a mass or even an elite following. A superficial review of the steady ascent of Christianity to control of the Empire by the fourth century would suggest that Jesus won. But closer examination of this struggle reveals that this first match between Socrates and Jesus ended in a draw.

The emergence of the Roman Empire during Jesus' lifetime represented the triumph of cosmopolitan Hellenism over the more martial, almost tribal culture of the Roman Republic. Indeed, rather than considering Hellenism as a degenerate interlude between the glory that was Greece and the grandeur that was Rome, it would be more accurate to say that the Hellenistic civilization founded by Alexander the Great lasted for a thousand years, spreading to Western Europe and persisting well into what we call the Early Middle Ages.

There was some truth to the charge of degeneracy during the first two centuries of Hellenism; while major advances occurred in science and philosophy, mass Hellenistic culture was overrun with superficiality, a rhetorical emphasis on style over substance, superstition, fear, and perhaps most costly, carelessness in preserving its heritage. Tarn sadly explains the loss of all but fragments of the great history of Hieronymus of Cardia on the grounds that "He neglected style and therefore perished" (*Hellenistic Civilization*, 284). The emphasis on style and rhetorical excess over substance seems a true charge against the early years of Hellenism, although it might be much mitigated if we had the evidence destroyed by the great fire that consumed the Library of Alexandria. Perhaps the greatest catastrophe in the history of human knowledge, the loss of the greatest collection of documents in the classical world has immeasurably impoverished our understanding not only of early Hellenism, but of Persian, Egyptian, Babylonian and Middle Eastern history, literature, religion, and philosophy, going back to very ancient times.

The Roman Republic bequeathed the Empire stable provincial governments (except in times of excessively greedy governors or civil war), an enduring infrastructure, generally sound finances, and a magnificent highway system. But it was to the Hellenistic states with their god–kings, efficient bureaucracies, and bustling commerce that Rome turned when it sought a template for Empire. The Roman genius for imperial government provided an effective distribution system, first for Hellenistic culture, and second for that child of Hellenism, Christianity. Although Latin remained the language of government, law, and religion, the *lingua franca* of the Empire and its successor states was demotic Greek, and this remained true even in Western Europe until the seventh century.

The impact of Hellenism on Roman culture resulted not only in a more Oriental style of government, but also in a gradual defensive retreat by Latin literature in the face of Greek "plain speech." A study of the most influential Latin writers and philosophers from the late Republic to the end of the second century suggests that a form of Stoicism, modified by elements of Cynicism and Epicureanism, was well on the way to becoming the dominant belief system of the Empire. Catullus, Ovid, Seneca, Martial, Horace, Tacitus, Juvenal, the Plinys, and others all drew on the main strands of post-Socratic philosophy to offer alternately a noble vision of a rational humanity, a witty critique of contemporary society, and a skeptical view of divinity. Cicero was no original thinker, although history owes him a debt of gratitude for his elegant and careful summaries of the various Greek philosophical schools. Virgil's early poems and the *Aeneid* self-consciously import into Latin the elegiac, pastoral, and epic achievements of the ancient Greeks. The second century Emperor Marcus Aurelius, in his *Meditations*, came as close as a philosopher probably could to providing directions for living a wise, happy, and productive life. He portrayed the universe as a divine, conscious being, evolving towards perfection, which introduced "the sense of an ending" (Empson's phrase) to Heavenly Eros. The Socratic tradition appeared to have triumphed, at least among the educated classes.

But read with hindsight, most of these writers were painfully aware that they were cutting against the real trends in popular culture, imitating the great Greeks or mocking the decadent present. They sound nostalgic or bitter, mostly orators, critics, propagandists, or journalists rather than original visionaries. They reported and synthesized the views of their great predecessors; they offered mordant insights into the foibles of a cosmopolitan society, but their work — even the great history of Tacitus or the sound and noble reflections of Aurelius — have a valedictory air. As Peter Gay writes of the second century:

> This age, which Gibbon singled out as the happiest and most prosperous period in history, offers melancholy evidence that while freedom and security may be favorable preconditions for artistic vitality, they do not guarantee it: under the Antonines, political stability and cultural weariness existed side by side.
>
> There was nothing new about this lassitude, this gradual return from thought to myth, from independence to nostalgia: symptoms of this "failure of nerve" (as Gilbert Murray has called it) were visible as early as the last years of the Republic. By the second century the symptoms were marked, and everywhere: the Roman Empire was swarming with Oriental superstitions and elaborate mystery religions; the masses and even educated men were overwhelmed by a disturbing feeling of sinfulness and of dependence on inscrutable powers, a growing desire for immortality and an obsessive fear of demons, a curiosity about religion that moved from intellectual inquiry to the pathetic hope for salvation. It seemed as though the traditional choice offered by the great philosophers — the life of reason, responsibility, autonomy, and freedom from dependence on myth — was too strenuous or too frightening.... The philosophers did not deign to educate the believers, and in time the believers overwhelmed the philosophers (*The Enlightenment*, New York, Knopf, 1966, 118–19).

It's interesting that as fine a historian as Gay would suggest that settled ages should provide the most fertile ground for great thought or art. To cite only three examples, the brilliant Athenian century was accomplished by a city of about a quarter of a million people in constant conflict and turmoil after the giddy triumph generated by victory over the Persians, the Medici Renaissance was achieved in a still smaller town riven by civic strife, and the genius of Elizabethan England occurred in a previously provincial country under constant threat from invasion and religious war. Great art and thought tends to be the product of heroic and dangerous ages. Perhaps because they lived at a peaceful time in a great cosmopolitan Empire, none of the Roman Stoics or wits provided a compelling vision of the purpose of life accessible to the average citizen. They exhibited that invariable sign of a late civilization best described by Northrup Frye: irony.

Ironic intellectuals were inevitably unable to develop mass appeal. The mystery religions that rushed into this gap derived equally from Platonism and the East. In the second and third centuries, crossbreeding between Neo-Platonist philosophers and Christian theologians caused the two systems — in competition for the same believers — to become more and more alike. Philosophers, most notably Plotinus, elaborated the gradations of Eros from man to God in a way that suggested a stairway to salvation. On the other side, Church Fathers from Origen to Augustine, in their efforts to develop a comprehensive theology, created a similar syncretic system with a strong Erotic component. They drew heavily on both Plato and the various strands of Neo-Platonism. Helpful intermediaries such as saints and angels were interposed as steps from man to God. It became common among orthodox Christian circles to celebrate a divine element in humanity, although this trend was even more pronounced in the many Christian Gnostic heresies that drew frankly on the currency of Neo-Platonism.

The struggle of the early Christian church with the classical tradition was importantly fought on the grounds of literary style and worked very much in favor of the Christians; plain speech, stripped of the class-bound shackles of late classical rhetoric, was well suited to conveying the style of the *Bible* and its concept of the relationship between man and God. Again, Auerbach is our guide. In *Mimesis*, he calls our attention to a sharp contrast between the rigid rhetorical categories of the Romans as contrasted to the common speech of the *Gospels*. He chooses as his Roman example a passage from Tacitus, describing the revolt of three legions when they received news that Augustus had died and Tiberius had succeeded to the imperial throne in 14 CE:

> Thus stood affairs at Rome when a sedition made its appearance in the legions of Pannonia, without any fresh grounds, save that the accession of a new prince promised impunity to tumult, and held out the hope of advantages to be derived from civil war.... From this beginning they waxed wanton and quarrelsome, lent their ears to the discourses of every profligate, and at last longed for a life of dissipation and idleness, and spurned all military discipline and labor. In the camp was one Percennius, formerly a busy leader of theatrical factions, after that a common soldier, of a petulant tongue, and from his experience in theatrical party zeal, well qualified to stir up the bad passions of a crowd.... [Percennius] asked [the troops], "Why did they obey, like slaves, a few centurions and fewer tribunes? When would they be bold enough to demand redress, unless they approached the prince, yet a novice, and tottering upon his throne, either with entreaties or with arms? Enough that they had erred in remaining passive through so many years, since decrepit with age and maimed with wounds, after a course of service of thirty or forty years, they were still doomed to carry arms; nor even to those who were discharged was there any end of service, but they were still kept to the colors, and under another name endured the same hardships. And if any of them survived so many dangers, still they were dragged into counties far remote, where, under the name of lands, they are presented with swampy fens, or mountain wastes (*Mimesis*, 34).

At first blush, it appears to the modern reader that Tacitus gives a fair hearing to the complaints of the common troops, but we must remember an important convention of classical writing: set speeches are not records of what someone actually said, but rather the author's idea of what such a *type* of person would say in such circumstances, a display of the historian's art rather than an attempt to report actual events. Auerbach comments:

> We must be careful not to read into [Percennius'] speech the admission that older grievances are justified. Nothing could be further from Tacitus' view. Time and again he dwells on the point that only the worst elements are ready to rebel; and as for the leader Percennius.... Tacitus feels only the most profound contempt for him.... So it becomes manifest that Tacitus' vivid recital of the soldiers' grievances and demands is by no means based on an understanding of those demands.... For Tacitus not only lacks understanding, he actually has no interest whatever in the facts underlying the soldiers' demands.

Aristocratic ethical considerations such as license and mob rule drive Tacitus' judgment, but the key point is that these essential aesthetic concerns are built into the style of classical rhetoric as a whole and control both what Tacitus can see, and how he reports it. This suggests an even larger and more interesting point: that classical rhetoric, as perfect a tool as it was for science, philosophy, and history, could not describe or empathize with the internal feelings or motives of human beings (matters of background). The rigid form it had attained in the Roman Empire may have prevented well-meaning writers from doing so either. Auerbach observes:

> Historiography in depth — that is, methodical research into the historical growth of social as well as intellectual movements — is a thing unknown to antiquity.... So Norden writes in his *Antike Kunstprosa*: "We must bear in mind that the historians of antiquity did not attain, and did not seek to attain, a presentation of general, world-moving ideas." And Tostovtzeff in his *Social and Economic History of the Roman Empire*: "The historians were not interested in the economic life of the Empire." These two statements, chosen at random, may at first sight appear to have little to do with each other, but what they express goes back to the same peculiarity of the ancients' ways of viewing things; it does not see forces, it sees vices and virtues, successes and mistakes.... Its formulation of problems is not concerned with historical developments either intellectual or material, but with ethical judgments (*Mimesis*, 38).

This emphasizes a point Auerbach suggested in his discussion of Odysseus' scar: Homer's foreground excludes not only the background of a separate, Divine world, but also the background of social forces and individual psychological causality. Directly tied to this inability to see historical forces at work, partly due to a conviction that all events proceeded from the gods or fate, existed an inability to see people as anything other than types that fit into the established rhetorical categories:

> Here we encounter a difficult principle which can not be circumvented. If the literature of antiquity was unable to represent everyday life seriously, that is, in full appreciation of its problems and with an eye for its historical background; if it could represent it only in the low style, comically or at best idyllically, statically and ahistorically, the implication is

that these things mark the limits not only of the realism of antiquity but of its historical consciousness as well (*Mimesis*, 33).

If tragedy could occur only to great men and if the life of common people could be represented only comically as dictated by rhetorical categories, we must confess, and it is largely true, that what we have in Roman literature is not characters, but types. Aesthetic categories are, by their nature, pre-programmed moral and political judgments as well.

We must not push Auerbach's distinction too far here. The classical Greeks had certainly found ways to express the inner feelings of men of all stations; consider Socrates' *Apology* — although it is still true that his sentiments are presented from the foreground, thoughts Socrates tells us he has had. Greek rhetoric at its height, informed as it was by the structure of Socratic reason, could convey empathy or motivation. Consider Pericles' Funeral Oration, which comprehends the conditions and sentiments of all Athenians, whatever their class. But by late Hellenistic and Roman times, as the rhetorical categories grew more and more rigidly tied to social status and stylistic display, they increasingly limited what one could see and feel.

For a counter-example to Tacitus' style, Auerbach turns to Peter's denial of Christ in the immediate aftermath of Jesus' conviction:

> And as Peter was beneath in the palace, there cometh one of the maids of the high priest:
>
> And when she saw Peter warming himself, she looked upon him, and said, And thou also was with Jesus of Nazareth.
>
> But he denied, saying, I know not, neither understand I what thou sayest. And he went out into the porch, and the cock crew.
>
> And a maid saw him again, and began to say to them that stood by, This is one of them.
>
> And he denied it again. And a little after, they that stood by said again to Peter, Surely thou art one of them: for thou art a Galilean, and thy speech agreed thereto.
>
> But he began to curse and swear, saying, I know not this man of whom you speak.
>
> And the second time the cock crew. And Peter recalled the words that Jesus said unto him, Before the cock crow twice, thou shalt deny me thrice. And when he thought thereon, he wept. (*Bible*, King James version, Mark, 14: 66–72.)

Auerbach observes:

> It is apparent that the rule of differentiated styles cannot possibly apply in this case. The incident, entirely realistic both in regard to locale and *dramatis personae* — note particularly their low social station — is replete

with problem and tragedy. Peter is no mere accessory figure serving as *illustrato* (or, type) like the soldiers Vibulenus and Percennius, who are represented as mere scoundrels and swindlers. He is the image of man in the highest and deepest and most tragic sense. Of course this mingling of styles was not dictated by an artistic purpose. On the contrary, it was rooted from the beginning in the character of Jewish–Christian literature; it was graphically and harshly dramatized through God's incarnation in a human being of the humblest social origins, through his existence on earth amid humble everyday people and conditions and through his Passion which, judged by earthly standards, was ignominious; and it naturally came to have — in view of the wide diffusion and strong effect of that literature in later ages — a most decisive bearing on man's conception of the tragic and the sublime (*Mimesis*, 41).

The figures of Christ or Peter simply could not have been portrayed in Roman literature with any degree of sympathy or understanding; no rhetorical category existed to contain the tragedy or triumph of common persons. This was one reason the startling originality of Christianity, especially the originality of style in the *New Testament*, blindsided Roman officialdom until the faith was firmly established. So we must bear in mind that in its competition both with the Roman Empire, and with its religious opponents, primarily the Mithraites, Christianity's plain style, appealing as it did to the needs and longings of the populous, had a tremendous advantage over the ever more hide-bound classical rhetoric.

The initial struggle between Neo-Platonism and Christianity — Eros and Agape — resulted in sporadic persecutions of Christians by the government, starting under Nero in the 60s and continuing for the better part of three centuries. Nothing unfamiliar about the deification of Christ caused these persecutions. Turning men into gods was big business in the Empire: most of the Emperors deified themselves and others they loved. The syncretic, cosmopolitan Roman sensibility did take offense at the fact that the Christians not only denied the divinity of other Gods; they actually considered them phantasms or devils. Polytheistic religions generally recognized versions of their own gods in other traditions, and Monotheism could be tolerated, as in the case of the Jews, as long as it wasn't trying to convert everyone else. But Christianity was a missionary religion that challenged the state by claiming to be the only way to lead a moral life. In addition, it held out the guarantee of salvation. And prompted by both Neo-Platonism and Christianity, salvation — the promise of a happier and more just afterlife — had become the hot spiritual property of the mature Roman Empire. A mass culture, after all, is both consumer-driven and an engine of rising expectations.

Most legally executed Christians were convicted on charges of failure to pay proper homage to either the Emperor or the traditional Roman gods, something all other competing popular religions were willing to do. Many Christians were slaughtered, often grotesquely, though not as many as would be slaughtered by other Christians in the century or two after the Catholic Church effectively assumed state power. When Constantine became the first Christian Emperor in the early fourth century, the now dominant Christians took the Western Empire into what amounted to a death embrace.

Christianity ultimately triumphed over pagan philosophy partly because it internalized important elements of it, but it simultaneously faced a serious challenge from another religion as well. Mithraism clearly derived from Zoroastrianism. Profoundly Gnostic, it formulated its theology at the same time as Christianity and for a period in the second and third centuries outpaced it. Its origins remain obscure; we first hear about it in the late first century CE. Almost uniquely among the major religions it boasts no charismatic founding prophet; Mithra himself was a purely legendary figure borrowed from the Zoroastrian *Avestas*. It first came to the attention of the modern world in Frank Cumont's *Texts and Illustrated Monuments Relating to the Mysteries of Mithra* (1894–1900). Early scholars believed the original cult was adapted from Iran, but subsequent investigations revealed that while Mithraism clearly owed a great deal to Zoroastrianism, no similar worship of Mithra or religious practices have ever been identified in Persia.

When we compare what we know about the origins of Mithraism to what we know about the origins of Christianity, we find the latter extremely well documented by comparison. While this can partly be attributed to the fact that after their final triumph over Mithraism in the late Empire, Christianity did everything it could to stamp out any memory of its rival, from converting *mithraea* (places of Mithraic worship) into Christian churches to destroying monuments and sacred texts. Still, we know a lot about other cults and religions Christianity superceded, if only from the surviving Christian attacks against them. The origins of Mithraism remain a mystery within a mystery and it appears the religion went out of its way to preserve secrecy in its beliefs and practices. Mithraism was the only major indigenous Roman mystery religion aside from Christianity and was managed with the oaths and secret ceremonies of a Masonic Lodge, rather like the Athenian ceremonies at Ephesus.

We can, however, piece together the basic Mithraic theology from the fragments that remain. In *The Early Christian Church*, J. D. Davies (Anchor Books, Garden City, New York, 1967) writes: "The appeal of Mithra ... lay not a little in the fact that he was represented as a savior who could release men from the hostile control of the Zodiac and the planets, the agents of unseeing fate." (42) Devotes performed sacrifices to this savior, including bathing in the blood of a slaughtered bull. This simple, manly religion (woman were excluded from its ceremonies) appealed to soldiers, whose lives were especially arbitrary and contingent; many in the Roman legions professed loyalty to it, including several third century

Emperors. Predominance in the military clearly provided one source of Mithraism's wide influence.

Its other major appeal could at least crudely be called spiritual. The Hellenistic astronomer, Hipparchus (flourished late second century BCE), had established correlations among the movements of the heavenly bodies, and crude astrological interpretations of his work gave birth to a widespread popular feeling that human life was predestined and governed by planetary forces entirely beyond any individual's control. During the period of Imperial Rome, this uneasy feeling became widespread and made incarnate in the "Goddess Fortuna," who arbitrarily spun men up or down on her wheel according to the inscrutable whims of the stars. The insecurity provoked by this Silenic vision spread throughout the early and middle Empire, generating a fascination with good luck charms, magic spells, and ceremonies to ward off evil. In this overheated atmosphere, Mithraism probably provided both theological and ritual comfort to its adherents, as well as the promise of a Savior who might be petitioned to avoid this mechanistic fate. Whether the Savior offered intervention in this life or relief in a better afterlife, we do not know.

The emergence of these two universal mystery religions at the same time speaks to a growing, if inchoate, longing for spiritual comfort among the working and middle classes in the mid and late Empire. Mithraism, like the work of the Stoics, prepared the ground for the triumph of Christianity.

Frank J. Frost in *Greek Society* captures the originality of the primitive Christian message and describes how, unlike Mithraism, it was transformed by its encounter with Greek philosophy:

> For more than a century, the movement spread throughout the empire with each congregation almost undisturbed in its interpretation of the new dynamic mystery. Doctrine was simple: basically all that was required was a baptism (a common sacrament among other cults); salvation would follow through faith in the Son of God, and grace through direct revelation. The novelty was the ethical code preserved in the sayings of Jesus, particularly in that oration called the Sermon on the Mount. In a world of violence and greed, the meek were to be blessed and the poor in spirit were to inherit the Kingdom of Heaven. One was to love not only one's friends, but enemies as well. Those who kept to the simple life, sharing their possessions with the needy, loving all around them, secure in their faith, could not be harmed. Of course, much of this was already familiar to followers of Socrates or Epicurus. The greater novelty was that the early Christians were willing to die for their beliefs. In the wake of the great fire in Rome in A. D. 64, most Romans would have been perfectly willing to believe Nero's claim that the Christians had spread the flame. But when the Roman mob saw the processions of Christian captives jubilantly singing hymns of exaltation as they were torn apart, or burned alive, or nailed to crosses, they felt a sudden revulsion for human cruelty and a wonder at this new God who could so inspire the souls of slaves, women, paupers, and criminals.... The exemplary conduct of the martyrs vastly expanded

the ranks of early Christians and began to bring the religion to the attention of the elite classes as well....

> But as the infant church began to be dominated more and more by a Hellenized elite, Greek philosophy began its struggle with revelation. The questions of fundamental importance, Greek Church members would say, were the nature of God, the Son, and the Holy Ghost, the nature of their energies, and their relationship to mortals. It was already apparent that these questions would challenge the most brilliant intellects Greek philosophy could produce — how absurd then to believe they could be left to the discussion of illiterate and uneducated Greek slum dwellers or Anatolian peasants.... Thus did the Greek preacher triumph over prophecy and revelation (190–193).

Christianity's openness to syncretism with classical thought gave it its decisive advantage over philosophy and other equally popular mystery religions such as Mithraism in the mid-Empire. Because it provided a universal explanation for the conduct and purpose of human life, Christianity attracted many of the best minds of the age. After Constantine's conversion, virtually all serious philosophical discussion occurred within the parameters of the developing Christian theology. But the incorporation of Socratic Eros into Christian theology also meant that the essential Christian mysteries would be subject to examination by erotic reason.

This attempt to reconcile Greek rationality with Judeo–Christian Agape took very different courses in the Western and Eastern parts of the crumbling Empire, as Frost points out:

> By the time Christianity was recognized in the fourth century and had become the official religion of the Roman Empire, its emphasis upon doctrine had become predominant. The greatest struggle was to enforce orthodoxy in the eastern, Greek part of the Empire, where philosophical disputation and, hence, theological disputation were so much a part of everyone's life.... Thorny points of doctrine evoked both stormy debates between bishops and riots in the streets of Alexandria, Antioch, and Constantinople. Such riots killed thousands of citizens who emerged from shops and tenements to do battle with the mobs going home from the hypodrome, fighting over matters such as the placement of one preposition in the liturgy (*Greek Society*, 193).

In the Eastern Empire, which would endure as Byzantium for a thousand years after its Western counterpart collapsed, Socratic reason applied to a mystery such as the trinity inevitably created factions, much like the previous quarrelling schools of Greek philosophy in the previous centuries. The issue of whether Christ was mostly man, mostly God, or a co-equal synthesis of the two provided sects including the Arians and the Monophysites with endless fodder for theological arguments that were often aligned with political factions or rival claimants to the Imperial throne. This situation actually persisted in the eastern Orthodox Church until the fall of the Byzantine Empire; dynamic preachers and even whole dynasties were branded as heretic; banished leaders of the Church and state were recalled from heretic status to become the new orthodoxy until another rival orthodoxy overthrew them, all carried out with a judicious mixture of philosophical argument and mob violence.

The Western Catholic Church of the late Empire was, like Eastern Orthodoxy, a shotgun marriage between Eros and Agape, but its development took a very different course. By all sorts of means — its emphasis on prayer (as distinct from the early Christian witnessing to God's grace), suggestions that the human soul was immortal and contained a spark of the divine, the forgiveness of sins which culminated in the selling of indulgences, the identification of the Church as mediator between God and man, the emphasis on reason as way to understanding God — Roman Catholicism imported major elements of Heavenly Eros into its practical theology. But it did so in a manner much less completely and disputatiously than the Greeks, partly because the West lacked an ancient tradition of philosophical disputation, and partly, as Frost points out, from necessity:

> As East and West drew apart under the onslaught of barbarian invasions in the fifth and sixth centuries, the Western church assumed the usual pragmatic Roman attitudes in its approach to Christianity. Doctrine was less important than survival, and Roman clergymen were impatient with paradoxical points of theology. In the ensuing centuries, the pastoral mission of the church was to become paramount in the Latin West and was essential to preserving some vestiges of civil authority. In the Greek East, the philosophical aspects remained fascinating, exasperating, gloriously satisfying to the soul, an eternal resource to challenge the Greek intellect and to stimulate the sort of civic disorder the Greeks regarded almost as a normal pastime (*Greek Society*, 193–4).

The Eastern Empire retained enough strength and resources as a civilization and a polity to afford these arguments. At the same time, the Empire, as personified by the Emperor on the throne, was subject to vigorous political and theological winds; in effect, to be Emperor was to be Orthodox; state and church were inextricably commingled. This was not the situation of the increasingly assertive Papacy in the West, where civil authority withered.

Frost concludes his treatment of the Eastern Empire with a vivid image:

> A thousand years later (1453), with the barbarian at the gate, and the Greek church discussing a compromise in matters of doctrine with the Roman church in return for military aid, dissenting priests let the Turks inside the walls of Constantinople, preferring Orthodoxy under foreign rule to a shameful corruption of what they considered the logical and therefore the only possible form of the Christian faith.

By contrast, the Roman Church found relative stability in its combination of Augustinian theology and the institution of the Papacy, beginning its long slow rise to preeminence in Western Europe.

Why did Christianity beat out Neo-Platonism in this contest for hearts, minds, and political power during the late Empire? While Christians constituted perhaps 10% of the Roman population at the time of Constantine's conversion, Rodney Stark calculates that the number rose to nearly 34 million in 350 CE, about 57% of the total population (cited in *Newsweek*, March 28, 2005). Although the Empire, aside from the second century, was often badly led and sometimes ruled by terror, a generally competent bureaucracy functioned until well after the fall of the last Western Emperor in 476. As a result, the Roman world became the first mature mass culture in human history, distinct from the great eastern Empires in that it had a concept of citizenship, a reasonable level of literacy, at least the sporadic rule of law, competing systems of philosophical and religious belief available to some extent even to the least fortunate, an entrepreneurial marketplace, a popular culture, and an abundance of both information and misinformation.

In a mass culture, where a rough form of democracy or at least public opinion is at work, history suggests a religion will always exert more mass appeal than a philosophy over the long term. Successful religions create a sense of community, of belonging — in the case of Christianity, by its worship, its rituals, its communal feasts and celebrations, its promise of salvation, its disregard for social status or ethnicity, its answer to death; in short, its unique emphasis on universal and eternal fellowship — all unavailable to a philosophy, which is bound to be academic, argumentative, and primarily the province of the highly educated. Mithraism's military orientation, uncertain salvation, primitive rituals, and exclusion of women could not offer a similar sense of cosmopolitan community. Initially dismissed by the elite as a "slave religion," Christianity conquered through the support of the lowest classes.

Daniel Dennett in *Breaking the Spell: Religion as a Natural Phenomenon* (New York, Viking Press, 2006) attributes the origins of religion to the human discovery of agency, that is, the awareness that other humans' actions arise from their desires, motivations, and intentions. Once the human mind grasped this concept, he argues, it was a natural evolutionary step to identify super-human agents behind all natural phenomena: the weather, the seasons, crop cycles, floods and tides, the sun, the moon, and the stars. While it was a long road from elves and fairies through antique polytheism to a monotheistic Almighty agent, the path was clear. Human beings, creatures of intention, are likely to seek out intention everywhere.

In recent years, evolutionary science has increasingly argued that natural selection operates through groups — whether they be gene pools or social units — as well as individuals. Allen Orr (*The New Yorker*, April 3, 2006) writes, citing David Sloan Wilson:

Religion is ... a collection of beliefs and behaviors that bring people together, coordinates their activities, and, in the end, allows groups to accomplish tasks that would otherwise be impossible. If my group's religion is better at this than yours, my group and its religion will spread and yours will recede. Wilson suggested, for instance, that the early Christian Church succeeded against all odds because its creed of selflessness provided its adherents with a sort of welfare state. Christians banded together, aiding each other through illness, famine, and war. The resulting biological edge, he thinks, played a part in the unexpected success of this once obscure mystery cult (81).

A critical element in group success — observable in ants, guppies, and early Christians facing gladiators or mass immolation — consists in the willingness to sacrifice individuals for the greater good of the group. Christianity demonstrated this inclusive communal quality far more forcefully and vividly than either of its main competitors for the hearts and minds of the Roman world, philosophy or Mithraism.

Of the major causes for the Western Empire's fall — exhaustion, perpetual civil war over who should be Emperor, farming out the military to barbarian recruits, a mass culture's tendency to infantilize the population, even lead poisoning from the water pipes — the least-commonly discussed (since Gibbon) is perhaps the most important. Successive Christian Emperors — with the late fourth-century exception of the renegade Neo-Platonist Julian — diverted increasing State resources to the Church. This was reinforced by a brain drain as the most capable minds, men like Jerome, Ambrose, and Augustine, devoted their lives to the priesthood rather than to the government or military. By the time Augustine completed his grand summary of Christian orthodoxy in the early fifth century, the Western Empire had become a hollow shell incapable of fighting off the routine crises and invasions that Rome had handled with aplomb and blood for six hundred years. The Christian conviction that the end of the world was at hand wasn't just reinforced by the collapse of Western civilization; it helped bring it about.

McLuhan quotes Toynbee citing an apparently trivial point of style that speaks volumes about why the Roman Empire collapsed:

> In his *Study of History*, Toynbee notes a great many reversals of form and dynamic, as when, in the middle of the fourth century A.D., the Germans began abruptly to be proud of their tribal names and to retain them. Such a moment marked a new confidence born of saturation with Roman values, and it was marked by the complementary Roman swing toward primitive values.... Just as the barbarians got to the top of the Roman social ladder, the Romans themselves were disposed to assume the dress and manners of the tribesmen out of the same frivolous and snobbish spirit that attached to the French court of Louis XVI to the world of shepherds and shepherdesses (*Understanding Media*, 49).

THE AUGUSTINIAN SYNTHESIS

Augustine (354–430) doesn't claim Socrates for Christianity as other Church Fathers did, and his work marks the beginning of the decline in Socrates' reputation that would last for a thousand years. Yet it was he who put Eros and Agape under the same yoke, much as Nietzsche describes the Athenian wedding of Apollo and Dionysus. We know more about Augustine than any other late Roman figure because he did something startling and virtually unprecedented: he wrote an autobiography, the *Confessions*. Rich in personal detail and psychological insight, though clearly polemical in intent, this remarkable work traces his spiritual odyssey from mysticism through higher paganism to Christianity.

Augustine was born near Carthage in North Africa to a pagan father whom he disliked and a Christian mother whom he adored, making him a very representative late Roman, except for the fact that he was a Berber of full African blood. He was eager to denounce the sins of his youth in the *Confessions*; it's clear that in the context of his maturity as a Christian, his main purpose was to make theological points. As Norman Cantor (*Medieval History*, New York, the Macmillan Company, 1963) puts it:

> In describing his selfishness as an infant, Augustine was expounding the doctrine of original sin. In the famous story of the theft of the pears the child Augustine steals fruit even though he is not hungry, merely to build up his reputation in the eyes of his friends. The purpose of this anecdote is to demonstrate the nature of sin as rebellion. All we know of the young Augustine indicates he was a studious, serious, and in fact a rather priggish lad. Augustine also pictures his young self as deeply bothered by an uncontrollable libido. Here again there is a theological argument, for sex, to Augustine, most clearly reveals both the inability of reason to control will and the resulting weakness of human nature. Yet, if Augustine was ever guilty of sin in the commonsense use of the word, it was in the direction of concupiscence, and this only to a moderate degree. After his ambitious and doting parents had sent the youth to Carthage to study rhetoric, the necessary gateway to success in law and public life, he acquired a mistress, kept her for fifteen years, fathered a son by her, and abandoned her after his later conversion to Christianity (83).

In Carthage, Augustine experienced the first of several spiritual crises. According to his mother's wishes, he had been preparing for baptism but his training in the classical writers, especially Cicero (who was heavily influenced by Socrates via Plato), made Christianity seem by comparison crude, ahistorical, and irrational. Instead, he converted to Manichaeism, a Christian version of Persian Zoroastrianism popular in the late Empire which postulated a battle between the forces of darkness and the forces of light. In this system, Christ was the God of Light. This was a frankly Gnostic doctrine, not only in its stark dualism but also in its gradations of the Elect, from those who possessed full Gnosis, or knowledge, through adepts and followers, down to those who lived in perpetual darkness.

This version of Christianity could be supported by selections from the *New Testament*, especially the more ecstatic passages of Paul and John, as well as by *Thomas*. It was probably during this period that Augustine made the famous comment: "Give me chastity God, but not yet." Gnostic cults right through the Middle Ages and beyond tended to indulge the sexual desires of its non-Elect followers, partly out of a Neo-Platonic conviction that the sensual could lead to the divine.

Augustine pursued his career as a professor of classical rhetoric and rose through the ranks quickly, but he gradually became convinced that Manichaeism failed to provide a convincing explanation for the existence of evil in the world. He underwent a second conversion, to Neo-Platonism. Cantor continues:

> Augustine's solution to the problem of evil is derived not from Manichaeism but rather from Neoplatonic doctrines that he took up shortly after his arrival in Italy in 383. He was ... destined for a great career in public life when he experienced another of his intellectual earthquakes. He left his job, turned his back on the world, and devoted himself to Neoplatonic spiritual exercises. In the end, he found Neoplatonic catharsis (oneness with Plato's Beauty) impossible; he was too much of a sensual man to become entirely Godlike and enter into mystical union with the deity. But Neoplatonism taught him that all God's creation was good and that evil was only a perversion of the good, the falling away from God. Later, he incorporated this Neoplatonic doctrine into his theology, and it became the common teaching of the medieval and modern church on the nature of evil (*Medieval History*, 85).

Clearly, the belief that evil equals error is fundamentally Socratic and alien to Pauline Christianity's emphasis on original sin. We find Augustine's contemporary, the Eastern patriarch Athanasius, saying, "God was made man so we might be made gods" — surely an Erotic construction.

In the *Confessions*, Augustine claimed that one day while meditating in a garden, a child approached him and recommended that he "take up the *Bible*." He fell naturally upon passages from Paul that would have been familiar to him from his Gnostic days. He was especially struck by the phrase "Put on Jesus Christ and make no provisions for the flesh in concupiscence." Augustine concluded that only through Christ could one escape the demands of the flesh and achieve oneness with God.

Once he converted, Augustine set out to give Christianity the coherence and splendor of classical philosophy, and he succeeded. In his later works, especially *The City of God*, Augustine preserved much of his former Manichaeism by arguing that the world was indeed dualistic, on the one hand earthly, sensual, and corrupt, on the other, heavenly, spiritual, and pure. Only Christ could redeem one from the fallen City of Man to the risen City of God. One would think that this final conversion would have turned Augustine decisively against his Neo-Platonic convictions, and, superficially, it did. This absolute gap between a vile world and an ineffable divinity coheres perfectly with Jesus' version of Agape. But as Nygren unanswerably writes:

> Although Augustine means to take a Christian point of view of his development in the *Confessions* he provides in fact a singularly clear example of what Plato calls "the right way of Eros." Augustine's earlier development is particularly dramatic; he passionately embraces a doctrine and as abruptly abandons it. Yet running through this apparently aimless veerings from one point of view to another, there is a remarkably strong continuity ... it is the Eros point of view. It was not Neoplatonism that introduced him to it; he had it from the beginning, and it dominates him equally as a Manichaean, as a Neoplatonist and as a Christian (*Agape and Eros*, 464–65).

Nygren points out that Augustine included Agape too in his doctrine, especially in his emphasis on grace and predestination, both of which can proceed only from an almighty and loving God. Augustine, more than any of the other great Church Fathers, except perhaps Jerome, emphasizes the worthless and undeserving state of fallen man. But pagan Socratic Eros has survived the triumph of Christianity and persists, not on the fringes, but at the heart of Catholic teaching.

Augustine in his Christian incarnation became Bishop of Hippo in North Africa and spent the rest of his life defending the Catholic church against various and rampant heresies, many of which he himself defined. One of these was Pelagianism, named after a British monk who maintained man's radical free will to choose good or evil — a position too close to Socrates' heavenly Eros even for Augustine. But later, during the High Middle Ages, the Pelagian insistence that man could find his way to God would become increasingly intertwined with Augustine's teachings, partly because the idea was inherent in his synthesis.

Augustine's battles for his version of orthodoxy included the role he played in the repression of the common Christian "Agape love feasts." These were generally held at marriages, funerals, and celebrations, and consisted originally of fellowship meals which consecrated the congregation's unity in Christ's love. As converts flocked into the church during the fourth century, however (now that it had become the official religion of the Empire), these occasions often became social entertainment for the rich and, at their extremes, borderline orgies. Gregory of Nazianzus railed, "If we come together to satisfy the belly and to enjoy the changing and fleeting pleasures, and so turn this place of temperance into one of gluttony and satiety ... I do not see how our conduct corresponds with the occasion" (J.G. Davies, *The Early Christian Church*, Anchor Books, New York, 1967, 364). Augustine's intervention was decisive in putting an end to these "love feasts," so ironically suggestive of the erotic Orphic cults. Augustine, following Paul in this respect, successfully cut off religious ecstasy from its sexual root, or at least managed to repress the connection for centuries.

Although Agape and Eros coexist uncomfortably in Augustine, he acknowledges little struggle in yoking them together. He calls the union "Caritas," which can be generally defined as God's love refracting among men and then back to Him. He never really acknowledges his profound debt to Plato, perhaps because, as the literary critic Harold Bloom argues, every great poet represses his most powerful predecessor due to "the anxiety of influence" and the determination to appear original. He allowed Apollonian reason into his system while banning Dionysius, and with him, the sensory world. This imported Paul's horror of sexuality into mainstream Christianity, a situation that has persisted to the current day. It also meant the death of science in the West for a millennium. Nothing could prove more clearly the truth of Socrates' profound connection between sensual attraction and the searching intellect. Distrustful of his own sensuality, Augustine set the Judeo–Christian Word as strict guardian over the disruptive pagan Eye.

Catholic theology remained essentially what Augustine had made of it through the early Middle Ages and that theology was as much Eros as Agape, called by another name. Imagery was confined to the iconic and memorial, and Christian vestments were consciously designed to de-sex. Socrates' reputation was suppressed for a thousand years, but still his contribution of "Higher Eros" remained central to Western Christianity and often dominated over primitive Christian Agape.

8. Socrates and Jesus in the Middle Ages

Although it's generally taught that the final collapse of the Western Empire in 476 plunged Europe immediately to the barbarism of the Dark Ages, Henri Pirenne long ago debunked this cliché. The Germanic conquerors adopted and perpetuated Rome's Hellenistic culture and government, though in a degraded form. New barbarian Kings insisted on holding their titles from the remaining Roman Emperor in Constantinople and maintained secular states; they wanted to join the Empire, not replace it. Pirenne claims the real Dark Ages came two centuries later when, under the inspiration of Mohammed's message, triumphant Islam burst out of Arabia and converted a vast territory stretching from the Middle East across North Africa to Spain. This restricted shipping in the Western Mediterranean, cutting Western Europe off from the commercial prosperity and the ideas of the East. Learning all but vanished and even bare literacy, previously widespread, survived only sporadically, mostly in the monasteries. Governmental power and the economy retreated into feudalism, manorialism, and subsistence agriculture.

Subsequent historians have modified Pirenne's conclusions, pointing out that trends towards lordship and local manorial economies were well advanced before the final collapse of the Western Empire. But it's certainly true that the advance of Islam provoked the final break between the emerging barbarian Kingdoms and the Papacy on the one hand, and the Byzantine remnant of the Roman Empire on the other. Only around 700 did what we call Western Europe begin to emerge as a distinctive and self-sufficient culture, culminating in the alliance between the Papacy and Charlemagne around 800.

The one Roman institution to survive during this period was the church, and persistent efforts by the Papacy led to the gradual conversion of most barbarian kingdoms west of the Rhine. This effort was assisted by a brief but dramatic resurgence of learning in eighth-century England that recovered the rudiments of learning, dispatched remarkable scholars to the Continent, and produced the only real writing and history in Western Europe during the Dark Ages. The Christianity practiced among the general population during this period amounted to little more than a superstitious mix of tribal traditions and rudimentary Christian ritual. Still, by 1000, most Europeans had some concept of Christ, and the Church played an important role in restoring a semblance of civilization and internationalism. Virtually no one for five hundred years, however, knew a thing about Socrates. Agape, with its simple faith, its submission to divine will, and its belief in the imminent end of the world ruled Western Europe more decisively than at any time before or since. The Venerable Bede, in his lovely eighth-century history of the English church, provides the most touching account of Agape in action during the Dark Ages.

Paradoxically, the force that galvanized the West and sowed the seeds for the rebirth of theology and philosophy was what had helped destroy it: militant Islam. Buoyed by faith and success, the desert Arabs and their converts rapidly established stable governments, great cities, and important centers of learning from India to Spain. By the mid-eighth century, Islamic forces threatened to conquer France. It was a rare moment, when history truly could have gone either way. Christianity faced the only potentially mortal challenge in its mature history. But it turned out the one thing the primitive Frankish kingdom knew how to do was fight.

As defeat loomed, the Carolingian family, who already controlled the government, completely usurped the authority of the decadent Merovingian dynasty and in a series of battles under the leadership of Charles Martel, managed to drive the Muslims back. Much like the Athenian victory over the Persians at Marathon, the French success sparked an upsurge in political confidence. By 800, Martel's grandson Charlemagne ruled France, Germany, and northern Italy, and was crowned Holy Roman Emperor by the Pope. This marks the real invention of Western Europe because for the first time its leader derived his authority not from the Byzantine Emperor but from the Pope. A crude international system had been reestablished, and though it took its knocks over the next two centuries, the Holy Roman Empire (which ended up ruling Germany) and the states that began to establish something approaching a national identity, including France, England, the Low Countries, and many city–states in Italy, formed a functioning community that began to lay the foundations for the social, cultural, and intellectual recovery that led to the High Middle Ages.

For two centuries and more, however, the Popes made little use of this potential power: from the ninth through the eleventh centuries the government of the Roman Catholic Church was thoroughly corrupt and the papacy no more than the plaything of thuggish aristocratic factions who competed for leadership of the city of Rome. The life of the church retreated into the monasteries, the last ecclesiastical structures to preserve some organization, integrity, and intellectual vigor. The great church figures of this period were Abbots. Carolingian monasticism began to take form as early as 817, when Louis the Pious, Charlemagne's heir, recognized the monastic constitution drawn up by Benedict of Aniane and appointed Benedict as head of all the monasteries in Carolingian territory.

Benedict drew hundreds of monasteries, many of which had little connection to each other or their surrounding communities, into a wider orbit and gave them for the first time a clear and unified sense of mission. Henceforth, their responsibilities included not only liturgical functions, but also important educational, social, and economic responsibilities in the lay world. The Benedictine Order became the focus of what social stability existed in these extremely perilous and contingent times, and by the middle of the tenth century, one of these monasteries, Cluny in Burgundy, had begun to attract other monasteries to its mission, founded client sister monasteries in areas of Europe that previously had little or no church presence, and initiated reforms that made Cluniac monasteries the centers of social welfare and education in their regions. Norman Cantor observes:

> Cluny's success must be partly attributed to the fact that it had obtained immunity from both lay and Episcopal interference and was directly subject to the Pope, and since the papacy, until the middle of the eleventh century, was in a state of complete decrepitude, the monks of Cluny were entirely free to work out the destiny of their own community. They chose a succession of extremely able abbots, usually men with the highest aristocratic, or even princely, backgrounds, who led the Burgundians to a position of eminence in the affairs of Europe.... Cluny demanded of its brothers and of affiliated monasteries the full observance of the Benedictine rule as amended by Benedict of Aniane. The monks of Cluny became famous for the extent and beauty of their liturgical devotions. Kings and nobles from all over Europe who had come to take seriously the teachings of the church and who were concerned for the salvation of their own souls and those of their relatives were eager to give Cluny rich endowments in order to be named in Cluniac prayers (*Medieval History*, 267–8).

The Cluniac monasteries returned the favor, providing the emerging secular governments with educated officials to run royal chanceries. Often these officials were eventually rewarded with bishoprics, further spreading the civilizing influence. Lay piety became more and more the norm throughout Western Europe.

Aided importantly by the monks in their service, the secular leaders in the tenth and eleventh centuries began to extend their authority, and with it, some semblance of the rule of law. West of the Rhine, the Carolingian family had exercised virtually no authority over the feudal lords for a century and in 987, with the support of the clergy, Hugh Capet seized the throne of France and founded a new dynasty. At first the authority of the Capetians scarcely extended beyond

Paris, but the Capetians and their descendents were tenacious, and by 1100 much of what is now France came under at least their titular control.

In 911 a Scandinavian adventurer, Rollo, conquered Normandy and founded a Duchy in defiance of the Carolingian King of France. Rollo and his successors rapidly built a new sort of state, highly centralized around the principal of feudal loyalty and steadied by a competent bureaucracy. In the 980s, the Norman Dukes were instrumental in setting Hugh Capet on the French throne. Rollo's distinguished descendant, William, though a bastard, achieved the title of Duke, completed the construction of the powerful Norman state, and in 1066 conquered England, where he immediately imposed the orderly Norman system. Other Norman pirates ventured further afield, finding rich but decadent states in south Italy that they conquered and reorganized in their feudal–bureaucratic style.

Carolingian rule proved equally ineffective east of the Rhine, leading to the rise of local Dukes who exercised unchecked power in their territories. In 911, the last Carolingian died and the Dukes elected Conrad of Franconia King. This electoral principle remained in force theoretically for the next six centuries. A strong King could almost always ensure his son's election the throne, but if a given dynasty failed or grew degenerate, the Dukes would step in and elect a new one. This system brought Henry, the Duke of Saxony to the throne in 918 and his dynasty, which came to be known as the Ottonian, found its first effective ruler in Otto the Great, who ruled from 936 to 973. He consolidated royal authority, in part by insisting on anointment by the Archbishop of Mainz at Charlemagne's old capital of Aachen. This alliance allowed him gradually to assert control over the German church, and with its backing, in turn curtail the power of the Dukes. In 955, Otto further increased his power and prestige with his total victory over the invading Magyars at the Battle of Lechfeld. This was the real foundation of the German Empire, which would remain the dominant state in Europe for the next three centuries.

During this period, the monastic and secular powers were building the social and political structures that laid the foundation for the High Middle Ages and their work had begun to pay off: Western Europe's population was growing, the germ of a merchant class independent of feudal authority was developing in towns from northern Italy to the Low Countries, and construction, especially of cathedrals and monasteries, boomed. But where was the papacy during this period? Theoretically, the Pope was the font of all secular authority, the religious and political leader of Western Europe, but for two centuries the papal government had exercised no power outside of the decrepit city of Rome itself. This changed when the German Emperor Henry III decided to revive the papacy by arranging for a kinsman to be elected Pope, a decision the dynasty was soon to regret.

Leo IX was genuinely devoted to bringing the spiritual reforms fostered by the monasteries and the managerial skills developed by the secular governments to bear on the renovation of the Papacy. But more important, he brought with him a group of young cardinals who had more radical reform in mind. Due to a series of strong Popes who emerged from this group and their Italian allies, Cantor observes:

> The period from 1050 to 1130 was dominated by an attempt at world revolution which influenced in highly effective ways the other aspects of social change. It seems, in retrospect, that it was almost necessary for a revolutionary onslaught to shake to its foundations the order of the early middle ages, in order that new political, economic, and intellectual forces be given the opportunity to develop in the face of the old institutions and ideas (*Medieval History*, 299).

Later called the Gregorians after one of their number, Hildebrand, was elected Pope as Gregory VII, the new Cardinals began their reforms with a deceptively procedural papal degree: henceforth only the college of cardinals would be involved in electing the Pope. This immediately excluded the previously preponderant influence of the Roman people and the German Emperor. From the start, these cardinals had a program to elevate the papacy from the streets of Rome to the real leadership of Europe, and they succeeded.

Hildebrand, while not the most original mind in the group, was a terrific organizer and administrator. Born Roman, and a student of canon law, he despised the German Emperor's intervention in Italian and papal affairs. Soon after he was elected Gregory VII, he issued a statement on papal power.

> The *Dictus Papae* asserted that the Roman church was founded by God alone, that only the papal office was universal in its authority and that the Pope alone could depose bishops, reinstate them, or transfer them from one see to another. No church council was canonical without papal approval.... Furthermore, the pope was said to be beyond the judgment of any human being; his actions were to be judged by God alone" (*Medieval History*, 314).

This breathtaking assertion of authority denied secular leaders the right to exert any influence over the church in their territories, a right they had held without challenge from time immemorial. In fact the German Dukes and their counterparts in other countries could legitimately claim that they, not the papacy, had built these monasteries and churches and nourished them for centuries. The northern clergy could make the same argument; bishops who had ruled great territories could now be fired or transferred on the whim of the Pope. *Dictus Papae* fell like a thunderclap over the whole political, social, and religious structure of Western Europe.

Gregory had based his claims primarily on the Donation of Constantine, an ancient but forged document in which the first Christian Emperor had purportedly deeded all his secular power to the Pope. We have no reason to believe Gregory knew the document to be a forgery, but at no time in history had any Pope ever held the power Gregory was claiming. In earlier or later years, secular rulers would have rejected his claim out of hand and an army surrounding Rome would have made him change his mind. But the revived piety of the eleventh century gave him a constituency: millions of believers agreed with Gregory that rulers were essentially enthroned thugs and that only a revived Church militant could improve their condition in this world and the next. Cantor points out: "Whatever Gregory's intentions in his emphasis on the spiritual superiority of poor Christians, his teachings were bound to give encouragement to the underprivileged and ambitious classes of the European cities" (*Medieval History*, 318).

This crisis, which came to be called the Investiture Controversy, called secular authority into question so radically that it demanded resolution, and events proceeded rapidly. The German Emperor, Henry IV, a very capable man and the most powerful leader in Europe, had recently won a struggle against the powerful German Dukes and consolidated his power. He acted with dispatch. In 1076, with the help of his clerical staff, he prepared and sent a letter to Rome denouncing Hildebrand as "not pope but false monk." The stage was set for a European-wide debate about values and the structure of society for the first time since the Roman Empire.

Gregory might be a fiery ideologue, but he was also a practical politician. He realized that the expanding Norman states were the second most powerful secular entity in Europe and that they especially craved legitimization for their conquests in south Italy. Confident that the cities of Europe, the defeated German Dukes, and the Normans were on his side, Gregory summarily deposed Henry IV on receipt of his letter. Furthermore, he notified the German bishops and abbots that they would be excommunicated if they supported Henry. Since most of the troops at Henry's disposal came from ecclesiastic lands, he suddenly found himself without an army. Meanwhile the German nobles, gleeful at Henry's predicament, set about the process of electing a new King who would be more amenable to their traditional independence. They went so far as to invite Gregory to the assembly of the nobility that would conduct the election.

Meanwhile, Henry's advisers convinced him that only submission to the Pope could save his throne and a race evolved that would have been comical if the stakes were not so high. Henry headed south with a relatively small force of loyalists, all that he could assemble at the last minute. Meanwhile, Gregory and his entourage proceeded north to attend the election of the new German King. The two parties encountered each other at the Castle of Canossa in northern Italy. Cantor summarizes the result:

> The events which occurred at Canossa in the winter of 1077 constitute one of the great dramas of European history. Contemporary royalist chroniclers describe, with pardonable exaggeration, how Henry stood in the snow for three days until at last the pope was willing to give him an audience and receive his penitent pleas for forgiveness and absolution (*Medieval History*, 327).

Gregory remained uncertain about his course of action because while he could not refuse the pleas for absolution of a genuinely penitent supplicant, he had good reason to doubt Henry's sincerity. In the end, the appearance at Canossa of Abbot Hugh of Cluny changed Gregory's mind. This testifies not only to the influence Cluny had gained by this time, but probably also to the fact that the monasteries, unlike the Roman clergy, were acutely aware of their dependence on the favor of secular rulers. Gregory's practical political side prevailed at a moment when he could have forced an absolute triumph, a testimony to his statesmanship. He was aware that to alienate the entire monastic movement might have catastrophic results. He heard Henry's confession, absolved him, and restored him to his throne.

Canossa had all sorts of consequences for the relations between Church and State. Many in Europe began to doubt the wisdom of untrammeled papal authority. At the same time, Gregory had demonstrated that the papacy intended to be the leading European power in both secular and religious affairs, as indeed it became for the next two centuries. But perhaps the most important consequence of Canossa was that it taught Western Europe to see itself as a whole, a community, for the first time. The stage was set for the great accomplishments of the High Middle Ages.

Due to its long struggle with Islam, the reviving West began to recover some knowledge of the classical era, leading to a rebirth of original thought. The Muslim armies had been driven back into Spain but Spain had great universities by the standards of the time, and Christian scholars like Aeneus Silvius, who became Pope around 1000, and Peter Abelard (1079–1142) began to learn of Aristotle through the work of Muslim Islamic scholars such as Averroes and Avicenna. The Crusades augmented this rudimentary knowledge of classical philosophy and sparked awareness that flourishing non-Christian cultures existed in the world. Begun in 1096 as an attempt by the papacy to expand its prestige by retaking the Holy Land from Islam, the Crusades rapidly degenerated into plundering expeditions by surplus European knights who took Jerusalem, lost it, and sacked Byzantium, the remnant of the Eastern Roman Empire, turning it into easy prey for the Muslim Turks. In the process, however, many crusaders grew more cosmopolitan through their contacts with the vibrant culture of the east, and some returned to Europe with translations of post-Socratic works from the Arabic, especially Aristotle. Mediterranean trade in goods began to revive as well.

Peter Abelard, a difficult, tortured genius, laid the foundations for high medieval thought. Abelard had lived an interesting life for a cleric; Cantor observes:

> Abelard was the son of a minor lord in Brittany, a wild frontier region which was accustomed to producing savage warriors but not scholars and philosophers. The tremendous social impact of the new learning may be gauged by the attractions it presented to this obscure nobleman. He was recognized from the beginning as an exceptionally brilliant student, and

he mastered the new dialectical methods rapidly, but he was also a difficult person, entirely inner-directed, arrogant, disagreeable, hypercritical, and gauche. After completing a course, it was his custom to set himself up as a lecturer on the subject in competition with his former teacher. He was not the kind of scholar who makes a pleasant academic colleague; such a type was as bound to get into trouble in the twelfth century as in the twentieth. Nevertheless, it was a personal scandal which, by his own account, if it may be believed, got him into trouble. He seduced a certain Heloise, the niece of a prominent cathedral canon in Paris. He tells us that her family punished him by "cutting off those parts of my body with which I had done that which was the cause of their sorrow" (*Medieval History*, 396).

Abelard's *History of My Calamities*, the first serious autobiography since Augustine, reintroduced the idea of personality after centuries of religious collectivism and by implication attacked the Platonic concept of the absorption of the individual into the universal. In *Sic et Non* (Yes and No) Abelard used Aristotelian dialectical reasoning to reveal glaring contradictions among the Church Fathers. Following the Spanish Muslim scholar Averroes, he proclaimed his famous "double truth" doctrine: reason and faith were separate and irreconcilable domains, each with its own type of truth. When he began to question traditional doctrine on the trinity, he was put on trial for heresy and was lucky to survive with his life. His prosecutor, St. Bernard, put the case against him crisply, saying that it was "blameable" to seek knowledge "merely that they may know." Socratic reason as developed by Aristotle had gone to war against Socratic Heavenly Eros as propagated by Plato and Augustine. Western thought had begun again. But Bernard's injunction suggested a perpetual challenge for the future of Christianity: could one believe only if there were things one refused to know? The Church's resistance to fact over the next few centuries actually provoked the efflorescence of Western science in the ancient battle between Eros and Agape.

THE HIGH MIDDLE AGES AND THE SYNTHESIS OF AQUINAS

These imports from the Muslim world were rapidly supplemented by other classical texts that had been moldering, virtually unread, in monastic libraries for centuries. The Arabs had favored Aristotle largely because he had opened the way to practical science. But he suited the medieval scholastics' purposes for another reason, well summarized by Nygren:

> The relation between the Aristotelian and Platonic theory of Eros might be formulated briefly as follows: Aristotle presents us with an expansion of the Platonic theory, in which the idea of Eros achieves cosmic significance. In Plato, Eros is the soul's striving after the object of its desire, its urge towards the ultimately beautiful and desirable, the expression of a deep homesickness for its heavenly fatherland. In Aristotle, this conception is given a wider reference and applied, in so far as it can be applied, even to the physical world. "Platonic love as modified by Aristotle," says Scholz (in *Eros and Caritas*), "is thus a striving after that which is worth

striving after, and is so conceived that the existence of this love is claimed, not only for individuals with souls in our sense of the term, but for all the elements of the cosmos." Accordingly, in order to see the significance of the idea of Eros in Aristotle, we must turn not so much to his ethics as to his metaphysics, and especially to his doctrine of motion ... It is the Pure Form that in the last resort sets the whole process (of the universe) in motion, but it does so without being itself involved in any motion or change; itself unmoved, it is the principle of all movement. But how is it possible for that which itself is completely unmoved to set anything else in motion? Aristotle's answer is the famous ... "it moves by being loved...." *We thus find the Eros of Plato raised to the level of a cosmic force.* However different Aristotle may otherwise be from Plato, with regards to the idea of Eros he is Plato's faithful disciple (*Agape and Eros*, 182–84).

Hence, the central high medieval concept of God as the "unmoved mover." Aristotle's development of Plato builds on Socrates' identification of Heavenly Eros as the motive force of the universe. All activity arises from desire, however thwarted or misguided, to approach the ideal, the form of forms. Aristotle is faithful here not only to Plato, but also to the essential Orphic message of Socrates: that the spark of the divine in us longs to go home and naturally, out of self-interest, seeks union with the highest Good. This position constitutes a fundamental challenge to Augustine's uneasy yoking of Eros with Agape in Caritas. God does not miraculously intervene to redeem a worthless humanity; a cosmic magnetism, in effect, draws man inexorably towards an essentially indifferent God. The concept of God as the unmoved mover represents a triumph of Socratic thought over Jesus' teachings, although the great medieval philosopher/theologians rarely mention Socrates' name and certainly (except perhaps for Abelard) didn't see it that way.

This complete transformation of Christianity's central message from Caritas to Eros had been thoroughly prepared for by the only force that had held some semblance of learning together through the Dark Ages — monasticism. Frequently Gnostic in its original manifestations during the Roman Empire, systematized by Benedict in the sixth century, and made socially relevant by the Cluniacs, medieval monasticism instilled a series of practices designed to lead man to God. Benedict himself had written: "If we wish to attain the pinnacle of the highest humility and quickly come to that heavenly exaltation to which the ascent is made by humility of the present life, then we must by our upward-striving works erect that ladder which was revealed to Jacob in the dream" (*Monastic Regulations*). Here we see one of the most influential figures in the history of Christianity looking to the *Old Testament* — not to Jesus of Nazareth — to justify an entirely Erotic concept of humankind's relation to the divine.

A sixth century forger, Dionysius, whose work the Catholic Church adopted as canonical, had fed this process by attributing Neo-Platonic gradations from man to God, derived from Plotinus, to a close associate of St. Paul (the Church didn't admit these documents were fakes until the nineteenth century). Jesus had taught that God had come to man unsought in his person. But the High Middle Ages, a period of increasing social diversification and stratification, had discovered in practice that only by emphasizing salvation by works (Eros) as opposed to salvation by faith (Agape) could humanity be productively organized. Agape was preserved in the writings of medieval mystics who claimed personal visitations from Jesus, but these ecstatic eccentrics were generally marginalized by the Church bureaucracy, then canonized after they were safely dead. Christian Agape, as Jesus had intended, could be completely disruptive of hierarchical social order. Ecstatic Agape created an increasing undercurrent of disruptive spirituality during the twelfth through fourteenth centuries that periodically erupted in Gnostic cults, such as the Albigensien movement in Provence or the poor peoples' and children's' crusades that set tens of thousands of people walking to Jerusalem to liberate the Holy Land. Such outbursts invariably resulted in mass slaughter at the hands of the French government, the Byzantine Empire, the Turks, or simply hostile local communities along the way.

It was the Spanish Muslim Averroes' assertion of a "double truth" — one in science and another in faith — as developed by Abelard — that set Thomas Aquinas (1225–1272) on his great mission to prove the essential Christian doctrines by reason. He entirely adopted Aristotelian Eros and methodology in his grand synthesis of high medieval philosophy, the *Summa Theologica*. God was the unmoved mover, his existence could be proved by the fact that everything had to have a cause, and it was humankind's job to climb the ladder towards Him. Aquinas made full use of Aristotelian dialectical reasoning, although unlike Abelard, he always resolved his Sics and Nons into orthodox conclusions — sometimes by force. Aristotle's influence on Aquinas restored the erotic connection between sensuality and science that Augustine had banned, opening a way for Socrates' return to the Western Pantheon. The cat was out of the bag.

If the greatest theologian of the era agreed that faith required the support of reason, then reason could also be legitimately applied to examining the phenomena of the natural world, as had been done in classical times, particularly by Aristotle and his successors. Equally important, the claims of faith must be subject to the tests of reason. Over time, the Church generally accepted Aquinas' solutions, creating an intellectual and political climate that made the Renaissance possible, starting with the relatively independent states in northern Italy. The rise of a mercantile middle class there had created a literate citizenry with a serious say in the government and the power to hold off the great northern monarchs on the one hand, and the Church on the other. This opened an imperiled but expanding zone of free thought. Into this breech, Socrates reemerged not only as an underground influence, but also as a revered mentor.

DANTE

The Florentine Dante Alighieri (1265–1321), a resident of the most intellectually independent city in Europe, took the fullest advantage of Aquinas's innovations. It's often said that his *Divine Comedy* put the *Summa Theologica* into verse, and to some extent that's true. As Cantor observes:

> [*The Divine Comedy*] has been viewed as the summation of medieval orthodox religious thought and also as a presentation in allegorical and poetical form of the chief teaching of (Aquinas). There is much to commend this interpretation. Dante describes how he was led on a journey from the depths of Hell, through Purgatory and Heaven, to the glory of the beatific vision.... There is a rough parallel between this scheme of religious pilgrimage and Thomistic doctrine.... There are some aspects of *The Divine Comedy*, however, which are sharply at variance with its generally orthodox and traditional teaching ... (including) many expressions of hostility to the claims of the papacy (*Medieval History*, 551–53).

Subtly in *The Divine Comedy* and more overtly in political essays such as *On Monarchy*, Dante introduces an argument that will carry the day over the next centuries: that there should be a separation of powers between civil authority and the Church. We can see this as the resurgence — and ultimate triumph — of the Averroes/Abelard "double truth" argument: reason and faith are separate and often contradictory, reason has its own natural sphere in science and public affairs, and no legitimate case can be made for temporal authority on the part of the Church. Western intellectuals and rulers alike began to push back against Hildebrand's extreme claims of papal authority.

In the whole body of his work, then, Dante doesn't fulfill the Thomist synthesis of reason and faith; he overthrows it. Separation of Church and State began the end of the Middle Ages. It's even possible that Dante, a man of breathtaking intelligence and erudition, intentionally literalized the gradations between man and God to explode Aquinas's system and the claims of the Church to universal rule. I'm unaware of anyone who has systematically interpreted the *Comedy* as intentionally satiric, but it seems likely Dante was subverting contemporary orthodoxies much as Swift later did in *Gulliver's Travels*. Walter Benjamin once said, "Every great work destroys an era or founds one." Dante did both.

For the first time since the Roman Empire, fact and reason had reemerged as sovereign goods, and with them reappeared their greatest champion: Socrates. Sensitive to the still enormous powers of the Church, Dante could not, as he might have liked, assign Socrates to Heaven in *The Divine Comedy*; fundamental Catholic theology taught that no one could be in direct communication with God who had not come to him through Jesus Christ. Even Virgil, whom many theologians believed had prefigured Christ in several poems (that in fact are flatteries of Augustus Caesar), and clearly represents reason, could conduct Dante only as far as the lower stages of Purgatory. So Dante did the next best thing: he assigned Socrates to Limbo, the eternal dwelling of blessed pagans, where he presides perpetually over a convocation of the greatest philosophers. This restoration of Socrates' reputation gradually permeated all corners of European culture: by the fifteenth century, we see Marsilio Ficino, the Florentine Platonist, comparing Socrates' martyrdom to Christ's, and Erasmus in the Netherlands writing "Saint Socrates, pray for us."

The debt of the subsequent Renaissance to Dante can hardly be overestimated. Over and above even his resurrection of reason, in *The Divine Comedy* he had invented modern Italian, bequeathing, in Ezra Pound's phrase, "a language to think in," which in turn transformed Europe over the next century. Increasingly, literature and philosophy were written in the emerging vernaculars.

Dante's journey from the depths of Hell to the Divine presence provides the most beautiful and comprehensive summary of high medieval moral cosmology and eschatology. As McLuhan might say, it could be seen most perfectly as it was vanishing. During Dante's lifetime, it could be argued that the messy compromise between the governmental traditions of the mature barbarian tribes who actually ruled Western Europe and the Catholic Church, with its Augustinian marriage of pagan and Judeo–Christian culture, was finally working. The major countries and city–states had gelled into coherent political units, growing increasingly efficient and populous. The rule of law prevailed more often than not; it was possible if not always safe to travel from London to the Mid-East for purposes of commerce or pilgrimage (Marco Polo made it to China and back). Educational institutions, while confined to the larger cities, increasingly took in students of all classes. Under a series of competent and often idealistic Popes and monastic leaders, the Church had earned a certain moral ascendency and generally used it wisely, ameliorating the plight of the oppressed, urging more humane standards of warfare, and providing an effective clearinghouse for international relations. The stable, divinely ordered late medieval hierarchy — from peasant to merchant to landowner to knight to aristocracy to King to God — probably rang true to most residents of Europe around 1300.

The Black Death of 1348, however, fractured this fragile synthesis into its component parts. At least a third of the population of Europe died horribly in the course of a year or so. Nakedness, disease, and corruption were everywhere; God's mercy was visible nowhere. Many observed that the good and the healthy were the first to die. Social bonds collapsed as family members deserted each other, priests refused to visit infected areas, local authorities and governmental institutions proved unable to meet the challenge. In the aftermath, peasants, suddenly scarce, were able to bargain for better wages; "hedge priests" and political agitators roamed among the laboring classes offering millennial visions of secular utopia and the authority of the Church suffered a continental shock.

The Black Death directly generated the skepticism, crisis of faith, activism, and social mobility that led to the birth of the early modern era. Augustine's Caritas compromise finally broke apart: pagan Socratic Eros presiding over the Renaissance and stern Christian Agape over the Reformation. Monarchs and even cities felt increasingly free to defy the will of the Church, while Popes grew increasingly luxurious and corrupt, seduced by the pagan Eye. The more complicated era to come was foreshadowed early in the 14th century when the King of France sent a gang of thugs to kidnap the Pope, got away with it, and set up his own papacy in Avignon. Never again would the Papacy preside unchallenged over Western Europe.

With Eros and Agape, State and Church, once again in a contest of equals, religious, artistic, political, economic, and philosophical debates could rekindle and Western civilization again began to lurch forward. By the sixteenth century, Western Europe had regained the intellectual and economic ground it had lost during the previous millennium. Over the next century it would match or surpass its predecessors in every field, if often by imitation. All these factors combined to produce the greatest outburst of art and thought since ancient Greece.

9. Socrates, Jesus, and the Renaissance

Reflecting the collapse of Aquinas' late-medieval consensus, fifteenth century Europe experienced endless dynastic wars, social dislocation, plagues, and the outbreak of apocalyptic religious movements. But in northern Italy, and to a lesser extent in the Low Countries, the early Renaissance saw Socratic philosophy reemerge as an equal competitor with the Christian Caritas compromise that had dominated the Middle Ages.

Nygren comments:

> During the whole Middle Ages, Eros had been a living reality — but it was *imprisoned* in the Caritas-synthesis. As perhaps the most important element in this synthesis, Eros had largely molded the interpretation of Christianity without anyone realizing what a transformation in Christianity it effected. In default of direct contact with the Greek sources for the Agape or Eros outlook, the modificatory influence which each of these two motifs exercised upon the other was generally unperceived.... Owing to the stream of Greek refugees, who in the middle of the fifteenth century came to Italy when the Turks conquered Constantinople, the West came into direct contact with [ancient] Greek culture and language. The result was a greatly increased study of the Classics, and not least of ancient philosophy (*Agape and Eros*, 667–68).

The fact that Dante and his successors had developed the rationale for a secular sphere independent of the Church provided a motive for monarchs and other rulers to ally with the emerging humanists. The secular philosophers had developed workable theories, based on their classical studies, of how to govern effectively. They encouraged the growth of an increasingly rational international economic system, importantly promoted by Italian bankers. Gradually these developments spread northward across Europe, encouraging the growth of a merchant class independent of the feudal strictures of the Middle Ages. First in isolated enclaves, and by 1500 more generally, Europe enjoyed some degree of free trade in goods and ideas for the first time since the seventh century, abetting the rise of great cities. Populations boomed; export industries flourished; guilds of merchants and artisans multiplied. The emerging middle class valued hard facts and craved a nourishing, entertaining, and more ostentatious secular culture. In capitals such as London and Paris they gained influence; in a number of city–states in Italy and the Low Countries, they ruled.

Cosimo de Medici (1389–1464)

The penetration of Greek scholarship into the city–states of northern Italy had actually begun earlier than Nygren suggests, through Venice, which controlled large chunks of the decadent Byzantine Empire, and most importantly under the sponsorship of the Medici family, which, with a few interruptions, ruled Florence from the fifteenth to the mid-eighteenth centuries.

Although the Medicis had been prominent in Florentine politics since around 1300 and were among the city" leading banking families, Cosimo initiated their central role in Florentine government and culture. He rarely held public office, but his character, his extensive international banking connections, and his modest good judgment made him the man with the last word in Florence from his middle years until the time of his death. Christopher Hibbert (*The House of Medici*, New York, William Morrow and Company, 1975) describes him in terms that help explain why he became one of the most extraordinary men in European history:

> He had received his early education at the school of the Camaldolese monastery of Santa Maria degli Angeli, where he had begun to learn German and French, as well as Latin and a smattering of Hebrew, Greek, and Arabic. Later, together with the young sons of other rich Florentine families, he had attended the lectures and lessons of Roberto de' Rossi, one of the leading scholars of the day and himself a member of an old and wealthy Florentine family. Under Roberto de'Rossi's enlightened guidance, and thereafter in discussion groups at the Santa Maria degli Angeli monastery which he continued to attend in his middle age, Cosimo acquired and developed deep respect for classical learning and classical ideals, combined with an interest in man's life on earth which was to remain with him forever. He became, in fact, a humanist.... Certainly there were few Florentine humanists with a wider knowledge of classical manuscripts that he began to collect at an early age, and there were scarcely any who were more intensely concerned with the importance of humanistic ideals in the conduct of public life. Although he himself never became a master of those arts and disciplines, such as rhetoric, which the humanist was taught to practice, he never questioned the right of those who did master them to occupy the most honored positions in Florentine society (37–38).

This thumbnail sketch tells us how much had changed in the century since Aquinas. First, a broad, largely secular education grounded in classical philosophy was available to families of means, even through institutions of the Church. Second, such an education was valued as a badge of honor by the leading families of the city. Third, cultural leadership had become a way to — in fact, a prerequisite for — political power. Such conditions had not obtained in Western Europe for a thousand years. Rich from trade, increasingly literate, with a burgeoning middle class, largely in control of their own destinies because of the standoff between the Church and the newly confident monarchies to the north, the Italian city–states, especially Florence, were plundering the ancient past in search of *how to be human rather than (or in conjunction with) how to be saved.* The focus had shifted from the next life to this one, mostly because this one had become far more tolerable, secure, and interesting than it had been since the Roman Empire.

As trustee of the Studio Fiorentino, the Florentine university, Cosimo added professors of moral philosophy, rhetoric, and poetry to the standard medieval faculty. He turned Florence into the Academy of Europe, and his family generally kept up that practice for three hundred years. The Medicis celebrated the tradition of Socratic Heavenly Eros as newly and directly available through translations of Plato.

Sometimes groups count for more than individual geniuses in the advancement of science and philosophy, and this was often true during the Renaissance. The key members of Cosimo's humanist circle included:

Niccolo Nicoli. Nicoli was obsessed with antiquity and assembled the greatest collection of classical manuscripts in his day. He developed a cursive script that permitted easy transcription and set the standard for italics in early Italian printing. He became, in effect, the first modern publisher.

Poggio Bracciolini. Whereas Nicoli sought out primarily Eastern classical texts, Bracciolini raided the monasteries of Europe, discovering previously unknown manuscripts such as Lucretius' *On the Nature of Things* as well as complete copies of major classical works previously known only in fragments. He encouraged the study of archeology and excelled as a scholar, essayist, historian, and raconteur. He also developed the model for modern handwriting and printing.

Leonardo Bruni. Bruni, translator and orator, was "the greatest Latinist of his age," and apparently a brilliant, haughty, avaricious character. His main contributions fell in the areas of ideology and practical politics. He help create a unique sense of mission for Florence by insisting that it was the modern heir to the great classical republics and he summoned it to become Europe's cultural capital. Bruni served as the state's Chancellor from 1427 until his death in 1444.

Gemistus Pletho. A Byzantine scholar who settled in Florence in 1439, Pletho had read deeply in the work of Plato and apparently inspired Cosimo to found the great Platonic Academy.

While none of these men could be classified as geniuses on the order of Aquinas or Dante, they demonstrated that a collaborative group of scholars could create a body of work that would change the direction of Western civilization. Bracciolini and Bruni came from extremely humble backgrounds, which emphasizes the remarkable social and intellectual mobility encouraged by the Medicis in fifteenth century Florence — another tradition Cosimo's family was to continue. The qualities of personality and individual accomplishment — Nietzsche's *principium individuationis* — had become available to any man of talent in early Renaissance Florence.

The Platonic Academy in particular decisively influenced the future of European thought. Led by Marsilio Ficino (1433–99) and Pico della Mirandola (1463–99), it translated all the essential works of Plato into Latin and promoted a climate of free inquiry. Constantly protected by Cosimo, and later by his grandson Lorenzo "the Magnificent," the Academy created an impetus that would drive scholastic Aristotelianism out of the major European academic institutions within a couple of generations. Ficino presented the first installment of his translations from Plato to Cosimo months before the great old man's death in 1464. Nygren writes:

> Ficino's admiration for Plato knew no bounds…. In such circumstances it is not surprising that Platonic dualism and Neoplatonic mysticism occupy a large place in Ficino's thought. The soul is a stranger and sojourner here on earth, and man's misfortune is that this immortal divine soul is imprisoned in a mortal body…. Philosophy is a Way of salvation, the way of Eros…. But it would be quite wrong … to assume from this that Ficino merely revives Neoplatonism. It is true that Ficino himself liked to regard his work in this light, but there are elements in his thought which point in a very different direction … It is a question of the new emphasis which is laid on man in his temporal existence: empirical man is made, in a way such as never before, the center of the universe. In a word, it is a question of *the human god* (*Agape and Eros*, 669–71).

Augustine's Platonism and Aquinas' Aristotelianism had always contained their Socratic lines of thought in uneasy alliance with prevailing Christian orthodoxy. But Ficino's position represented unadulterated Eros and, by the standards of the Church, rank heresy on several grounds. Its version of Neo-Platonism flaunted its Gnostisism in both its dualism and its mysticism. Its suggestion that any man other than Christ might become godlike could not be countenanced by even the most liberal Christian orthodox traditions. Empirical man could know only by verifying, that is, by means of reason, science, and the senses. Philosophy, in other words, no longer claimed to be another truth, separate from the equal truth found through faith. The only truth, it overthrew the truth of the Church. No such speculation could have been pursued without the protection of a patron as powerful as Cosimo de Medici.

Nygren's reservations aside, the claim that men could become gods was entirely consonant with the antique spirit and contained the suggestion that godlike men were as close to God as we could get. The idea of individuality awakened by Abelard and dramatized by Dante burst into full flower. Cosimo put his philosophy into practical action by sponsoring not only scholars, but also Brunelleschi, who erected the Duomo over Florence's great cathedral; Ghilberti, who sculpted the Baptistry doors which Michelangelo later called the "gateway to heaven"; Donatello; della Robbia; Fra Angelico; Filippo Lippi; Uccello; and many others. Self-manifesting individuals flooded into Western history. As far away as England, Chaucer, who had visited Italy and read Boccaccio, created a series of indelible types — if not personalities — in his *Canterbury Tales*. Artists began signing their paintings and became celebrities. Indeed artistic achievement was the key to the Renaissance, often driven by an Apollonian homosexual aesthetic that had been repressed since the triumph of Christianity. It represented the return of the pagan Eye, the triumph of the individual, visual, and the sensual over the communal, oral, and ascetic. Equally, the pagan Eye invited scientific examination of the sensible world.

As Camille Paglia writes in *Sexual Personae*:

> The sudden intellectual and geographical expansion of culture inaugurated three centuries of psychological turbulence. Renaissance style was spectacle and display, a pagan ostentation. The Renaissance liberated the Western eye, repressed by the Christian Middle Ages. In that eye, sex and aggression are amorally fused.... At the Renaissance, says Jacob Burckhardt, there was an "awakening of personality." Renaissance art teems with personalities, arrogant, seductive, vivacious. Italy restores the pagan theatricality of Western identity.... What would have been vanity and sybaritism in the Middle Ages becomes the public language of personae.... The white marble of the Florentine Duomo is crossed with red and green, hallucinatory vibrations in the Italian sun (140–141).

This "burst of color" (in Paglia's phrase) represented the spirit that unleashed the Renaissance and the modern era. It accompanied the re-enthronement of Socrates foreshadowed by Dante.

LORENZO DE MEDICI (1449–92)

James Cleugh writes of Cosimo's grandson Lorenzo:

> Lorenzo embodied the ideal of what might be called "the Renaissance man" — that is, the man to whom nothing human is foreign.... He was famous as a poet, and still more famous as a statesman. In the domain of agriculture, as well as in that of music and architecture, his interests went beyond contemplation to action. He could judge a painting or sculpture as well as any professional of his day. He collected books and manuscripts with taste and discrimination. He bred racehorses expertly. He loved hunting, pageantry, and also less pretentious forms of entertainment. He could work all day and half the night at the problems of public affairs. He could turn easily from a romp with his children, who were characteristically encouraged never to call him anything but "Lorenzo," or his boon companions, to attend Mass or debate with a great theologian. And whether the head of the Republic was being ribald or deadly serious, he

expressed his views with a grace and precision that few of his contemporaries ... could rival. In private he lived simply, but his public appearances were usually ceremonious in the high Renaissance manner, although they consistently avoided flamboyance in manner of dress.... Finally, the practically effective help, in particular financial relief that he gave to friends in trouble is illustrated again and again in contemporary chronicles (*The Medicis*, New York, Dorset Press, 1975, 175).

As the most respected man in Italy, perhaps in all Europe, Lorenzo regularly used his influence to broker peace among the peninsula's welter of warring states.

Lorenzo, in Ficino's phrase, was a god-like man and he spawned a seeming race of them. He immediately recognized the genius of working-class boys such as Leonardo Da Vinci and Michelangelo and took them under his wing. The number of philosophers, scholars, artists, architects, archeologists, engineers, and scientists that he sponsored, educated, and patronized would take pages to list, but they included Ficino, Pico, Donatello, Verrocchio, Michelangelo, Da Vinci, and Botticelli. All of them enacted the Platonic Academy's doctrine that "physical beauty is love's emanation, and so identical with it" (*The Medicis*, 174), and they proceeded to put this conviction to work in the greatest outburst of thought and art since ancient Athens.

Heavenly Eros, and its Socratic twin, Reason, had burst the fetters of Agape, and the genie would never again be put back into the bottle. Sexual attraction and its Socratic ally reason henceforth repulsed every attempt to repress it in the name of divine revelation. The greatest scientists, writers, philosophers, artists, and engineers (in the cases of Michelangelo and Leonardo Da Vinci combined in the same persons) were indeed regarded as "god-like men." When Michelangelo visited Clement VII, the Pope (a Medici) would always sit down at once because, he said, "Otherwise he would sit down before me." In the last years of his life, the King of France, simply for the delight and honor of his conversation, accorded Leonardo Da Vinci the status of a fellow sovereign.

For all his sponsorship of secular thought and art — degenerate paganism in the eyes of the more rigorous religious orders, if not usually to the increasingly worldly Papacy — Lorenzo maintained at least the appearance of a deep conventional Christian piety. This was enough to save him during his lifetime, though so much radical change in so short a time was certain to produce a reaction. On his deathbed, Lorenzo turned to the consolations of a popular monk, Savonarola, who had been preaching fire and brimstone to huge crowds under the Duomo. It was said that all Italy, even his political enemies, mourned Lorenzo when he died, and feared much worse days were to come. The Pope exclaimed, "The peace of Italy is at an end."

SAVONAROLA (1452–98)

Although Lorenzo's son Pietro inherited his father's informal position as head of the Republic after his death, power was now within the grasp of Savonarola due to his control over the masses. This fact — that a previously unknown monk could control a great state through popular support — marks a new stage in European history. Often portrayed after his brief career and spectacular death as "the mad monk," Savonarola was in fact a brilliant and complex figure of considerable historical importance. Hibbert provides a brief portrait of him:

> Savonarola had convinced himself that he was gifted with foreknowledge of the future, that his words were divinely inspired and that to deny their truth was to deny the wisdom of God. "It is not I who preach," he said, "but God who speaks through me." After prolonged periods of fasting and meditations, visions of the future had been vouchsafed to him. He knew the Church was to be scourged, then regenerated, and that "these things would come quickly to pass." He knew, too, that unless the people of Italy and, in particular the people of Florence, mended their ways they would be punished dreadfully. Only a return to the simplicity of the early Christian Church could save them. They must turn their back on Aristotle and Plato, who were now rotting in hell; they must abandon the luxuries and sensual pleasures that were destroying their souls, abolish gambling and card games, dissolute carnivals and palio races, fine clothes and scent, powder and paint; and they must give the money they saved to the poor. They must blot out all those pictures so wantonly painted that they made "the Virgin Mary look like a harlot." They must chastise prostitutes — those "pieces of meat with eyes" — and burn sodomites alive. They must reform their political institutions (*The House of Medici*, 180).

Savonarola's battle, then, was not just against the open triumph of Eros in Florence, but more importantly against the covert triumph of Eros in the whole Catholic Church. Other reformers had preceded him such as Wycliffe in England and Jan Hus in the Holy Roman Empire, but neither had controlled a powerful state in the heart of Italy, and neither had Savonarola's hypnotic powers as a preacher or his fanatical popular following. Decades later, as an old man, Michelangelo said his could still hear the Dominican friar's voice ringing in his ears.

Although Savonarola didn't favor the loving and forgiving elements in Jesus' message, there is no doubt that he was recalling Christianity to the apocalyptic vision of the primitive Christian Church. The end was near, material things must be put off, and only total submission to God's stern love could save mankind from hell in the coming judgment. Savonarola represented more than a backlash against the concept of a secular society; he personified, quite consciously, the revenge of Agape on Eros and foreshadowed the more thoughtful reformers who would break the Catholic Church's monopoly on faith in Europe within a generation.

After Pietro de Medici conspicuously failed to stave off an invasion of Italy by the King of France in 1494, he fled into exile. Savonarola assumed the formal leadership of Florence and ruled as a popular tyrant for four years. Nor did he fail to put his apocalyptic program of salvation into action:

> With crucifix in hand, he urged the people to put to death all those who advocated the restoration of the Medici. God had called him to reform the city and the Church, and God's will would be done. There must be continual fasting; the golden ornaments and illuminated books, the silver chalices and candlesticks and jewelled crucifixes must be removed from the convents and monasteries. "Blessed Bands" of children, their hair cut short, must march through the streets, singing hymns, collecting alms for the poor, and seeking out those rouge-pots and looking-glasses, those lascivious pictures and immoral books, all those "vanities" which were the Devil's invitation to vice (*The House of Medici*, 191).

Savonarola was nothing if not sincere. At the peak of his power, he summoned all Florence to a true "Bonfire of the Vanities." Erecting an enormous scaffold in the Piazza della Signoria decorated with fine clothing, all sorts of cosmetics, jewelry, games, paintings, and books by, among others, Plato and Aristotle, he put everything to the flame. What finally brought him down was his continued assault on the corruption of the papacy and the Catholic Church as a whole. A combination of revolted Florentines and papal agents burnt him at the stake on the same spot where he had torched all the symbols and manifestations of Eros.

After a period of revolving governments, the Medicis were brought back to rule Florence as heads of a formally Republican state. For the most part they continued their traditional role as protectors of knowledge, secular rule, and the arts, sponsoring the work of, among others, Galileo (1564–1642), who more than anyone else founded modern science. During this period, the Florentine formulation of Socrates as a master of secular wisdom spread throughout Europe, and with it knowledge of his life, his legend, his devotion to reason, and his example of martyrdom to objective truth. To Montaigne, writing in the sixteenth century, Socrates "was not a Christ-like figure, but a paradigm of natural virtue and wisdom, and the supernatural elements in the ancient portrayal, particularly the divine sign, were to be explained in naturalistic terms; the sign was perhaps a faculty of instinctive, unreasoned decision, facilitated by his settled habits of wisdom and virtue" (Taylor, *Socrates*, 89). Socrates, in other words had become the secular saint and mentor for the early modern empirical world. This was bound to produce the continental reaction that Savonarola had anticipated.

The spread of the Renaissance throughout Northern Europe lies outside the scope of this work, but one exception must be made. The Renaissance arrived latest in England, still a provincial country compared to the leading states of Italy or France, but it burned there with a gem-like flame. Its presiding spirit, Shakespeare, it could be argued, married Apollo and Dionysius in his mind and work more happily than any thinker since Socrates or any writer since Plato.

SHAKESPEARE (1564–1616)

Almost uniquely among great world figures, Shakespeare's biography is of little interest in considering his work. He married young, left home to work in the theater in London, acted, wrote plays, became a partner in his companies, and at the peak of his career retired, a wealthy man, to the life of a well-respected gentleman in his hometown of Stratford. His romantic life, as best we can tell, was bisexual in the Greek Erotic tradition.

What matters are the plays. Harold Bloom, our greatest living literary critic, claims Shakespeare "invented the human," and while this may be a pardonable exaggeration, it's certainly true that Shakespeare not only captured the Renaissance explosion of individual personality, he expanded its possibilities in reach, in depth, in language, in style, and in action. Although conventional religious figures appear in many Shakespeare plays, the atmosphere, and often the setting, is pagan.

In would be impossible in a study of this type to survey his staggering body of work in detail, but consider just this one play as a synecdoche:

The Tempest, the last play written entirely by Shakespeare (1611), takes the entire human universe for its subject. In it, this most self-aware of all writers encapsulates all the themes he has addressed over the greatest career in literature. Its structure embodies his trope of the "green world," central to many other plays such as *As you Like It*, where characters retreat from the corrupted city to a simpler and more wholesome place, bring the human hierarchy into correspondence with the natural order, and at the play's end return this purified vision to the larger world. It is a masque in the sense that its great pageantry is set to music. It is a history in the sense that it aims ultimately at a political resolution. It is a comedy in the sense that love triumphs and right governance is restored. It is a tragedy in the sense that great sacrifices must be offered to achieve this reunion of the human and the divine.

It tells much that the plays opens in disaster and confusion as the shipwrecked mariners emerge dripping from the sea. The sea — its flux, its solemn power, the endless lapping of waves — is everywhere in *The Tempest*. It represents the primordial ooze from which mankind was crafted, and to which that re-invention of the Renaissance, the individual personality, is destined to return. Gradually, a microcosm of human society is elaborated on this special island: from the oafish evil of a Caliban, who represents the final reduction of Shakespeare's villains, to the ethereal Ariel, a curiously willful and resentful "spright" who must be captured to serve human purposes and longs only for freedom. Between these two poles fall the other characters, with their mixed motives, their loves, their ambitions, and their moral dislocations. Ultimately, Shakespeare tells us, divinity must be enslaved if it is to serve human purposes, and even a restored natural order on earth will remain provisional, that is, human.

Music provides the central imagery of the play in consonance with the Renaissance idea, derived from the Greeks, that it represented the highest of the arts, the "music of the spheres." Lyrics by Shakespeare and melodies originally by Robert Johnson — "solemne and strange Musicke" — urge on the social harmony toward which the play tends. We are reminded that Greek comedy and tragedy — indeed all of Western poetry — emerged from the "goat dances" held in Athens to commemorate the Eleusinian Mystery Cycle of death and rebirth.

Over this brilliant, limited, magical world presides Prospero, arguably a surrogate for Shakespeare himself. As Peter Ackroyd writes in *Shakespeare, a Biography*, "Shakespeare has created the most artificial of all plays that becomes a meditation upon artifice itself." Artifice here must be taken most seriously as the art of creating meaning, ways in which we understand our world more deeply. When Prospero says "Our revels are now ended," and frees Ariel, he abandons most importantly his power to create a magical world — the world of Shakespeare's plays.

In an interview with Eleanor Wachtel Bloom notes:

> Shakespeare is universal. Shakespeare is the true multicultural author. He exists in all languages. He is put on stage everywhere. Everyone feels they are represented by him on the stage ... I don't know who Shakespeare was. He has hidden himself behind all of these extraordinary men and women.... One cares about wisdom, and in the end one wants to be judged by wisdom. If one hasn't got it, one has to ask the biblical question "Where shall wisdom be found?" And I suppose for me, the answer is: wisdom is to be found in Shakespeare, provided you get at it in the right way (*Queen's Quarterly*, v 102, #3, Fall, 1995, 609–19).

10. The Resurgence of Agape During the Protestant Reformation

The Reformation, based in Luther's close reading of Paul, echoed the chiliastic view of Savonarola. It introduced unadulterated Agape back into the mainstream of Western Christianity. Once more believers, like *Old Testament* Jews, quivered as sinners in the hands of an angry God who loved them despite their inherent worthlessness. Nygren observes, "Augustine finds the synthesis of (Eros and Agape) in his doctrine of Caritas, and it is this very synthesis that Luther smashes to pieces" (560). Or, more delicately: "The Middle Ages made the best they could of the doctrine of Caritas; they followed the path of Caritas as far as it ever led. But it was reserved for Luther to see that this path was impracticable, to abandon the idea of Caritas, and to rediscover primitive Christian Agape as the only legitimate point of departure for the Christian doctrine of love" (641). As Luther demonstrates beautifully, eruptions of pure Agape change society to its roots rapidly, orphicly; they signify a radical shift of sensibility. Just as rapidly, the creative inspiration of Agape is channeled into daily behaviors that have thrown off the shackles of the previous era and are proving practical in a new environment.

The Catholic Church's incorporation of Eros into its theology, stretching back to Augustine and before, had left the way open for precisely the sort of "Christian humanism" sponsored by the Medici and temporarily overthrown by Savonarola. With the Reformation, and Luther's radical reassertion of Judeo–Christian Agape, Socrates and Jesus were released from their forced marriage of convenience, and went, as most broken marriages do, to war. They have struggled for the soul of Western Civilization ever since.

Martin Luther (1483–1546)

Rather like Paul, Luther appears to have gone into Christ's service after being struck by lightning while traveling during a thunderstorm. He entered the Augustinian order of Eremites at Erfurt and prepared for ordination in its theological seminary. The Eremites emphasized the Erotic strain in Augustine's teachings but went further, drawing heavily on Augustine's opponent Pelagius, who had argued that man could approach God through good works even without divine grace. Luther, desperately concerned for his own salvation, wondered whether he was being severely enough judged. He put aside the prevalent teachings of the neo-scholastic (Aristotelian) theologians and undertook a radical rereading of the *New Testament*. There he rediscovered Agape in its purest form.

Harold J. Grimm, the Reformation historian, summarizes his spiritual development:

> Luther's difficulty did not lie in his failure to understand the teaching of the church concerning the importance of faith, works, and grace, but in his inability to accept them and to believe with assurance that a righteous God would save him. When he examined his life, as he was required to do constantly as a monk, he found he was not leading a perfect life of love for God; and when he pondered over this problem in terms of scholastic theology, he could not bow without question to the authority of the Church.... Despite his faithful use of the sacrament of penance, he was aware of his natural proclivities toward imperfect spiritual attitudes, such as pride and anger, and could not be certain that God as his stern judge would find enough merits, either his own or those of God and the saints, to save him from eternal damnation.... Luther was searching for absolute certainty that a righteous God would accept him, and this he could not find until he had discarded the doctrine of merits and developed the emphasis of Paul upon God's righteousness as justifying man by faith (*The Reformation Era*, New York, the MacMillan Company, 1967, 99–100).

These views were reinforced when Luther served on a mission to Rome, governed in 1510 by the luxurious, militaristic, and secular Pope Julius II, a great patron of the Renaissance. As Grimm comments, "[H]e did not find in Rome the certainty of salvation, the lack of which lay at the bottom of his religious anxieties" (*The Reformation Era*, 101). Rather, Luther became convinced, the Catholic Church had corrupted Jesus' vision of a God-centered love into a near-pagan man-centered — even self-centered — love. He must have found evidence for this all around him in his visit to Italy: the profusion of pagan art even within the Vatican itself; the worldliness, political ambition, greed, and lasciviousness of the papacy; and the tolerance of frankly pagan philosophers such as Ficino and his successors. Intellectual revolutions tend to come from the cultural provinces; Luther was, and remained, determinedly provincial. He realized Europe was religiously and politically ill, trying to shed an old skin, much as he himself was. But his channeling of the age resulted in a far different world than he expected.

On October 31, 1517, Luther posted his famous 95 Theses on the door of the Castle Church in Wittenberg. At this time, and for many years afterwards, he sought not to break with the Catholic Church but rather to reform it from within. He first aimed at a target large and easy to hit: selling indulgences, largely to the poor, which would remit past sins. Indulgences provided a major source of income for the papacy, and hucksters sponsored by the Pope were raffling them off all over Europe without any defensible theological justification. The sixteenth century Popes generally needed this money to buy more pagan art and to set their relatives up as rulers throughout Italy.

Luther initially asserted that if the Pope had the power to remit sin (which he doubted) he should do it freely out of Christian charity. He gradually expanded this critique to include the selling of ecclesiastical offices where favored prelates received the income from a benefice without having to provide any service or religious guidance. Outrage over these egregious abuses of credulity also became widespread among the growing reading and thinking public, most especially among the Catholic humanists, whose leader, Erasmus, had already mounted a serious although discrete critique of Church corruption within academic circles. It was said, "Luther hatched the egg that Erasmus had laid."

Luther himself had probably intended to launch a debate among Church scholars, but he was far more pugnacious than Erasmus and desperately concerned about the state of his soul. The charges he made in the Theses, subsequent pamphlets, and theological disputations spread widely, fueled by Gutenberg's recent invention of the printing press. He rapidly developed a mass following and simultaneously garnered protection from several powerful German leaders who recognized that the spread of Luther's doctrines would reduce the power of the Church in their territories and consequently strengthen their own.

While it was his attacks on obvious abuses that propelled Luther's doctrines into the cultural and political mainstream, they linked inextricably to his call for a return to the primitive Pauline Christianity cataloged in the *New Testament*. The Catholic Church might have been able to stem the tide of reformation by curtailing indulgences and the sale of benefices (as it belatedly did in the Counter-Reformation), but it could never accept Luther's rejection of over a millennium of Caritas theology and papal tradition. Luther's critique, echoing Dante, also questioned the Pope's claims to any temporal authority.

Pauline justification by faith meant, essentially, that the individual Christian didn't need the apparatus of the Church to approach God. The enormous implications of this theological revolution — grounded by Luther in prodigious scholarship — included the right of every Christian to read and interpret the *Bible* (consequently, rapid translations of the *Old* and *New Testaments* into every major European language, preeminently Luther's and the British *King James* versions), a rapid shift of power (including power over religious belief and practice) to the states, and the radical principle that the individual had a responsibility to participate in her or his own religious, economic, and political fate. This concept laid the foundations for the spread of education, the rise of secular states, the growth of an increasingly prosperous middle class, and, ultimately, the emergence of mass movements and democracy as real forces in European politics.

Luther's revolution moved very quickly through European society through the medium of the newly available printed word and not only because printing made distribution plentiful and cheap. As Marshall McLuhan points out, people suffer a sort of defenselessness in the face of a new medium: it creates both the opportunity and the need for new sorts of communities that appear almost without their members being aware that they and the world have changed.

REFORMATION AND REVOLUTION

Luther's unleashing of primitive Christian Agape with its emphasis upon individual responsibility had four enormous and counter-intuitive consequences, first religious, second, economic, third political, and fourth, cultural:

Religious Consequences of the Reformation. Contrary to his expectation, Luther's insistence that every person should have a personal relationship with the Divine and bear responsibility for his or her own salvation rapidly generated a bewildering variety of dissenters, all of whom claimed to possess the only true reading of the Bible.

Although numerous Protestant leaders and sects sprang up from England to Italy, John Calvin achieved the most influential refinement of Luther. He took Luther's emphasis on the primacy of faith to its logical extreme: humans were worthless sinners in the hands of an angry God who had predestined their fate before they had even been born. While Luther had stressed many of the loving and forgiving elements of Christ's message, Calvin emphasized a judgmental, *Old Testament* God and delighted in depicting the hellish tortures facing the vast majority of human beings in the afterlife. This went beyond even Savonarola's insistence that everyone must repent to be saved, which still suggested the possibility of salvation by works and faith.

While Luther preferred to cooperate with supportive political leaders, Calvin decided to become one. He took over Geneva, and, like Savonarola, tried to convert it into a saved heaven on earth through ruthless persecution and the judicial murder of religious and political opponents. Calvin's bleak version of Protestantism, through its influence in England, Scotland, the Low Countries, and, ultimately, North America, generated the widespread practice of capitalism, fueled the cult of individualism, and propelled the gradual rise of democracy that came to characterize the modern Western world.

Calvinism succeeded for two important reasons. First, Calvin's doctrine of predestination, which denied that any good works could benefit one in the afterlife, paradoxically generated a conviction that you could prove that you were already saved by doing well — especially financially — in this world. This was, in essence, Weber's "Protestant work ethic." Although a corruption of Calvin's doctrine, this appealed to the mercantile Swiss, and Calvin, or at least his successors, went along with it, because otherwise followers might decide you should enjoy the here-and-now while you could since your fate in the afterlife was already decided. Many Calvinist sects in fact developed in hedonistic or Epicurean directions; utopian cults sprung up in Europe and in the North American colonies. Second, if human beings could enforce heaven on earth, all sovereign individuals were essentially equal before God, and should have a say in how they were governed.

Economic consequences of the Reformation. A more subtle interpretation can be developed of the Protestant work ethic, however. Calvinism was incubated in Geneva, and the Swiss were by this time the most mercantile people in Europe. As Calvinism spread throughout northern Europe and America, it brought with it the values and practices of the Swiss merchants and bankers: thrift, hard work, and an entrepreneurial spirit. Perhaps most important, the Calvinists rejected the Roman Catholic strictures against usury, that is, lending money for profit. People who were "sovereign selves" were more comfortable than the Catholic faithful with making money, taking risks, and running their own businesses. Capital began to flow more freely. Finally, the opening of the world to trade by Portuguese, Spanish, Dutch, and English exploration created vast new markets and resources.

The "Dutch finance" model of capitalism, involving a stock market to provide investment first for global trade and then for domestic manufacturing, eventually migrated to Britain, taking form in the Bank of England in the late seventeenth century, and since World War Two has made its home (at least until very recently) on Wall Street. Capitalism experienced its first popped bubble in the Netherlands when the vast profits being made in the tulip trade finally collapsed. Other venture capital experiments such as the British "South Sea Bubble," based in the spice trade, encouraged hysterical speculation, bidding up prices of investments far over their true value, but on balance, and compared to their Catholic counterparts, the Protestant capitalist economies produced rapid population growth, the opportunity to develop new types of expertise (creating new jobs), and rising standards of living.

Political Consequences of the Reformation. The proliferation of Protestant sects, many with local government support, created not only vigorous international debate, but also safe havens for almost any point of view. Many rulers, whether out of political prudence or far-sightedness, practiced religious tolerance and gave broad latitude to the distinguished humanists who decorated their courts. Calvin's theocracy in Geneva might be executing Protestant "heretics" with an enthusiasm worthy of the Catholic Inquisition, but almost anything could be believed, said, or published in parts of northern Italy and the Low Countries.

Breaking the stranglehold of the Catholic Church on religious authority naturally called all other authority into question as well, and transformed the political landscape of Europe. Fired up by millennial preachers, German peasants rose in a social revolt, and Luther determined the future of his Church as a state religion by siding with the powers that be. In northern Germany, many rulers simply converted to Lutheranism, assumed control of the Church in their territory, disestablished the Catholic Church, and seized its property. This drastically increased secular power and was soon imitated by Henry VIII in England. The belated Catholic Counter-Reformation responded by purging the Church of its most unpopular and egregious practices while simultaneously enforcing an increasingly heavy-handed orthodoxy where it was still strong, especially in Spain and much of Italy. France, with its strong Protestant Huguenot movement, ultimately remained Catholic in form but maintained effective independence from the papacy.

International and civil conflicts were increasingly conducted along the religious fault lines. France burst into a long and brutal religious civil war, and a century after Luther's death a coalition of radical Protestant factions temporarily toppled the British monarchy. In this situation, religious debates naturally spilled over into discussions of right governance. France groped towards a national Catholic church, while in England, the temporarily victorious Puritans (1649–1660) experimented with and discussed a wider variety of political systems and theories than had been considered since ancient Greece. The English Revolutions inaugurated the discussion of serious political theory in both England and France and eerily prefigured both the French Revolution and the emergence in the next century of workable national representative governments.

The English Civil War originated in a religious dispute: the attempt by the King and the Archbishop of Canterbury to impose Protestant Anglicanism, which in some ways resembled Catholicism without the Pope, on the fiercely Calvinist and fundamentalist Scottish Presbyterians. The repression of the resulting Scottish rebellion nearly bankrupted the government, and as a result King Charles I was forced to convene a session of Parliament, whose sole major power at this time involved controlling the purse strings. The Short Parliament of 1640 resulted in a standoff between the royalists and the low-church Puritans who were deeply concerned about creeping Catholicism in the monarchy and the established church, but the Long Parliament that followed proved increasingly restive. It executed the King's chief military defender, the Earl of Strafford, and imprisoned the Archbishop of Canterbury, William Laud (who was eventually executed in 1645). Emboldened by these successes, Parliament went on to pass a series of revolutionary acts significantly expanding its powers: it decreed that it could not be dissolved without its own consent, required that Parliament be summoned into session every three years, abolished certain royal taxes regarded as illegal, and closed those courts considered to be tools of royal absolutism. The City of London rallied to the Parliamentary cause.

Charles at first conceded these points, but in January 1642 he committed a dreadful strategic blunder, invading Parliament but failing to capture the dissenting leaders who, forewarned, escaped. Parliament demanded control of the military and some executive royal powers, the King fled London, and in August the Civil War began. Parliament reconciled with the Scots, created its own army, and passed regulations turning the established Anglican Church in the direction of Presbyterian Calvinism. In the course of the early battles, the Parliamentary "New Model" army (the Roundheads) won several decisive victories over the royal forces (the Cavaliers) and produced its own leader in the previously obscure but consistently victorious country squire and General Oliver Cromwell.

Cromwell's army became a seething hotbed of social and religious reform and clashed repeatedly with the by now considerably more conservative Parliament. Defeated, the King fled to Scotland and surrendered. Cromwell sincerely engaged in negotiations with the King to restore a limited monarchy, but when Charles perfidiously rallied to the cause of Scottish Presbyterians and led an invasion of England, Cromwell had had enough. He purged Parliament of all elements except his supporters, who consisted mostly of dissenting religious denominations that wanted neither Anglicanism nor Presbyterianism but rather at least a limited freedom of religious conscience (limited, at least in that it did not include Catholicism). This significant leftward shift turned the Civil War from an essentially religious and political to a social revolution. The King was captured, tried, and finally executed in January of 1649. For a time Parliament really ruled England, but eventually, disgusted by its factions and increasing corruption, Cromwell dispersed Parliament and ruled as Lord Protector, a near-monarchical position, with the support of the radicalized army. He remained in power until his death in 1658 and governed very effectively, brutally suppressing an Irish revolt and strengthening England's position both domestically and internationally.

During the successive phases which led from royal absolutism to a proto-democratic Commonwealth and finally to effective power sharing between the restored King and Parliament, perhaps the most remarkable outburst of free speech occurred since classical times. Leaders, intellectuals, and even organized groups of common citizens and soldiers argued the merits of universal suffrage, the separation of powers, women's rights, the value of labor, and even communism. The gains of the first English revolution were consolidated thirty years later by the Glorious Revolution (1688), which finally deposed the proto-Catholic Stuarts and consolidated the active role of Parliament in the government. The development of a constitutional monarchy encouraged the spread of the rule of law, which in turn enabled the emergence of stable financial markets where risks were quantifiable. The creation of the Bank of England, which made it possible to manage the national debt, also encouraged private investment in mercantile and early industrial efforts.

Luther, who had originally intended to call a united Catholic Europe back to Christian first principles, could not have intended these results. The Protestant eruption of Agape into Western Civilization, rather than restoring a unified primitive Christianity, resulted in a Europe more diverse, more secular, more pagan, more Erotic, more Socratic than at any time since the mid-Roman Empire. By 1600, the ideas of the Medici Renaissance had become the cultural currency of all Western Europe.

Cultural Consequences of the Reformation. Political diversity and debate created many new opportunities for rational inquiry and reinterpretation of the Socratic tradition. Authorized to read and think for themselves, large numbers of educated people in Northern Europe began to study not only the *Bible*, but also the proliferating number of classical and contemporary texts. Grimm writes:

> Probably the most serious defection from the ranks of the early reformers was that of the humanists who had originally hailed Luther's bold stance against papal authority and ecclesiastical abuses, but who were gradually alienated by his dogmatic stand on religious questions. Such a parting of the ways should cause no surprise, however, for the differences between Luther and the humanists were fundamental. Whereas Luther, with his overwhelming sense of sin, stressed the absolute corruption of human nature and the complete dependence of man on the grace of God, the humanists emphasized the goodness and dignity of man (*The Reformation Era*, 165).

Luther's radical assertion of Agape, in other words, forced the humanist movement to acknowledge its roots in Socratic teaching. Direct experience of Heavenly Eros became the property not just of a handful of Italian city-states and a few northern humanists; suddenly the fruits of Florentine High-Renaissance paganism were available to intellectuals in Paris or pamphleteers in London. In France, philosophers began to lay the foundations for the Enlightenment. England produced the most concentrated explosion of great literature since fifth century BCE Athens. The wide distribution of classical and contemporary science led to rapid advances in cosmology, physics, chemistry, medicine, geography, navigation, and architecture. It's a Hegelian irony that Luther's reassertion of Agape, by finally smashing the medieval Caritas consensus, ushered pagan Socratic Eros back into a dominant role in European culture.

11. Reason and Nightmare: The Enlightenment

Between the Reformation and the late eighteenth century, Europe experienced its most profound and rapid change since the collapse of the Roman Empire. Economic and cultural dominance passed from south to north. The countries truly under the control of the Catholic Church, such as Spain and much of Italy, were reduced to backwaters. France, while nominally Catholic, was actually ruled by an absolute monarchy confident enough to tolerate and even encourage wide (though selective) freedom of thought and expression. England, following its chaotic but astonishingly creative revolutions, had a semi-representative parliament that actually and increasingly participated in governing. By 1800, Europe had explored most of the globe; its influence controlled the Americas and went from strength to strength in Asia and the Pacific. Before the end of century, the United States had established a successful democratic Republic.

This had all been made possible by sophisticated philosophies of government derived from a study of the classics, the increasing separation of Church and State, rapid advances in the sciences, a free flow of information, rapid population growth, radical improvements in naval technology, and the expansion of an educated middle class. Philosophy, science, art, and literature had become the province of a significant segment of the population, and even the peasants and working classes had begun to demand a say in society and governance. The spirit of Socrates presided over this Enlightenment.

Camille Paglia writes:

> The Enlightenment, developing Renaissance innovations in science and technology, was ruled by the Apollonian mind. Not since Greek high classicism had clarity and logic been so promoted as intellectual and moral values, determining the mathematical form of poetry, art, ar-

chitecture, and music. "ORDER is heav'n's first law," says Pope, from the cold beauty of Descartes and Newton's mechanical universe (Essay on Man, IV.49). The Enlightenment, as Peter Gay asserts, used pagan science to free European culture from Judeo–Christian theology. Reason, not faith, created the modern world. But overstress of any faculty causes a rebound to the other extreme. The Apollonian Enlightenment produced the counter reaction of irrationalism and demonism which is Romanticism (*Sexual Personae*, 230).

It's customary to treat the Enlightenment as an eighteenth century phenomenon and Romanticism as the nineteenth-century reaction to it, but this is a teaching convenience; in fact the two were as intertwined as a double helix. Voltaire, the prototypical Classicist, and Rousseau, the prototypical "Romantic," for example, each commanded Europe-wide audiences for anything they wrote. Voltaire's rationalism, cynicism, omnivorousness, and faith in science personified the Enlightenment. Rousseau's pantheistic celebration of nature with its undercurrents of Orphic horror and sexual compulsion defined Romanticism. When that triumph of the Enlightenment, the first phase of French Revolution, liberated the Bastille, one of the handful of prisoners released was the Marquis de Sade (although he made it out just before the populace stormed this hated symbol of aristocratic tyranny).

This polarity offers a useful image suggesting how the mirror-image values of the Enlightenment and Romanticism would struggle for the soul of Europe over the next two centuries, but it dilutes the achievements of its two chief protagonists into useful caricatures. It was Voltaire, not Rousseau, who truly "cultivated his garden" and made domesticating nature popular throughout Europe. And although Rousseau achieved fame as a celebrator of the innocence of childhood and the state of nature, he was a sadomasochist who made his mistress abandon every one of their newborn children to wretched orphanages. More importantly, Rousseau's and Voltaire's philosophies converged in important ways. Voltaire's mission to scour the world of inherited myth, while essentially destructive, helped clear the way for the staggering triumphs of reason up to the current day. Read as a whole, Rousseau argues not for a return to a mythically joyous and innocent primitivism, but rather for a liberal, representative government that respects individual rights, and for appreciation of the natural world's aesthetic — if not moral — beauty.

Most important to our thesis, both Voltaire and Rousseau were equally acolytes of Socratic Heavenly Eros. Their disagreements were not between Eros and Agape, but between Apollo and Dionysius. Rationalism — with its tendency towards sterility, and pantheism — with its tendency towards the Orphic dissolution inherent in nature — are the thesis and antithesis of Socrates' philosophy. For the first time in European history, both sides of the central debate about the meaning of human existence were Socratic, because Socrates himself was equally

Apollonian and Dionysiac. Agape was in full retreat; reacting against two centuries of brutal religious wars, the dominant forces in society, while all professing some sort of Christianity, had relegated revealed religion to a social convention.

The burden of being an individual and figuring out the meaning of life moved forward in lock step with the advance of the Enlightenment, resulting in the Romantic discovery of the interior self. Although he idealized the situation, Marx's famous observation that during the Middle Ages, people were primarily defined by their roles and felt included in a continuum from their stratified society to an egalitarian afterlife had a grain of truth to it. The Enlightenment inexorably generated the alienation of the individual personality that is the mark of modernism. Everyone became a "personality." Fiction from the 16th to the late 18th century is filled with archetypes from Rabelais' Gargantua and Pantagruel through Milton and Racine to Voltaire's Candide or Rousseau's Heloise — always excepting Shakespeare, who was not only ahead of his own time, but ahead of our own. As early as 1774, however, Goethe's *The Sorrows of Young Werther* reintroduced the tragically self-absorbed youth to Western literature, and Werther's fictional suicide was imitated by many real young men across the continent in response to the stress of self-hood.

Although generally regarded as primarily the product of French *philosophes*, the Enlightenment was importantly a result of the English Revolutions of 1640–1688. Often treated as a provincial anomaly or a dress-rehearsal for the far more important French Revolution, the twenty-year battle for power between parliament and the monarchy, mirroring the last phases of the Reformation struggle between Protestants and Catholics, set the agenda for the greatest intellectual revolution in Europe since the Medicis' achievements during the High Renaissance, which crucially prepared for it.

An important side effect of the Puritan Revolution and its aftermath was the development of public opinion — something totally different from the random peasants', students', or workers' protests during times of hardship, which had existed since the Middle Ages — as a force to be considered in English government. This tendency gradually spread to the Continent. A passion for rational discourse, free expression of ideas, religious freedom, and broad popular participation in government pervaded Northern Europe. It's a fine irony that bears repeating: the resurgence of Agape that characterized the Reformation inevitably generated a Socratic reaction: the proliferation of people who wanted to think for themselves.

Peter Gay appropriately subtitles his magisterial *The Enlightenment* (New York, Alfred A. Knopf, 1966) "The Rise of Modern Paganism." He writes:

> There were many *philosophes* in the eighteenth century, but there was only one Enlightenment. A loose, informal, wholly unorganized coalition of cultural critics, religious skeptics, and political reformers from Edin-

burgh to Naples, Paris to Berlin, Boston to Philadelphia, the *philosophes* made up a clamorous chorus, and there were some discordant voices among them, but what is striking is their general harmony, not their occasional discord. The men of the Enlightenment united on a vastly ambitious program, a program of secularism, humanity, cosmopolitanism, and freedom, above all, freedom in its many forms — freedom from arbitrary power, freedom of speech, freedom of trade, freedom to realize one's talents, freedom of aesthetic response, freedom, in a word, of moral man to make his own way in the world. In 1784, when the Enlightenment had done most of its work, Kant defined it as man's emergence from his self-imposed tutelage, and offered as its motto *Sapere aude* — "Dare to know": take the risk of discovery, exercise the right of unfettered criticism, accept the loneliness of autonomy (3).

Nothing defines the curve of the Enlightenment better than the fact that Descartes (1596–1650) believed that pagan logic could prove the existence of the Christian God, while Kant (1724–1804), who would dearly have liked to do the same, reluctantly concluded that pagan reason and Christian faith led to different conclusions.

DESCARTES (1596–1650)

If one figure could be considered to have sparked the northern European Enlightenment more than any other, it must be Descartes. Descartes, perhaps more profoundly than anyone since Socrates asked the question: how do we know?, reviving the philosophical discipline of epistemology. To illustrate his subject, he considers the properties of a piece of wax. His senses tell him that it has a particular size, shape, color, smell and weight. Then he holds the wax to a flame, and many of these properties change, yet, to his mind, it is still wax. From this, he concludes that to grasp the nature of wax, his mind must intervene to correct the evidence of his senses. This leads him to conclude that perception is unreliable, and that truth can be arrived at only through the mental process of deduction.

But deduction can begin only if, like Archimedes, the thinker can find a place to stand, a certainty on which he can begin to build his deductive argument. He does so in his famous statement *cogito ergo sum*, "I think therefore I am." This certainty authorizes him to reach conclusions about the nature of reality so long as he employs a purely deductive methodology such as mathematics or geometry. John A. Garraty and Peter Gay follow Descartes' thread here:

> According to him, the certainty of mathematics flows from the certainty with which we can directly intuit the clear and distinct component ideas involved in those of number and figure and then demonstrate further properties of extension (existence in space) that are not immediately apparent. But he also maintains that the fundamental properties of bodies are their extensive ones, all others (such as weight, hardness, or color) being reducible to modes of extension, so that anything in the world, insofar as it is extended, is a proper subject for mathematical analysis. In consonance

with this view, Descartes presented in outline a universal mechanics that attributed all changes in the motions of bodies to impacts between them (*The Columbia History of the World*, New York, Harper and Row, 1972, 688).

Descartes' philosophy had its most profound impact on the future of epistemology from Locke and Hume to the present day, but an epistemological framework was necessary to the development of the natural sciences as well, and here Descartes made important contributions in the areas of physics, analytical geometry, mechanics, and optics. His development of the principle of inertia and his position on the mechanical nature of the refraction of light led directly to Newton's first two laws of motion. His attempt to put his discoveries in service of proving the existence of God, however, were tortured and unsuccessful, ultimately depending upon an a priori assumption that God must exist. But perhaps even more important than his specific contributions to natural science was the change he wrought, first among other scientists and philosophers, and then gradually among the general population, in the standards of rational and scientific truth. It was importantly because of the radically different views in how the Greeks and the Jews, Eros and Agape, Socrates and Jesus, perceived the world and defined value that made epistemology central to the revived Western philosophical debate. After Descartes, speculation or appeal to higher authority could no longer call itself science.

We must make a distinction here between the broad achievements of the Enlightenment as a whole and the very influential *philosophes*, a relatively narrow group mostly centered on Paris. Many of the profound thinkers of the Enlightenment were British. Heirs to the English Revolution's tradition of free-thinking and mixed government, the British philosophers operated in an liberal intellectual climate that was the envy, indeed the goal, of their French counterparts. They concentrated predominately on the physical and social sciences, and were left free to so because their revolution had already happened. Peter Gay observes:

> [W]hile Paris was the modern Athens, the preceptor of Europe, it was the pupil as well. French *philosophes* were the great Popularizers, transmitting in graceful language the discoveries of English natural philosophers and Dutch physicians. As early as 1706, Lord Shaftesbury wrote to Jean Le Clerc: "There is a mighty light which spreads itself over the world, especially in those two free nations of England and Holland, on whom all the affairs of Europe now turn (*The Enlightenment*, 11).

Three key figures can be considered as representative of the British intellectual revolution:

Thomas Hobbes (1588–1679)

Hobbes, in his strange, difficult, and often contradictory book *Leviathan* (1651), was the first modern historian to conduct a systematic, rational analysis of the nature of man and the construction of states. During the English Civil War, he adhered to the Royalist faction and consequently spent much of the conflict with other exiles in Paris. Beginning from a mechanistic understanding of human history, and no doubt influenced by the bloody conflict he had witnessed before leaving England, he concluded that in the state of nature man was in a condition of a "war of all against all," in which life was certain to be "nasty, brutish, and short."

Based on this grim assessment, he developed a social contract theory that influenced Rousseau: appalled by constant violence and selfishness, mankind gathered together and ceded some of their personal rights to a state, thereby inventing government. The book was shocking for its time and context, and its secular bias was especially offensive both to the Anglican royals and the French Catholics. Ejected from the exiled royalist circles, he had no choice but to take his chances with the Puritans who now governed England. They proved more tolerant, and after submission to Oliver Cromwell's Council of State, he was allowed to remain in England.

Curiously, especially considering his revival of the ancient Greek concept of the social contract, Hobbes ultimately concluded that the only workable government was an absolute monarchy in which the sovereign retains total authority over the civil, military, and ecclesiastical powers. Much of *Leviathan* is couched in such obscure terms, perhaps because of his delicate position vis-à-vis the politics of the day, that analysts are arguing to this day what Hobbes really believed. But his great work opened up wide areas of exploration for anthropology, philosophy, government, and religion.

ISAAC NEWTON (1642–1727)

Newton studied at Cambridge in the immediate aftermath of the English Civil War and succeeded his mentor as Lucasian professor of mathematics in 1669. His greatest work, as is the case with many world-shaking geniuses, occurred early. During a two year period (1664–66) during which the University was closed due to the political turmoil accompanying the restoration of the monarchy, he developed his theory of universal gravitation, discovered that white light was composed of all the colors of the spectrum, and roughed out the principles of calculus, the tool that would enable mathematicians to complete the task the Greeks had begun of understanding celestial motion. These achievements represent perhaps the greatest single creative eruption in the history of science, comparable only to Einstein's *annus mirabilis* in his Swiss patent office, 1915–16.

After many years working out the implications of his startling insights, Newton gathered them together in the *Principia Mathematica* (1687). Here he detailed how the principle of gravitation — that bodies are attracted to each other according to their masses — explained everything from why an apple fell to earth to why celestial bodies orbited each other elliptically — the point on which the great Greek mathematicians had foundered. He also developed his famous three laws of motion which demonstrated decisively that things on earth and things in the heavens, contrary to almost all previous philosophical speculation except Epicurus', operated according to the same laws. In *Opticks* (1704), he followed up his insight into the spectrum and developed his corpuscular (particle) theory of light. Although this was displaced by the wave theory in the nineteenth century, Einstein, Plank, and Heisenberg later combined the two to produce the quantum theory. Curiously from our perspective, Newton spent his later years acting as the Warden of the English royal mint and turned most of his private time to fruit-less alchemical experiments.

Although Newton believed his discoveries revealed the simple and elegant laws of God's universe, as his work spread rapidly across Europe, others saw things differently. If a complete explanation of the universe's operations had been achieved, where did that leave God? Figures well known in their time but obscure to later ages such as Thomas Woolston and Anthony Collins built on Newton's work to construct a cosmology that came to be known as Deism, which held that the universe ran mechanically, like a clock, according to Newton's laws. While there might be a God, at best he had created the universe and then stepped aside. Deism, the first widely held philosophy that argued against the existence of any divine intervention in human or celestial affairs, thus opened the door to atheism. Widely popular on the Continent, Deism was the preferred "religion" of most prominent intellectuals; Voltaire was an early convert and considered himself a Deist his entire life.

DAVID HUME (1711–1776)

David Hume, who is most important for bringing empiricism to an impasse, was most notorious in his own day for applying pure reason to religion. Hume followed the work of previous empiricists to its logical conclusion, reducing being to the status of a purely subjective phenomenon. Garraty and Gay observe:

> Hume pursued his motive of asking, first, what grounds there were in experience for believing the imperfect world we see is matched by a perfect one hereafter. On earth we see men treated not according to their deserts; what evidence is there that a just ruler will later correct these injustices? It is all "mere possibility and hypothesis." But observe: we do not know and cannot reasonably infer the existence of a Creator. The analogy to a watch takes us nowhere, for we have seen a watch being made, but we have no good reason to think that a universe is also and similarly "made...." Hume suggests that the order we find might be accidental; chaos would be equally natural. Besides, there is every reason to suppose the world finite. Why then expect a finite product to have an infinite cause? For all we know, its maker may have been a limited, fallible being like ourselves, or he may be dead, or he may have worked with one or more other gods of either sex, each or none of them concerned with good or evil.

Hume's last word of doubt on religion carries with it such a doubt about the mind of man that the certainty of science goes down in shipwreck too. In its ultimate phase in Hume, the psychology of sensation turns upon and destroys itself. For Hume's last word is that there is no warrant for believing in the existence of anything but the sensations we receive (*Columbia History of the World*, 719).

In his "Natural History of Religion," a chapter added to a late edition of his magisterial *Enquiry Concerning Human Understanding* (1748), Hume wrote, "(U)pon the whole, we may conclude, that the Christian Religion not only at the first was attended with miracles, but even at this day cannot be believed by any reasonable person without one."

Many of the other figures of the English Enlightenment deserve mention here; to name but four:

Francis Bacon (1561–1626), a precursor of the Enlightenment proper, imported the latest thinking of Renaissance Italian philosophers into English discourse, and wrote, "We are much beholden to Machiavelli and other writers of that class, who openly and unfeignedly declare or describe what men do, and not what they ought to do."

John Locke (1632–1704) reacted against Descartes' belief that some ideas are innate in the human intellect, insisting that the mind was a *tabula rasa* or blank slate until it was acted upon by experience. Locke distinguished between intuitive knowledge such as "two plus two equals four," demonstrative knowledge, such as the existence of God by the proof of causality, and sensational knowledge such as awareness of the natural world, but he was unable to resolve the contradiction between his desire to assert knowledge of the phenomenal world and his insistence that all apprehensions were subjective impressions contained in the mind. Perhaps Locke's most important and immediately useful contribution was his formulation of classical liberalism based in the fundamental rights of life, liberty, and property that had long-term implications for the future of British democracy and importantly influenced the leaders of the American Revolution.

Edward Gibbon (1737–94) in his enormous and wonderfully readable life-work, *The Decline and Fall of the Roman Empire*, applied strictly rational and empirical standards to researching the past and produced the greatest historical writing since Thucydides. By implication he also put contemporary civilization into context as a phase in the march of Western history as a whole, providing a template for future prophets of cultural decline.

Adam Smith (1732–1790) in *The Wealth of Nations* (1776) raised economics to a legitimate field of study. He was the first to carry the complaints of tradesmen and merchants — high road tolls, inefficient taxation that fell heavily on the manufacturing process, export and import duties, arbitrary laws from one province or country to the next — into the sphere of intellectual and political discourse. He analyzed the workings of a capitalist economy, and made a convincing argument that everyone would benefit if the maze of restrictions — largely holdovers from a feudal era — were eliminated, facilitating trade.

The French *philosophes*, by comparison to the English, had primarily political work to do; they lived in an absolute monarchy and were regularly harassed or hindered by the arbitrary powers of a still essentially feudal state and church. Their job was not construction, but destruction of the old order, the *ancient regime*. It's instructive that the great *philosophes*, organizers and popularizers of so much of ancient and modern knowledge, with the exception of Rousseau, bestowed on the future so few great works of literature, science, or even philosophy. In this they were analogous to Cosimo Medici's scholars who laid the foundations for the Renaissance. Voltaire's plays and poems are essentially political journalism, Diderot's and Samuel Johnson's most important contributions were encyclopedias, and only Rousseau's *Confessions* and *Nouvelle Heloise* and Voltaire's *Candide* stand out as good reads today, in other words, as works of enduring art.

This lack of great work shouldn't surprise us, because what the core *philosophes* were really up to was a brilliant campaign of intellectual propaganda. Their program aimed to marshal the sophisticated paganism of the late Republic and early Empire — especially the Stoics, Skeptics, and Epicureans — against what they regarded as a dark millennium of Christian mythmaking that still held Europe in its grip. Their goal was not to make great discoveries in philosophy or science or create permanent works of art, but rather to generate the conditions in which intelligent individuals could live morally without faith. In this they were remarkably successful. The fact that their mission was essentially destructive explains why wit and satire — perishable commodities — were their main weapons. They blew away the cobwebs of received religious and political opinion; they established a useable body of knowledge; they popularized the Roman classics; they created a space where fact trumped received myth.

The *philosophes* derived their critique of the Christian millennium from the relatively minor, syncretic thinkers and artists of Rome — Cicero, Juvenal, Horace. These writers were, like the *philosophes*, a combination of satirists and propagandists. Why did the eighteenth century thinkers rarely derive their primary impulse from the greater Greeks, all of whom they knew? The glib but most likely explanation is that — like the Augustan Romans, in awe of their towering predecessors — the *philosophes* knew they lived in a Silver, not a Golden, Age. As Gay observes, "For the Enlightenment ... the organized habit of criticism was the most far-reaching invention of classical antiquity" (*The Enlightenment*, 121).

The rapidly growing number of educated people in the second half of the eighteenth century, from aristocrats and merchants to teachers, ministers, and priests, wrestled personally with the existential mission of Western civilization known as modernity: How should we govern ourselves, what provides defensible foundations for morality or knowledge, what is the structure of the human personality who dares to know, what are truth, beauty, or love? These are the great Socratic questions that cleared the ground for the enormous political, scientific and artistic achievements of the late eighteenth and nineteenth centuries. They created a climate in which every educated person had to examine what it meant to be an individual in a universe expanding in time and space, the origin and purpose of which was uncertain and perhaps unknowable.

While we can point out interesting inconsistencies between the convictions and the lives of the two greatest *philosophes*, there is no doubt that they held radically different points of view, both of which would go into action in Western history.

Voltaire (1696–1778)

Voltaire, the son of a notary and minor government official, was born in Paris, and despite many travels and extended exiles he remained all his life a product and creature of that city. Although he dabbled at law as a career, from his very early years he wrote satire in verse, essays, plays, and many other forms. His targets were invariably the government or the Church. As early as 1717 he became involved in a conspiracy against the Regent of France and received a year's sentence in the Bastille. There he wrote his first play, *Oedipe*, which made him famous. Voltaire's career, among other things, demonstrates the endemic ambivalence of the French Monarchy about free speech: while throughout his life the state regularly jailed or exiled him, usually for brief periods, it never did what it could have done: shut him up. The King, while concerned to protect his prerogatives, was at the same time sensitive to criticism that he was acting tyrannically and proud of the artistic ornaments of France, of which Voltaire was the greatest.

Voltaire prudently took what precautions he could against state censure, formulating his attacks as witty satires, setting his critiques in remote or fictional locations, and occasionally trimming his sails, but he remained relentlessly devoted to his central project: exposing the government and conventional piety to a withering critique. Following his imprisonment he was exiled to England for two years and found himself intrigued by the idea of constitutional monarchy, impressed by the relative freedom of religion and speech, and interested in English literature, especially Shakespeare, whom he helped popularize on the Continent. On his return to Paris, he published *Letters philosophiques sur les Anglaise* (1728) which suggested none too subtly what was to become a central theme of the *philosophes*: that free thought flourished most vigorously in Protestant, proto-democratic countries such as England and Holland. He became a staunch devotee of Newton's work, a champion of pure science and reason, in short, a Deist. Here the English Revolution and its aftermath was working its way into the mainstream of European discourse. From this point on, Voltaire never let up in his attacks on the willful ignorance of the French Catholic Church.

For fifteen years, Voltaire found shelter in a tripartite relationship with Emilie le Tonnelier de Breteuil (as her lover) and her husband, the Marquise de Chatelet (as his partner in historical studies and scientific experiments) at their chateau in the provinces. The Marquise possessed an enormous library of which Voltaire made full use. Here Voltaire formulated his mature positions on issues such as the existence of God and the separation of Church and State.

On his return to Paris, Voltaire published a biography of King Charles XII, in which he first openly criticized religions in general. Curiously, if characteristically for France, this resulted in an appointment as court historian (perhaps to bring him inside the tent). In 1751 he accepted an invitation from his friend Frederick the Great of Prussia and moved to Potsdam but he soon became involved in a feud with the head of the Berlin Academy of Sciences and wrote a satire on the subject. Promptly arrested and expelled by Frederick and temporarily banned from Paris by Louis XV, he retreated first to Geneva and then in 1758 across the French border to Ferney, where he remained for virtually the rest of his life. Here he wrote *Candide*, a satire on Leibnitz's assertion that we live in the "best of all possible worlds," received distinguished guests from all over Europe, and published a mature summary of his iconoclastic view on religion and the State, the *Dictionnaire philosophique*. During this period it became fashionable to observe that Paris was wherever Voltaire resided.

Peter Gay writes:

> [A]round 1760 ... Voltaire discarded all compromises and threw away much of his caution. A great deal had happened both to the (*philosophe*) movement and to him. Radical writers were being persecuted, and hardworking *Encyclopedists* harassed; the tempo of the anti-Christian crusade had quickened. Voltaire was ready: after long wandering he was safely settled at Ferney, just a short ride away from Genevan territory. He was old, rich, world-famous, and almost, if not quite, immune from prosecution.... And he did not like to see the leadership of the movement pass into younger hands.... Man was born for action — he had said that in the *Lettres philosophiques* — and now the time for action had come. Long before, in 1738, he had written to a friend, "I know how to hate because I know how to love." In the 1760s he translated this to mean that destruction must precede construction: many ask, he wrote, what shall we put in the place of Christianity? "What? A ferocious animal has sucked the blood of my family; I tell you to get rid of that beast, and you ask me, What shall we put in its place?" To get rid of that beast Voltaire made himself into the unofficial advisor to the underground army arrayed against it: he began to use the phrase *Ecrasez l'infame*.... He had his reward: the little flock recognized his preeminence. In 1762, Diderot affectionately saluted him as his "sublime, honorable, and dear Anti-Christ...." Voltaire added for maximum journalistic effect: "Every sensible man, every honorable man, must hold the Christian sect in horror.... May this great God who is listening to me, this God who surely could not have been born of a virgin, or have died on the gallows, or been eaten in a piece of dough, or have inspired these books filled with contradictions, madness, and horror — may this God, creator of all the worlds, have pity on this sect of Christians who blaspheme him!" (*The Enlightenment*, 390–91).

Here Voltaire reveals both the extent of his genius and its limitations. Christianity, whatever its foibles, had not existed for nearly two millennia without fulfilling some important human needs. His critics were right in one regard. Voltaire's talent and mission was destruction, but he was not far-seeing enough to realize that once he had destroyed the Christian Beast, something more substantial than a vague Deism would have to take its place.

ROUSSEAU

Rousseau was born in Geneva Switzerland in 1712 to a declining middle class family, and always considered himself a citizen of that wealthy, well-educated, and secretively run city. He faced tragedy early: his mother died soon after his birth, and his father left Geneva and remarried when Rousseau was ten, farming him out as a sort of supplicant to various members of his extended family. Early on, he developed a passionate interest in the classics, and especially favored Plutarch, whose biographies of Greek and Roman heroes convinced him to be a great man. After brief apprenticeships as a notary and an engraver, he fled Geneva at fifteen, was taken in by a Catholic priest, and through him met Françoise-Louise de Warrens, 29, a noblewoman who had left her husband and worked to bring Protestants back to the true Catholic faith. Under their influence, he converted.

The teenaged Rousseau, now totally abandoned by his family, supported himself as a secretary and tutor in various locations throughout northern Italy and southern France. He briefly considered becoming a priest. Throughout this period he lived frequently with de Warens, whom he regarded as his mother. Eventually, de Warens invited him into her bed, which she also shared with her steward. We can only guess what combination of passion, guilt, sexual desire, and self-loathing accompanied this affair with his adopted mother, but for the rest of his life Rousseau regarded de Warens as his greatest love. She moved in sophisticated intellectual circles, and Rousseau was exposed to the larger world of serious philosophical debate. While suffering numerous real and imagined illnesses, Rousseau engaged in his own course of study, delving seriously into mathematics, history, music, and what social analysis was available.

His introduction to Paris was unlikely: he moved there to present a theory of musical notations to the Academy of Sciences; although he left Paris to work for the French ambassador to Venice, he was back within the year, only to become enamored of a seamstress, Therese Levasseur. Soon he was supporting much of her family. He and Therese remained lovers for the rest of their lives despite Rousseau's constant affairs and social entanglements. They had several children, all of whom were disposed of as described above. In their late years they finally married.

Gay captures a critical moment in Rousseau's development:

> The *philosophes*, weary of oppressive schedules, mechanical regularity, and hateful discipline, on occasion exalted imprecision into a virtue. In

the winter of 1750, Jean-Jacques Rousseau threw away his watch. "Thank heavens," he remembered exclaiming after this sublime gesture, "I shall no longer need to know what time it is." With this single impulsive act Rousseau overthrew, for himself at least, the tyranny of the absolute, objective Newtonian time (*The Enlightenment*, 245).

Rousseau, the son of a watchmaker who had rejected him, was overthrowing more than his family or even the tyranny of Newtonian time. He was throwing out as well the Deist clockwork universe with its mechanical operations and demands, in favor of a more organic relationship with nature, human development, society, and politics.

In Paris, Rousseau met Diderot and began to contribute to the composition of the great Encyclopedia that gentleman was assembling with D'Alembert. His great break came when he submitted an article to *The Journal of Arts and Sciences* that argued mankind had become degraded in the process of acquiring property and culture. This radical view, which he later qualified considerably, made him a notable figure in Parisian intellectual circles, and founded his reputation as a "child of nature." Tangled social and sexual relations, however, led to an ugly break with Diderot. At the root of this quarrel probably lay Rousseau's disagreement with the Encyclopedists' insistence on a mechanical, Deistic universe that Rousseau saw as essentially atheist. Although he had reconverted to Calvinism to regain his Genevan citizenship, for the rest of his career he maintained his faith in man's spiritual origin and the divinity of the universe, which was consistent with Calvinism, and in man's essential goodness, which was not.

His ejection from the Encyclopedists provoked Rousseau's greatest work. His image as a child of nature was reinforced by his publication of *Julie, ou la nouvelle Heloise* (1761), which with its elegant sentiments and spectacular portrayals of the Swiss countryside made him famous. The Pagan Eye — which had flourished vividly during Italian Renaissance but not yet penetrated the fogs and snows of northern Europe — awoke, and English poets began to rediscover the beauties of the natural landscape, a territory already mapped out by Shakespeare and Spenser. The French began to paint their lives and visions.

Rousseau followed up with *The Social Contract* (1762) and its striking opening lines, "Man is born free and he is everywhere in chains. One man thinks himself the master of others, but remains more of a slave than they." These words, more than any other, led in a direct line from the French Revolution through the Paris Commune to Marxism in all its twentieth century manifestations. And yet, read as a whole, *The Social Contract* is not a summons back to a state of nature, or the adoption of a radical leftist ideology, but rather an endorsement of classical republicanism.

Rousseau claimed in fact that the state of nature consisted of chaos and lawlessness that human beings left voluntarily to create a cooperative, moral community a la Hobbes. Naturally, as society grew more complex, divisions of labor and private property required the development of law. This law was valid so long as it proceeded from the general will of the people as expressed through an ideal city-state rather like Plato's Republic, or perhaps an idealized version of his native Geneva. Rousseau objected not to government in and of itself, but to the erection of a tyrannous state that could override the peoples' will as expressed in the law.

Finally, in an essay disguised as a novel, *Emile*, Rousseau outlined an ideal system of education including an age-appropriate curriculum, non-coercive learning, giving the student opportunities to learn for herself including making mistakes, and many other features that have had a profound effect on the field until the present day. The book is especially notable for a chapter, "The Confession of Faith of a Priest from Savoy," which argues that faith is not the proper object of scientific investigation because it originates outside the realm of the measurable, in man's religious impulse. Effectively, but from the other side, Rousseau was restoring here Abelard's doctrine of "double truth." Kant was to follow a similar course not long after.

For a philosopher, Rousseau's impact was unusually immediate and direct on how people lived their lives. Because of his writings, large numbers of Europeans began to explore the beauties of the Swiss countryside, stand in awe of towering mountains, in short to cultivate an aesthetic appreciation of nature in all its grandeur. Women of all classes began to breast feed their babies, a practice often previously relegated to a wet nurse. Most important, a sentiment spread throughout France, especially among the educated classes, that a people should have a say in how it was governed. Intermittently mad in his last years, Rousseau died in 1778. Eleven years later France went into revolution largely in defense of the principles he had promulgated.

The emerging French republican movement received an enormous boost from the events that resulted in American independence. The invention of the United States by a national movement including Deist *philosophes* like Jefferson and Franklin, created the first continental (as opposed to city-state) republican government since the Romans. The English American colonies had been founded primarily by Protestants, with their proto-democratic proclivities, habits of life, and history of democratic assemblies. The principles of the American Constitution represented a fusion of Protestant community democracy as developed during the Puritan and Glorious revolutions, and Enlightenment political philosophers such as Montesquieu, who had thought through the Roman model that, in its ideal state, separated the powers of the executive, the legislative, and the judiciary, and Locke, who had grounded classical liberalism in the fundamental rights of individuals in relation to the state. A number of republican-inclined Frenchmen such as Lafayette served in the American Revolution, and returned to France convinced the job could be done there too.

Tracing this process in which the *philosophes* grounded their criticism and re-construction of contemporary society in the surviving Roman texts, Gay writes:

> If there was any one figure that dramatized what was best in that long evolution, it was Socrates. A folk hero to the *philosophes* as he had been to antiquity, Socrates became the subject, in the eighteenth century, of plays, paintings, apostrophes, and slightly uneasy jokes by literary men who admired his irony without wishing to share his fate. Rousseau singled out the Delphic maxim, which Socrates had quoted, and indeed lived by as "a precept more important and more difficult than all the fat volumes of the moralists" (*The Enlightenment*, 81).

That precept was "Know thyself," and the *philosophes* correctly read it as "a critical moment in the history of man's mind, a laconic invitation to moral self-mastery."

That the writers of the eighteenth century preferred the relatively diluted Roman summaries of Socrates' teaching to the Greek originals was due to a necessary limitation of their own project. Their goal was to demolish once and forever the dominance of religious myth over humanity, and here they partly succeeded. This in turn led them to reject or ignore the work of Socrates' two most important interpreters: Plato, who constantly stressed the creative tension between rationality and spirituality in Socrates' teachings, and Aristotle, who had been the model for the Augustinian scholasticism that the *philosophes* rightly believed had paralyzed the human intellect for centuries (quite contrarily, it must be said, to Aristotle's original intentions). Nevertheless, Plato deeply infiltrated the thinking of the *philosophes* although most would have denied it; as Gay points out:

> Despite this condescension, the Enlightenment was permeated with Platonic ideas. The Stoics, who taught the *philosophes* a great deal, had studied Plato closely, and had adopted many of his teachings. The Neoplatonist had adopted others, and Augustine transmitted their system in large part.... Traveling through the ages incognito, Plato found himself welcomed by *philosophes* who did not recognize him: they borrowed better than they knew" (*The Enlightenment*, 83).

Thus was a sanitized Socrates incarnated as the secular saint of the Enlightenment. By emphasizing the Apollonian side of Socratic teaching, the *philosophes* achieved their greatest triumph: creating a free climate for scientific inquiry and the discussion of rational government. The dividends were enormous.

But the Orphic whisperings in his ear which Socrates himself always acknowledged had haunted the *philosophes* as soon as they began their Promethean project of demonstrating that rationality and criticism of existing culture alone could alone create a sound basis for universal ethical behavior. This they could have discovered from their Roman sources, whose much-imitated wit and cynicism signaled their awareness that they were belated writers, temporarily holding the fort against the rising tide of mysticism and irrationality which would ultimately result in the Christian takeover of the Empire. Most of the *philosophes* never grasped that things as easy to mock as faith or absolute monarchy could have roots deep in the human psyche, but some, especially Rousseau and Kant, knew it. The *philosophes'* faith in the essential goodness of enlightened human nature would become the nightmare of later Romanticism and the wellspring of the twentieth century's most brutal ideologies.

The political effect of the *philosophes'* efforts was indeed immediate: a decade after the deaths of Rousseau and Voltaire a relatively peaceful and triumphant French Revolution had proclaimed the utopian rights of man. But Thucydides could have foretold the result: successful revolutions against an entrenched autocracy usually move step by step to the left until stopped and reversed by the rise of a military dictator. Five years after the joyful triumph of the first National Assembly, Robespierre, in the name of Reason, presided over a Terror designed to force men to be equal whether they wanted to or not. Five years after that, Napoleon had entrenched himself as the popular tyrant of France. As he pursued his wars of domination throughout Europe, the liberal and intellectual classes on the Continent at first celebrated the approaching *liberté, égalité, et fraternité.*

To some extent, Napoleon met their expectations in the early phase of his rule. He rationalized the structure of the French government, personally headed the committee that wrote the greatest judicial code since Justinian's, and kept the trust of the French common people until he was overthrown. He swept aside rotten autocracies throughout Europe and installed more popular regimes. But as he increasingly imagined himself as the Emperor of the Continent and pursued dynastic ambitions, he began to seem more and more indistinguishable from the Bourbons he had replaced. By the time Napoleon fell, Europe was in ruins, and liberalism in retreat everywhere. Still, by one important measure, he was successful: the conservative regimes that succeeded him discovered that, try as they might, they could not go back to the old ways.

12. ROMANTICISM

In *Visionary Company* (revised 1971, New York, Cornell University Press), his great survey of the English poets from Wordsworth to Keats, Harold Bloom puts his finger on the central character of Romanticism:

> The useful term "Romantic," describing the literary period that was contemporary with the French Revolution, the Napoleonic wars, and the age of Castlereagh and Metternich afterwards ... has meant not only that cultural period, in England and on the Continent, but a kind of art that is timeless and recurrent as well, usually viewed as being in some kind of opposition to an art called classical or neoclassical. The word goes back to a literary form, the romance, the marvelous story suspended part way between myth and naturalistic representation.... [Romantic poetry] is in the tradition of Protestant dissent, the kind of non-conformist vision that descended from the Left Wing of England's Puritan movement.... Though it is a displaced Protestantism, or a Protestantism astonishingly transformed by different kinds of humanism or naturalism, the poetry of the English Romantics is a kind of religious poetry, and the religion is in the Protestant line, though Calvin or Luther would have been horrified to contemplate it. Indeed, the entire continuity of English poetry that T. S. Eliot and his followers attacked is a radical Protestant or displaced Protestant tradition. [The Romantics were] breaking away from Christianity and attempting to formulate personal religions in their poetry (Preface, xvi–xvii).

In breaking with traditional Christianity, the early Romantics remained true to the mission of their forefathers, the *philosophes*. At the same time, in contrast to the *philosophes*' conviction that critical reason could rapidly tidy up an irrationally constructed society, the Romantics wrestled to a draw with the irrational or super-rational impulses that drive the alienated human personality, government, religious belief, and nature at large.

Of all major artistic movements, Romanticism is the most obviously both the cause and consequence of an epochal political upheaval. If any one document led most directly to the French Revolution, it was Rousseau's *Social Contract*. After Napoleon's fall all *ancient regimes* had been discredited. Thrones had tumbled, and the people themselves had become contenders in the battle for sovereignty. Napoleon himself had based his legitimacy largely on a series of victories in popular plebiscites, although equally important to his longevity was his détente with the Catholic Church.

The field had been cleared: the last remnants of medieval politics and sensibility were undermined although not yet totally destroyed. A new world must eventually emerge, but in the absence of practical mechanisms for popular government, and terrified by the disorder and tyranny into which Napoleon's regime had degenerated, the remnants of the old order patched together a temporary and defensive conservative compromise that held for much of the nineteenth century. In a sense, Diderot's vision that human freedom would only arrive when the last King had been strangled with the entrails of the last priest had been briefly realized, but this had produced nothing like the restitution of unfallen humanity that the orthodox *philosophes* and the more naive early Romantics had foreseen. Moreover, Napoleon had bequeathed to future philosophy, art, and politics the dangerous example of the Great Man who could transform the world with the support of the masses.

Many disillusioned Romantic theorists — Goethe, Wordsworth, Hugo, Beethoven, Hegel — followed the reactionary post-Revolutionary tendency by adopting what could be called a pessimistic post-Romanticism. The gloomiest and most incisive of them was Schopenhauer, especially when he first fully showed his hand in *The World as Will and Idea* (1818). The early date of this book should not surprise: disenchanted Romanticism flowered in Europe rapidly in the wake of Napoleon's later depredations and defeat. On the Continent, the hopes for drastic social change raised by the French Revolution and, for a time, Napoleon himself, suffered an early winter. In England, the sole victor in the Napoleonic wars, Romantic optimism survived much longer under the guises of scientific progress, conservative social reform, and an increasingly wistful literature. The German Romantic philosophers exercised particular influence throughout Europe, and three deserve special mention here:

IMMANUEL KANT (1724–1804)

Kant is properly an Enlightenment figure, but we include him here because of his debt to Rousseau and his direct, profound influence on the German Romantic philosophers. Kant's starting point was Hume's rejection of any certainties about the origins of the universe or objective measurement of the phenomenal world. Kant accepted Hume's premise that we cannot establish the existence of God or the purpose of the universe by reason. Garraty and Gay write that, according to

Kant: "All these truths belong not to pure reason, but to practical reason. It was in the *Critique of Pure Reason* (1781) that by this distinction, Kant opened the way out of skepticism, renewed the possibility of religion and moralism, and slipped a fresh foundation under the work of science" (*Columbia History of the World*, 720).

Kant was influenced by the chapter in Rousseau's *Emile* in which the Savoyard priest argued that religious feeling was not an appropriate area of investigation for science because it was by its nature not subject to purely rational investigation, or "pure reason." Rather, the love of God or an instinctive belief in certain moral principles fall into the realm of "practical reason." Kant's acceptance of Abelard's "double truth" doctrine provided a firm intellectual foundation for Romantic writers and philosophers who were in rebellion against radical skepticism and anxious to investigate possible sources of truth inaccessible to scientific reason.

GEORG WILHELM FRIEDRICH HEGEL (1770–1831)

Hegel was a frank dualist who believed that history operates through conflicting forces, and this enabled him to retain some optimism in the face of the Napoleonic debacle. Hegel divided the political development of mankind into three steps: in the first, only one person, the King or tyrant is free, in the second, such as the middle ages, a number, composed of the nobility, are free, and in the modern world, all are free. Or, as John Garraty and Peter Gay write:

> All men, that is, were *to be* free: there was work yet to do, and Hegel has views on the process of historical evolution. The recent past has shown unmistakably that the idea of freedom realized itself in mankind through conflict. A force or thesis (which could be an idea-bearing group as well as an embattled institution or people) claimed or held power — only to be met by an antithesis or opposition, equally determined to prevail. The outcome of the struggle was that regardless of any victory, neither side conquered; rather a synthesis resulted, which fused elements from each set purpose into a higher expression of mankind's unconscious, brooding will (*The Columbia History of the World*, 866).

Since any synthesis was bound to produce a new antithesis, Hegel's concept of the dialectic was necessarily progressive; it appealed especially to the Romantics, and went into the mainstream of their thinking. Hegel believed the dialectical method was not only appropriate for explaining the working of history but also constituted a new and dynamic logical tool. Rather than simply analyzing history, the dialectic invaded history, transforming the thinking of the later English Romantics, the New England Transcendentalists and, most influentially, providing the template for Marx's dialectical materialist analysis of class conflict. It has also informed this essay's discussion of the struggle between the thesis of Greek reason and the antithesis of Judeo-Christian faith, although in a form of which Hegel might not have approved. While we have seen balances struck and compromises reached in the contest between the Greeks and the Jews, their radically opposed world views have continued to struggle for domination of the Western mind, at times one dominating, at times the other, sometimes reaching a balance, but never reaching a synthesis.

ARTHUR SCHOPENHAUER (1788–1860)

Schopenhauer started by disagreeing with Kant's premise that it is impossible to know "the thing in itself" by analyzing experience. Schopenhauer agreed Kant was right as far as the intellect went, but he pointed out that human beings also have bodies and a will:

> Will is therefore our reality ... because of the monistic concept of Schopenhauer (as distinct from the dualistic and dialectic Hegel), the reality which we are (will) must be extended to all things in nature. Thus the entire reality is will. The primordial will is a blind unreasoning impulse to self-preservation. In other words, primordial reality is the will to live. The blind impulse to life is the cause impelling the will to display itself in a multiplicity of natural beings, with the purpose of becoming conscious. Hence this impulse makes its appearance in natural bodies in the form of mechanical forces — in plants as vegetative life, in animals as instinct. Once consciousness is attained, knowledge appears as representation of the world.
>
> In such an irrational world, however, there exists a morality which is necessarily ascetic and nullifying. In a pessimistic morality there is no glorification of life, but nullification and destruction of the will to live. Indeed, if the root of all evil is the will to live, there is no other escape, no other remedy, than to suppress this will. The steps which make possible the suppression of the instinct to life are three: aesthetics, ethics, ascetics. Schopenhauer is inspired by Neo-Platonism in this regard....
>
> The moral teaching of Schopenhauer, culminating in his asceticism, the nullifier of life, is completely opposed to Hegel's mentality, which glorifies life. Both, however, are atheistic.... (radicalacademy.com/philschopenhauer)

Schopenhauer's finding his solution in asceticism and renunciation boarders on Buddhism and lies therefore outside the mainstream of Western culture, the wisdom of Silenus. But his depiction of blind will would have serious consequences for the future of Western philosophy and politics.

Others tried to make sense of the destruction of shared values and comfortable cosmologies and set about to build something to replace them, both by reimagining the human psyche and by asserting a Socratic faith in the possibilities of self actualization in a just state where the people were sovereign. In his defense of Romanticism against the charge of fostering twentieth century despair and totalitarianism, Jaques Barzun wrote:

> [M]an is first of all a creature lost in the universe, and he *makes* his shelter, physical, social, and intellectual. This was bound to be also the view of the later romanticists, who found themselves at odds with the remnants of the old regime, without protection from the universe, and forced

to build a new order" *Classic, Romantic, and Modern* (Chicago, University of Chicago Press, 1961, 16).

The presiding science of the early Enlightenment was mathematics, and the eighteenth century Deists in every medium imagined a perfect mechanical universe that ticked like a clock, but Romanticism rapidly complicated and enriched this purely rational approach. Barzun points out how rapidly the tidy Deist universe was overthrown by Romanticism:

> What happened ... can be summed up in the words which apply particularly to science: it was a Biological Revolution. The term says plainly enough that the absolute reign of physics and mathematics was over, and with it the dominance of Reason patterned upon these two sciences. By the end of the eighteenth century new branches of knowledge — the sciences of man — had come of age: anthropology, ethnology, and new modes of thought. Cartesian and Newtonian mechanics were taken for granted; the new principle was vitalism and the new theory, evolution. The mechanical materialism which had threatened to overcome all rival philosophies was in retreat" (*Classic, Romantic, and Modern*, 54).

Amidst the reactionary politics that inevitably followed Waterloo, many Romantics, their idealism in shreds, were crushed under the burden Pascal had predicted for them a century and a half before: creating a livable human world from the powers of their imaginations alone, with no recourse to divine certainties. Liberalism in retreat often took refuge in the utopian schemes developed by Fourier, Saint-Simon, Owen, the Transcendentalists and many others that gave birth to romantic socialism. Others, like Goethe and John Stuart Mill, transferred their faith to science.

As he does in his comparison of the *Odyssey* with *Genesis* or Tacitus with Mark, Auerbach finds a stylistic break that signals a profound change in world view between the language of the Enlightenment and that of the Romantics which he says originally provoked his search for earlier examples:

> I came to realize that the revolution early in the nineteenth century against the classical doctrine of levels of style could not possibly be the first of its kind. The barriers which the romanticists and the contemporary realists had torn down had been erected only towards the end of the sixteenth century and during the seventeenth by the advocates of a rigorous imitation of antique literature. Before that time, both during the Middle Ages and on through the Renaissance, a serious realism had existed. It had been possible in literature as well as in the visual arts to represent the most everyday phenomena of reality in a serious and significant context. The doctrine of levels of style had absolutely no validity (*Mimesis*, 554–5).

Auerbach is careful to point out that the break between Roman classicism and the plain style of the Middle Ages and the break between classical Enlightenment style and romanticism did not manifest themselves in the same forms:

> [I]f one compares the two breaks with the doctrine of stylistic levels, one cannot but see at once that they came about under completely differ-

ent conditions and yielded completely different results. The view of reality expressed in the Christian works of late antiquity and the Middle Ages
differs completely from that of modern realism.... I use the term figural to
identify the conception of reality in late antiquity and the Christian Middle Ages.... In this conception, an occurrence on earth signifies not only
itself, but at the same time another, which it predicts or confirms, without
prejudice to the power of its concrete reality here and now. The connection between occurrences is not regarded as primarily a chronological or
causal development but as a oneness with the divine plan, of which all
occurrences are parts and reflections (*Mimesis*, 555).

The Enlightenment's debt to classical rhetoric and the Socratic methodology it contained was enormous, and it produced, in relatively short order, the
greatest body of philosophical and scientific work since ancient Greece. But by
around 1800 it had reached an impasse, intellectually in the total skepticism of
David Hume and stylistically in the parodic tributes it offered to Napoleon in
both words and art. Auerbach is right to distinguish between the transition from
rigid Roman style levels to medieval common speech and the transition from Enlightenment rhetoric to romantic naturalism. But crucial similarities are in play
as well: the Christian background of a just universe tending towards redemption
manifested in the plainly-described events during the Middle Ages is not so different in kind from the morally much more ambiguous and threatening background that provided an intrusion of demons, ambiguous forces, and dread into
the style of Romantic realism. Both have background.

Although his works were not widely circulated until the late nineteenth century, and therefore could not have influenced the other great Romantic poets and
philosophers, William Blake (1759–1827), was the first poet or philosopher fully
to diagnose the crisis forced by the Enlightenment and the French Revolution
upon the individual. He did so in a self-consciously "plain style" drawn in his
early years from popular lyric poetry and in his later years from Christian mysticism. Basing his system on the Swedish mystic Swedenborg, who had earned
Kant's contempt as a "metaphysician," Blake described three constantly feuding
parts of the personality (strikingly predictive of Freud): the original Self, its Emanation — the projected parts of the self that represents our higher desires — and
the Spectre — sterile Reason, the solipsism which attempts to prevent the self
from reuniting with its Emanation. Camille Paglia writes:

> In Blake the soul has split, so that the prophetic poems ask what is
> the "true" self. This is a new question in history, more sweeping than the
> multiple impersonations of the Renaissance, where social order was still
> a moral value. In Blake, territorial war is waged among parts of the self.
> His characters are in identity crisis, Rousseau's invention. In his Spectres
> and Emanations, Blake is doing allegorically what the nineteenth century
> novel will do naturalistically, documenting the modulations of emotion.
> Blake rejected Judeo–Christian morality. Nevertheless, he wants to inte-
> grate sexuality with right action. But sex, which Christianity correctly as-

signs to the daemonic realm, always escapes moral control. The paradoxes of Blake's eerie Gothic psychodrama of Spectre and Emanation arise from the impossibility of his mission: to redeem sex from its miring in mother nature (*Sexual Personae*, 288).

Paglia has been criticized for overemphasizing the role of sexuality in driving the development of Western culture, but she is undoubtedly right. From the Platonic dialogues that argue attraction to a beautiful boy can be the first sensual intimation of the Good to twentieth-century cinema and commercial advertising, it's clear that the Orphic impulse to lose the self in another can fuel everything from the ecstatic worship of God to the impulse to buy things. One can trace the history of Romanticism (as Paglia has done) by examining how everyone from the first Romantic poets to the producers of contemporary sitcoms freight their characters with all the implications of alienated individuals defining and redefining their sexual roles, desires, and compulsions.

Blake, the oldest of the great Romantic poets, was also the first to notice another important side effect of the Enlightenment: the Industrial Revolution. While the Romantics, from Wordsworth and Coleridge to Shelley, Keats, and Byron, were celebrating Erotic pagan nature and mythologizing the Middle Ages as a time of romance, chivalry, and dangerous mystery, Blake bore witness to the costs of rising industrialism and excoriated its effects on the working population:

> London
> I wander through each charter'd street
> Near where the charter'd Thames does flow,
> And mark in every face I meet
> Marks of weakness, marks of woe.
>
> In every cry of every man
> In every Infant's cry of fear
> In every voice, in every ban
> The mind-forg'd manacles I hear.
>
> How the Chimney-sweeper's cry
> Every blackening church appalls;
> And the hapless Soldier's sigh
> Runs in blood down Palace Walls.
>
> But most thro' midnight streets I hear
> How the youthful Harlot's curse
> Blasts the new-born infant's tear
> And blights with plagues the Marriage hearse (1794).

Published several years before Wordsworth's and Coleridge's groundbreaking *Lyrical Ballads*, Blake's *Songs of Experience* dig beneath the early Romantic optimism that the infamy of human servitude had been erased by the early victories of the French Revolution and that mankind had achieved oneness with a benevolent, Rousseauesque Mother Nature. The "charter'd" streets and rivers had become private property, undermining the mutual communal responsibilities of an earlier order. Harlots represent the sad overflow of peasants who were drawn into the cities by the prospect of jobs, found none, and blasted the infant's tear with venereal disease. The Churches have blackened from industrial pollution — in fact, early observers of evidence for evolution began by noting that the birds perched on the various marble public buildings in London had turned from white to black in a human generation in order to preserve protective coloration. Of all the Romantic poets, Blake was by far the greatest Prophet.

On balance, the Industrial Revolution produced great gains for the people of Britain and the Netherlands; individual income and the gross national product rose in tandem significantly for the first time since the collapse of the Western Roman Empire. James Watt's invention of the steam engine revolutionized manufacturing and transportation. Blessed by its victory in the Napoleonic Wars because it had never been a battleground, and relatively unencumbered by the tariff and toll roads that constricted economic growth in France, England suddenly surged ahead of its rivals to become the first real global power. Historians have variously interpreted the fact that the Industrial Revolution began in Britain to the wealth it imported from its colonies, the enclosure (privatization) of public lands that made agriculture more efficient and created a labor surplus, or England's unique resources such as vast coal reserves, but these were at best contingent factors. The true explanation was cultural: the Protestant entrepreneurial spirit, the advances in the new science of economics including freedom of trade, carried out in the spirit of the Enlightenment largely by Scotsmen such as Adam Smith and David Hume, the relative stability of the laws (including the crucial invention of patents which ensured the inventor the fruit of his labors), and the mobility available to a relatively free people. One more factor must be added: like Athens after its victory in the Persian Wars, the English, who had stood alone against Napoleon and won, experienced a huge surge in self-confidence.

Of course the short-term social costs of the Industrial Revolution were high. Within a generation after Blake first noticed the privatization and blackening of London, the Chartist movement, made up largely of peasants and industrial workers, began to protest wretched living conditions, long hours, and even starvation. The benefits of the revolution were distributed unevenly, and the feudal compact between the manor and the peasants had finally broken down. Nevertheless, although mostly unheeded at the time, the demands of the Chartists set the agenda for working-class improvements throughout the nineteenth century and for the first time common laborers were beginning to organize into an effective political force.

The Industrial Revolution also transformed how people experienced their world in complex ways. Some were obvious: improvements in transportation not only made everything faster, it also drew communities whose lives had been essentially unchanged for centuries into a grid of new technologies and vastly increased sources of information. Mass production alienated individuals from the product of their labor. Marshall McLuhan has argued that every medium (writing, technology, radio, movies, television, etc.) has as its content a previous medium, and he starts with a lovely image that explains precisely why Rousseau was able to spark a fascination with spectacular vistas at the dawn of the Industrial Revolution: "The machine turned nature into an art form." He goes on:

> For the first time men began to regard Nature as a source of aesthetic and spiritual values. They began to marvel that earlier ages had been so unaware of the world of Nature as Art. Each new technology creates an environment that is regarded as corrupt or degrading. Yet the new one turns its predecessor into an art form. When writing was new, Plato turned the old oral dialogue into an art form. When printing was new, the Middle Ages became an art form. "The Elizabethan world view" was a view of the Middle Ages. And the industrial age turn the renaissance into an art form as seen in the work of Jacob Burckhardt (*Understanding Media*, Preface ix).

Wordsworth and Coleridge, the co-founders of English Romantic literature, personify the early Romantics' progress from a naive faith in nature to a conservative defense against Orphic immersion. Wordsworth started as a frank pantheist and his greatest poems such as "Tintern Abbey" celebrate a submission to the "something far more deeply interfused" in nature. Even by the end of this poem, however, in his invocation to his sister, we can see Wordsworth pulling back from this identification toward the sterile philosophising — Blake would say the Spectres — of his later poetry. Wordsworth had plumbed the clothonian depths of Rousseau's merging with Mother Nature and, shaken by the excesses in France, discovered that one could find much that was beautiful but little that was conventionally moral there. Nature, in other words, meant death as well as birth. Twenty years later, we find Wordsworth twitting Keats for realizing his own initial project — he called *Endymion*, the first major work of a nineteen-year-old boy, "a pretty piece of paganism." Coleridge at his best, as in "The Ancient Mariner," "Christabel," and "Kubla Khan," personifies female nature as an aggressive rapist of the moated, alienated individual personality.

Both Wordsworth and Coleridge retreated into Toryism and conventional Anglicanism, foreshadowing the identical reaction to full-blown Romanticism by early twentieth century modernists such as T. S. Eliot, who spent his whole career constructing an anti-Romantic canon composed mostly of non-English writers and minor English poets. As Harold Bloom and others have convincingly demonstrated, the major British literary tradition runs from Spenser through Shakespeare and Milton to the great Romantics. All of their works feature great personalities being condemned, deceived, or overwhelmed by mysterious or indifferent forces (Dante had foreseen this). As with the great Greek tragedies, the destruction of the moated personality always comes from within. A mind as transcendent as Socrates' could contain the Orphic wisdom of his whispering daimons within the larger framework of his Apollonian philosophy and acknowledge the creativity of the struggle between what Freud would later call the superego and the id. Few other writers or thinkers since him have proved so strong.

The essence of the Classical view, from Aristotle to the Enlightenment, was that art imitates nature. Aristotle's mimesis, however, consists in more than just "holding a mirror up to nature." It is designed to confront us with the "pity and terror" of existence more profoundly than reality itself usually does. Dr. Johnson delivered the classic 18th century formulation: "Imitations produce pain or pleasure, not because they are mistaken for realities, but because they bring realities to mind." Classic art takes us out of ourselves. The Romantic interpretation, by contrast, insists that the artist becomes a god by creating a new and enlarged reality, or, more precisely by projecting that reality from her divided interior self.

The enormous burden of this effort explains why Romanticism, overwhelmed by the voracious indifference of the nature it adored, rapidly slipped into mourning. In Keats, as in any number of late Romantic poets, beauty can be grasped only as it is slipping away into what Baudelaire later dubbed "the phosphorescence of deliquescence." This Romantic tendency, conjoined with the repeated post-Napoleonic defeats of political liberalism, took in art the forms of Decadence and Aestheticism — both rejections of the natural — that permeated the mid-and late-nineteenth century. Nietzsche's insistence that Apollonian beauty and meaning could only be coldly constructed over the geyser of Dionysiac energy that animated it was therefore an inevitable late-Romantic awareness. His whole mission, in fact, can be construed as a desperate attempt, entirely consonant with the work of the *philosophes*, to wrest heroic Greek Eros from the grip of "slave-myth" Christianity, finally to turn man into a God. This attempt to yoke Enlightenment Reason and Romantic Orphism eventually drove him mad.

J. M. Roberts (*Twentieth Century*, New York, Penguin Books, 2000) observes:

> Well before the nineteenth century was over the German seer and philosopher Nietzsche had already announced that "God is dead'; religious faith, he believed, was no longer possible for an intelligent human being, and the spirit-body dualism so long taken for granted in European culture could no longer be sustained. Whether this was true and, if it were, whether it was the result of a general loss of religious belief or of a changing view of what religion might be thought to imply and require is a harder question to clarify. So far as ecclesiastic authority went, almost all the Christian communions seemed in a measure touched by the intellectual

blight of one or another of these trends. If many Europeans could be found who still retained simple and literal beliefs in the dogmas of their faiths and the narratives of the *Bible*, so could others who contested the claims of revelation and questioned the authority of priest and pastor, and did so more strenuously and publicly. Traditional belief may indeed well have been most consciously and explicitly threatened and challenged among Europe's elites themselves (166–7).

This gap created a potentially dangerous situation in which Europe's masses and elites shared very different values, a Hegelian contradiction of which Marx and other, lesser theorists would make much. It turned out to be much easier to convert Europe's masses from religions to totalitarian ideologies than it would be to turn them into philosophers and rationalists. As Hegel and Marx both believed, radical social contradictions were generally resolved by war.

This rapid cycle — from classical rationalism and criticism through Romantic hubris, to alienation from both God and nature — reveals why the Romantics, from the start, were driven to explore the interior of the human personality; that is, the limitations of the conscious and unconscious perceptual apparatus through which we interpret the external world. It set the agenda for the next two centuries of philosophy, psychology, poetry, and hard science. The climax of creative Romantic decadence can be found in artists like Mallarme and especially Oscar Wilde. Wilde's ironic sense of displacement gave birth to a major sensibility of the next century, Camp, where vanity is everything, an insight perfectly attuned to the approaching onslaught of popular entertainment by means of journalism, recordings, stage, and screen. Romantic personae went electric, iconic, and ultimately cyber in the hundreds of millions, progressively more a created image than the representation of an actual person. As Camille Paglia observes:

> In Wilde ... gossip intensifies the aura of glamour that signifies prestige in the salon. Algernon says of a widow, "I hear her hair has turned quite gold from grief." A character in *A Woman of No Importance* remarks, "It is said, of course, that she ran away twice before she was married. But you know how unfair people often are. I myself don't believe she ran away more than once." A lord declares, "It is perfectly monstrous the way people go about nowadays, saying things behind one's back that are absolutely and entirely true."

> Oscar Wilde was the formulator of personal style for the modern male homosexual. Thus, for most of the century, the male homosexual world replicated the salon, even in dingy bars in provincial cities.... From Wilde's life and work came the aesthetic of high camp, an Apollonian mode of comedy and connoisseurship.... The male homosexual, by his Wildean self-conceptualization, carries on the work of Western imagination (*Sexual Personae*, 557).

We will see how camp, the ultimate erotic irony, while fading as a specifically male homosexual stance, contributed a wildly popular antidote to existential despair in the late twentieth century.

The presiding spirit of all these speculations and discoveries was still pagan and therefore Socratic. Nothing essential about the Enlightenment, the Romantics, or indeed nineteenth and twentieth century science or philosophy had been unanticipated by the tradition which stretched from Socrates through Thucydides, Plato, Aristotle, Zeno, Epicurus, Archimedes, and Democritus to Lucretius, Cicero and the writers of the Roman Empire, except, importantly, possession of a style and sensibility that could express historical consciousness and causality. The Romantic insistence on the interiority and multiplicity of the individuated personality predictably led to increasingly widespread psychic crisis. As Paglia writes:

> High Romanticism, thinking imagination alone can sustain the universe, is riven with anxieties. An excess of phenomena, no longer ordered by society or religion, floods consciousness. Late Romantic imagination contracts in fatigue, protecting itself with modes of closure. The world collapses into a heap of objects, honored by the Decadence for their morbid decay (*Sexual Personae*, 420).

Or, more succinctly: "Reality always falls short of imagination" (431). Romanticism embodied from the start the haunting wisdom of Silenus, the terror that no amount of Apollonian reason could demonstrate human life was meaningful once the old religious and social certainties had proven hollow. The Socratic Enlightenment would march on from triumph to triumph in science and governance to the present day, but the frustrated idealism of its twin, Romanticism, would produce a dreadful revenge of the repressed in the next century.

13. The Twentieth Century

While Dionysiac chaos, sexual frenzy, and despair haunted the darker corners of Romantic art and literature, foretelling things to come, the Apollonian Enlightenment presided over the governance, economy, and science of Europe from the final fall of Napoleon to the outbreak of the First World War. Rational, cynical statesman in the tradition of Machiavelli and Voltaire like Talleyrand and Metternich solved disputes through international conferences and the occasional tidy little war. Nation-states formed (Germany, Italy) or matured (France, Britain), defined their spheres of influence, developed rational economic programs, and moved cautiously towards representative government and its necessary corollary, the compassionate state. Smaller political units, especially in the Low Countries and the United States, served as laboratories for social experiments spurred by the French Revolution. The rights and entitlements of individual citizens multiplied except on the periphery: Spain, Eastern Europe, and Russia. Bordering territories and smaller countries were bartered, won, or lost, reminiscent of the Hellenistic period, but the integrity of no major power was threatened, at least from without. Understanding the justice — or at least the revolutionary potential — of pressures from the left, conservative statesmen like Bismarck and Disraeli extended the franchise and initiated a real social safety net. These developments gradually migrated to the exuberant United States.

This delicate international balance of power was fundamentally secular, rational, and, in the largest sense, Socratic. It generated an economic boom that continues to the present, an increasingly integrated national and international culture, and predominance over the globe by Western governments and ideologies.

Rapid advances in all the sciences created the foundation for a post-Newtonian revolution that married the mechanistic precision of the Enlightenment to the subjectivity of Romanticism. This had profound spiritual, scientific, and social consequences. Four key thinkers who laid the foundations for both the triumphs and the disasters of the century to follow can be cited as importantly responsible for the collapse of the Victorian world-view:

CHARLES DARWIN (1809–1882)

Charles Darwin's proof of the general outlines of evolution decisively relegated the biblical account of creation to the status of myth or beautiful allegory among most educated people. This completed Abelard's project of separating reason and faith; all the major European governments achieved a distinctly secular cast. The sciences continued to diversify into specialties; biology and its allies — medicine, anthropology, archeology, ethnology, and psychology — would henceforth hold their own as equals with mathematics, astronomy, physics, and chemistry in the search for human progress and meaning.

Darwin's view of evolution by natural selection, driven by scarce resources and shaped by random actions of climate, geography, and geology, was bound to provide a shock to the mid-Victorian consensus. Aware of this, Darwin held off publication from many years until colleagues kindly warned him that they would publish if he didn't. *The Origin of the Species by means of Natural Selection, or the Preservation of Favored Races in the struggle for Life* appeared in 1859. The challenges it posed to conventional theology, history, and many of the sciences was immediately appreciated and vigorously debated. Considering the conundrums the book posed to established religion in particular, however, the dialogue was respectful and largely conducted within the bounds of rational discourse, a tribute to mature Victorian civilization.

J. M. Roberts (*Twentieth Century*) observes:

> [Natural Selection] was vastly influential beyond the world of formal biology but all too soon was hideously misrepresented and misunderstood. In vulgarized form, it was taken to mean "the survival of the fittest" — a phrase Darwin did not use — and by the beginning of the twentieth century this notion was familiar enough to be widely misconstrued. It was, for example, taken to indicate a supposed superiority of white people over those of other colors. Like other secondary impacts of his ideas, it was almost certainly dwarfed by the almost casual blow he had given to the biblical account of creation .... Darwin's ultimate importance is scientific. He transformed biology as fundamentally as Newton had transformed cosmology [32–33].

Roberts touches only lightly here on the twisted uses perversions of Darwin's thinking would be put to in the twentieth century. Darwin himself had feared dreadful opprobrium. But he died a national hero, and was buried with great pomp in Westminster Abbey. Such broadmindedness in the debate between science and religion a century and a half ago should raise some questions about the maturity of at least American culture, not necessarily that maturity is always an unalloyed good.

KARL MARX (1818–1883)

Marx produced an analysis that, though flawed by cooked data, correctly emphasized the role of economic forces and classes in shaping history. This provided both the inevitable antithesis to classical free-market theory and a systematic socialist program that enabled the left to argue even conservatives into reform. It also bequeathed Robespierre's project of perfecting humanity here and now into the twentieth century.

Marx was an unusual figure to become the founder of one of the two major political movements of the twentieth century (the other being liberal democracy). He was not a popular leader, a great orator, or even really the builder of a movement. By nature he was a retiring writer and intellectual who spent most of his waking hours doing research in the reading room of the British Museum after his exile from Paris in 1849. There had been a Europe-wide leftist movement since the Jacobins took power during the French Revolution, but Marx did not fit the mold of his predecessors, figures like Robespierre, Alexander Herzen, Manzini, Proudhon, or Bakunin. These leftist theoreticians, as Isaiah Berlin points out,

> ...believed that there was little that could not be altered by the determined will of individuals; they believed, too, that powerfully held moral ends were sufficient springs of action, themselves justified by an appeal not to facts but to some universally accepted scale of values. It followed that it was proper first to ascertain what one wished the world to be: next one had to consider in the light of this how much of the existing social fabric should be retained, how much condemned: finally, one was obliged to find the most effective means of accomplishing the necessary transformation (*Karl Marx*, New York, Oxford University Press, 1963, 5).

Marx was not much impressed with eloquent socialist demagogues or idealists, up to and including Lenin. His studies had convinced him that at certain points in history, one class would inevitably displace another due to economic forces beyond any individual's control, as the bourgeoisie had replaced the aristocracy in the eighteenth century. Value was created by labor, and the class that produced the most value would inevitably come to power, take over the means of production, and become the dominant force in society. In his time, he believed, that class was the proletariat. This transformation would be accomplished not by a charismatic leader, but rather by the collective action of the workers themselves. His slogan, "Workers of the word, unite! You have nothing to lose but your chains" from the *Communist Manifesto*, written with Freidrich Engels during the French revolution of 1848, intentionally and directly refers to Rousseau.

Marx published the first volume his life work, *Das Kapital*, in 1867. Berlin observes:

The appearance of this book was an epoch-making event in the history of international socialism and Marx's own life. It was conceived as a comprehensive treatise on the laws and morphology of the economic organization of modern society, seeking to describe the processes of production, exchange, and distribution as they actually occur, to explain their present state as a particular stage in the development constituted by the movement of the class struggle, in Marx's own words, "to discover the economic law of motion of modern society" by establishing the natural laws that govern the history of classes. The result was an amalgam of economic theory, history, sociology, and propaganda which fits none of the accepted categories. Marx certainly regarded it primarily as a treatise on economic science (*Karl Marx*, 236).

Marx believed that as labor differentiated itself into specialties, the more gifted individuals managed to acquire the tools — or "means of production" — and were then able to hire other laborers who then became commodities, creating surplus value for their employers, the bourgeoisie. Gradually, as capital was concentrated in fewer hands, workers would be progressively impoverished. Marx predicted that as a result of these inequities, industrial strife would grow, increasingly destructive wars would break out, and eventually the proletariat would violently overthrow the bourgeoisie. Marx left vague exactly how this would or should occur, but it would result in a managed economy the guiding principle of which would be: "to everyone according to his needs, from everyone according to his capacity."

It's important to observe that Marx did not call for these events; he predicted them as historically inevitable. Of course they would occur first in the most advanced industrialized countries. In Marx's phrase, "The knell of history sounds. The expropriators are expropriated." It was Lenin, a man Marx knew and detested, who decided to force history's hand, and do so in the least industrialized country in Europe. Contrary to Marx's expectations, Communism came to power in the least developed, not the most developed counties. Those communist governments generally raised the standards of health, education, and productivity, but at the cost of tens of millions of lives sacrificed to a rigid doctrine.

Against his will, Marx ultimately imitated the socialist idealists he had rejected. He believed the proletarian revolution would result in a classless society of equals; instead it resulted in the destruction of anyone who refused to pretend that paradise on earth had been achieved. Marx was right on a central point: the working classes, broadly defined, would eventually govern. The power of his ideas provided a counterweight to traditional capitalism: the existing social and political structure grew to fear exactly the cataclysm he predicted, and often worked to ameliorate the conditions Marx had condemned. Socialist movements did form governments in the twenties in England and the thirties in France. What Marx never imagined was that pragmatic democratic governments, both left and right, would create a social safety net as a bulwark against revolution. Nor did he foresee the capacity of capitalism to generate one of the central phenomena of the twentieth century: the vast migration of the proletariat into the middle class. McLuhan puts it pithily: "Marx based his analysis untimely on the machine, just as the telegraph and other implosive forms began to reverse the mechanical dynamic" (*Understanding Media*, 49).

SIGMUND FREUD (1856–1939)

Freud forged the insights of recent psychology and literature into an analysis of the individuated human personality. His model emphasized that the (sometimes) rational ego was only one of several forces that determined human behavior. His descriptions of unconscious motivation, repression, the libido, mental geography, and neurosis gave a materialist and dynamic form to the insights of the Romantic poets and philosophers, helping to initiate both sexual and cultural revolutions. One can argue that psychoanalysis has withered in recent decades not only because of its failures or the advent of effective psychotropic drugs, but also because Western civilization as a whole has already been psychoanalyzed via the media. Many of Freud's once-startling insights have become commonplaces on television shows. But arguments about the details of his complexes and treatment methods aside, Freud's life work cumulatively changed Western humankind's understanding of itself.

In his later years, Freud increasingly turned the attention he had paid to the individual psyche on civilization itself. In *The Future of an Illusion* (1927), he allied himself with Voltaire in criticizing (in a much sadder but wiser tone) the effect of religion as a whole upon the Western world. But in *Civilization and its Discontents* (1930) he went much further. For Freud, this little book is atypically replete with hedges, self-doubt, and a pervasive suggestion that his conclusions are tentative and subject to challenge. It seems to have been suggested by a correspondence he shared with the French novelist Romain Rolland. Rolland wrote that while he agreed with the conclusions of *The Future of an Illusion*, he wondered whether Freud had penetrated to the source of humankind's need for the "particular feeling" of religious consolation.

Freud's great biographer, Peter Gay, on whom we have already depended heavily in our discussion of the Renaissance, writes:

> We human beings, (Freud argued), are unhappy: our bodies sicken and decay, external nature threatens us with destruction, our relations with others are a source of misery. Yet we all do our desperate utmost to escape that unhappiness. Under the sway of the pleasure principle, we seek "powerful diversions, which let us make light of our misery; substitute gratifications, which diminish it; intoxicating substances, which make us insensitive to it." Religion is just one of these palliative devices, no more effective, in many ways less effective, than others.... It is as though "the intention that man should be happy is not contained in the plan of "Creation.'"

The pathetic human quest for happiness, and its foreordained failure, have generated an astonishing point of view: the hatred of civilization. While he rejected this "surprising hostility to culture," Freud thought he could explain it. It had a long history; Christianity, which puts a low value on human life, was one of its most flamboyant symptoms. The voyagers who encountered primitive cultures during the age of exploration compounded that hostility by mistaking the life of these alien, seemingly uncivilized tribes as models of simplicity and well-being, a kind of reproach to Western civilization (*Freud*, New York, Doubleday, 1988, 554–5).

Here Freud was rejecting the view that humankind was born good and then corrupted. Surely this slap is aimed most directly at Rousseau, but Freud was undoubtedly aware that it applied equally to Leibnitz's "best of all possible worlds" and the Pelagian Christian heresy that held human beings were inherently good. Gay continues:

More recently, advances in the natural sciences and technology have produced disappointment in their turn. This was not a mood Freud was disposed to share; the recognition that modern inventions have not secured happiness should produce one single conclusion: "Power over nature is not the only precondition for human happiness, just as it is not the only aim of cultural endeavors...." Unquestionably, we do not feel comfortable in our present day civilization.

Still, this uneasiness should not obscure the fact that throughout history, civilization has been a vast effort at subduing the forces of nature. Humans have learned the use of tools and fire, tamed the waters and tilled the soil, invented powerful machines to lift and transport, corrected visual infirmities with eyeglasses, aided their memory with writing, photography, the phonograph. They have found the time to cultivate splendid useless things; to strive for order, cleanliness, and beauty; and to foster the most elevated capacities of the mind. Practically all the omnipotence they once attributed to the gods they have now engrossed for themselves. Freud condensed the case in a startling, deeply-felt metaphor: man has become a "prosthetic god" (*Freud*, 546).

And yet, according to Freud, Hobbes, who had said life in a state of nature would be "nasty, brutish, and short," was right: "man is as a wolf to other men." Only an imposed political structure that reserved the monopoly of power to the state could coerce individuals to sublimate desires, impulses, and needs that would tear society apart. These primal impulses to murder, rape, steal, commit incest, or dominate others, then, have been repressed but long to erupt and sometimes do. This constant tension, Freud claims, provides the perfect recipe for unhappiness. Gay concludes:

Freud's theory of civilization, then, views life in society as an imposed compromise and an insoluble predicament. The very institutions that work to protect mankind's survival also produce its discontents. Knowing this, Freud was ready to live with imperfection and with the most modest expectations for human betterment. It is significant that when the First World War was over and the German empire had collapsed, he expressed his satisfaction at seeing the new Germany reject Bolshevism. Thinking about politics, he was a prudent anti-utopian. But to qualify Freud simply as a conservative is to miss the tension in his thought and to slight his implicit radicalism. He was no Burkean respecter of tradition; it follows from his thinking that timid traditionalism needs to be analyzed no less than ruthless idealism. What is old, Freud could well have said with John Locke, is not therefore what is right. He was even willing to speculate that "a real alteration in the relation of mankind to property" was more likely than ethics or religion to bring some relief from modern discomforts (*Freud*, 547–8).

ALBERT EINSTEIN (1879–1955)

Einstein, by demonstrating relativity, revised Newton and opened the door to the triumphs and terrors of modern physics. His discoveries, however much against his own intentions and beliefs, translated in the popular mind into a meta-physics in which values, as well as the sensible world, could be seen to operate on relative principles, rather than being based in absolute revelation or a natural social order. Einstein defensively claimed that "God doesn't play dice," but he could never prove it, and his co-invention along with Plank and Heisenberg of quantum mechanics enthroned probabilities, rather than Einstein's hunger for certainties, as the royal road to what physical truth was available at the micro and macro levels.

Einstein's theory became wildly popular very quickly and combined with an endearing public personality to make him one of the most famous people in the world. While laymen and even most scientists couldn't do the math, the idea of relativity — in nature, ethics, social structures and even world affairs — could be roughly understood, and caught the temper of the times in the aftermath of World War One. In Europe especially, all the old certainties had been debunked. People and things floated about randomly, with no frame of meaning or fixed point of reference. The proscenium had collapsed, and no one was sure who was directing the play. The impact of relativity was especially immediate and wide-spread in the arts as representation in poems and painting gave way to analysis of relative points of view.

In his excellent biography, *Einstein: His Life and Universe*, Walter Isaacson captures the quality of mind millions of ordinary people intuited in Einstein:

> From his earliest days, Einstein's curiosity and imagination were expressed mainly through visual thinking — mental pictures and thought experiments — rather than verbally.... There was an aesthetic to Einstein's thinking, a sense of beauty. And one component to beauty, he felt, was simplicity. He had echoed Newton's dictum, "Nature is pleased with simplicity" in the creed he declared at Oxford the year he left Europe for America: "Nature is the realization of the simplest conceivable mathemat-

ical ideas...." He became like a gardener weeding a flowerbed. "I believe what allowed Einstein to achieve so much was a moral quality," said physicist Lee Smolin. "He simply cared far more than most of his colleagues that the laws of physics have to explain everything in nature clearly and consistently...." Perhaps the most important aspect of his personality was his willingness to be a nonconformist (*Einstein*, 549–50).

Content and even delighted with this image, Einstein remained an iconoclast to the end.

If we add a fifth figure to this list of geniuses, it should be Thomas Edison, supreme representative of the primarily American inventors and tinkerers (the Wright brothers, Ford, Westinghouse, Bell, and many others) who, in short order transformed the home, the towns and cities, transportation, and communication. The world crowded in on the individual materially as well as conceptually and spiritually. Massive gains in productivity offered vastly greater choices of creature comforts, mechanical conveniences, flexibility, wider horizons, and a constant bombardment of information and misinformation. The ideas and products of all these great thinkers and doers were transmitted indiscriminately to the general population much more rapidly if crudely than could have happened in any earlier age by means of journalism, advertising, the arts, radio, and, perhaps most important, cinema.

These revolutionary intellectual and mechanical developments, anticipated and echoed in all the arts, arose from an international culture that valued the free exchange of goods and ideas and trusted in reason over faith. But the apparent triumph of Eros or Agape is inevitably followed by the resurgence of the other. The "War to End All Wars" became a fight to the death, a European civil war, because the belligerents expected it to produce total peace. This enormous failure fragmented the Victorian synthesis, giving birth to disillusioned modernism. The enlightened discoveries of the late nineteenth and early twentieth centuries produced the seeds of their own antitheses and the soil in which those seeds could grow. A universe of ancient, uncertain origin and obscure purpose, governed by physical and moral relativities in which human beings were the pawns of large economic and industrial forces and deep instincts beyond their individual control frightened its master theoreticians. How much more did it terrify the emerging masses of the semi-educated public? Alienation became the property not just of the intellectual classes, but also the populations of Europe and the United States.

Predictably, new certainties based on faith rushed to fill the gap in the form of the totalitarian movements that so disfigured the twentieth century. Twisted, secular forms of Agape triumphed: The infallible ideology and the Great Leader who could reintegrate Western civilization into a community of certainties replaced God as the source of love and truth. Communism proposed to realize the Christian heaven here on earth by recreating all human beings as equals. Fascism held out the promise of belonging to a Master Race that would revive imagined past glories and dominate the world. Both came to prominence and power as a result of the First World War, a senseless orgy of self-destruction that can best be explained as an eruption of fury from a collective psyche strained beyond endurance in its effort to believe in something absolute.

Agape erupted from the chains of Eros, Dionysius from the classical restraint of Apollo; in Freud's terms, the repressed returned. Virulent forms of Romantic sadomasochism were to tyrannize much of the world throughout the twentieth century. Most elements of totalitarian control were already in place in William II's Germany and Czarist Russia, and these practical tools enabled the institutionalization of militant fascism and communism, much as Rome had served as a vehicle for Hellenism.

But secular Agape failed spectacularly in its fascist and communist forms both because it attempted to create a faith based on fake science and a concocted personality cult and because it tried to create an idealized human nature. It turned out you had to murder millions of people and terrify the rest to achieve the pretense of heaven on earth. If the currently fashionable version of Marxism called social constructionism were widely valid, some form of communism or fascism — government by secular Agape — would have worked in the modern European era. But there is something irreducible in post-Socratic humankind that resists reconstruction, refusing to conform entirely to any totalitarian concept of the greater good. Perhaps it's what Christians call "original sin" and Socrates identified as the rebellious determination to *know for oneself*, a peculiarly Western impulse and potent with hubris.

But the roots of a uniquely Western insolence go back much further than Socrates: Adam and Eve insisted on eating the apple; the Earth Titan Prometheus stole fire from the upstart Olympians and gave it to his own children, the humans. As we've discussed earlier (See Chapter VI), Agape and Eros emphasize, in contrast with all other belief-systems which have sustained major civilizations, that man and the ultimate are in contention, creating a discontinuity between the human and the divine. They just disagree on how that gap can be breeched, introducing the element of existential doubt now uniquely embedded in Western culture.

Literature and art of the first half of the twentieth century took, for the first time, a detached, indeed, increasingly ironic view of itself and of Western culture. English poetry turned from valediction (Yeats) to relative uncertainty (Eliot, Pound, Williams, Stevens, Auden, and Ashbery). Irony began to pervade high literature and art. The post-war sense of spiritual paralysis was captured perfectly by T. S. Eliot:

The Love Song of J. Alfred Prufrock

Let us go then, you and I,
While the evening is spread out against the sky
Like a patient, etherized, upon a table.
Let us go, through certain half-deserted streets,
The muttering retreats
Of restless nights in one-night cheap hotels
And sawdust restaurants with oyster shells:
Streets that follow like a tedious argument
Of insidious intent
To lead to you an overwhelming question ...
Oh, do not ask, "What is it?"
Let us go and make our visit.

In the room the women come and go
Talking of Michelangelo....

And indeed there will be time
To wonder, "Do I dare?" and "Do I dare?"
Time to turn back and descend the stair,
With a bald spot in the middle of my hair—
(They will say: "How his hair is growing thin!")
My morning coat, my collar mounted firmly to the chin
My necktie rich and modest, but asserted by a simple pin—
(They will say: "But how his arms and legs are thin!")
Do I dare
Disturb the universe?
In a minute there is time
For decisions and revisions which a minute will reverse.

For I have known them all already, known them all—
Have known the evenings, mornings, afternoons,
I have measured out my life with coffee spoons;
I know the voices dying with a dying fall
Beneath the music from a farther room.
So how should I presume?...

Shall I part my hair behind? Do I dare to eat a peach?
I shall wear white flannel trousers, and walk upon the beach.
I have heard the mermaids singing, each to each.
I do not think that they will sing to me.

I have seen them riding seaward on the waves
Combing the white hair of the waves blown back
When the wind blows the water white and black.

We have lingered in the chambers of the sea
By sea-girls wreathed with seaweed red and brown
Till human voices wake us, and we drown.

The action of the poem here is still as romantic (and Platonic) as an ode by John Keats: the imagination proceeds through the beautiful natural phenomena of this world to approach the Form, or Ideal truth. But in *Prufrock* the revelation never comes: "I do not think that they will sing to me." Eros rejects Eliot's suit. Eliot had written this prophetic poem in 1910, but amid the post-war ruins of Europe, many members of the cultivated and intellectual classes were experiencing a similar failure of nerve.

An instructive figure here is Northrup Frye, perhaps the only great twentieth century critic aside from Auerbach and Paglia who has suggested a comprehensive literary interpretation of Western civilization. In *The Anatomy of Criticism* (Princeton, New Jersey, Princeton University Press, 2000) Frye argued that any civilization goes through four literary, or more properly, mythic phases: the comic, the romantic, the tragic, and the ironic or satiric. I would alter the order a bit to remain faithful to linear history rather than, as Frye does, organize them according to the seasons, and add a fifth, the heroic, to produce the following scheme:

The heroic. This is the phase of a civilization that produces its founding myths, in the case of the Greeks, *The Iliad* and *The Odyssey*, in the case of the Jews, the books of the *Bible* from *Genesis* to *Exodus*. The culture identifies its essential values: the Greeks a warrior motif of conquest and exploration, the Jews, the return to the Promised Land, the metonymy of Eden. The culture, throughout its various mythic phases, will repeatedly drift away from, and then return to, these core values when it feels it has gone astray.

The tragic (Frye's autumn). This corresponds to the archaic period of a civilization, in the case of the Greeks from Hesiod to Sophocles, and in the case of the Jews, from the establishment of the Davidic Kingdom to the Exile in Babylon. It represents the phase in which cultures come to terms with their subjection to higher powers or forces beyond their control: in the case of the Greeks, the gods or fates, in the case of the Jews, Yahweh's rigorous otherness and insistence that any disloyalty will be punished by suffering and exile. This period is characterized by the development of strategies by which the founding myths can be

squared with life experience. For the Greeks, this represents the rise of philosophy, and in Israel, the age of the Prophets.

The comic (Frye's spring). Marx says that history always repeats itself, once
as tragedy and once as farce. In the Greek case, this period runs from the Persian
Wars to the death of Alexander. All the heroic myths are reenacted, but with a
heightened self-consciousness: Alexander, for example, scrupulously shapes his
life to fit the culture's founding myths but the civilization that results from his
efforts, while rich in variety and socially progressive, hardly lives up to its imagined heroic analogue. In the case of the Jews, the comic period stretches from
the return from exile in Babylon to the advent of the Romans. Jews reestablish a
state, but the Prophets cease to speak, and the Maccabees, the dynasty of Kings
and High Priest that reigned in the second and first centuries BCE, are mostly
intriguing politicians, parodies of the heroic founders. This phase is the great age
of record-keeping: the Greeks begin writing history and philosophy, the Jews
assemble their Holy Book by splicing the information remembered by those who
have returned from Babylon with the often variant traditions of the Jews who
have stayed in subject Israel.

The romantic (Frye's summer). This is a period of popular mass culture, satu-
rated with everything from the highest learning to the lowest superstition. In
the case of the Greeks, it corresponds to the Hellenistic period, when most of literature consisted of fabulous tales of romantic adventure or picaresque journeys
through the oddities and grotesqueries of contemporary culture. In the case of
the Jews, it corresponds to the period of Roman control, where the ruling families were not really Jewish and the literature alternated between apocalyptic pre-
dictions of a second coming and the sexual adventures of creatures like Herodias
and Salome. It is an age prone to the invention of syncretic gods, belief in the
operation of remote and uncaring forces, and outbursts of religious enthusiasm.

The ironic (Frye's winter). This is the phase where the culture's already shred-
ded heroic founding myths, and society in general, can be treated only satirically.
Absolutes have collapsed, and concepts like heroism, duty, order, and God(s) can
only be treated by the intellectual classes as objects of humorous mockery. In the
case of the Greeks, this phase occurred in the first centuries CE and, as we have
seen, rapidly permeated Roman culture as well. In the case of the Jews, it can be
treated as a prominent aspect of their culture from the time they were expelled
from the Holy Land by the Romans until the present day. Frye writes of the highest type of irony:

> [T]he incongruous and the inevitable, which are combined in tragedy,
> separate into opposite poles of irony. At one pole is the inevitable irony
> of human life. What happens to, say, the hero of Kafka's *Trial* is not the

result of what he has done, but the end of what he is, which is an "all to human" being. The archetype of the inevitably ironic is Adam, human nature under a sentence of death. At the other pole is the incongruous irony of human life, in which all attempts to transfer guilt to a victim give that victim something of the dignity of innocence. The archetype of the incongruously ironic is Christ, the perfectly innocent victim excluded from human society. Halfway between is the central figure of tragedy, who is human and yet of heroic size which often has in it the suggestion of divinity. His archetype is Prometheus, the immortal titan rejected by the gods for befriending men. The Book of Job is not a tragedy of the Promethean type, but a tragic irony in which the dialectic of the divine and human nature works itself out. By justifying himself as a victim of God, Job tries to make himself into a tragic Promethean figure, but he does not succeed (*Anatomy of Criticism*, 42).

Perhaps the signature image of an ironic age — think Kafka, Faulkner, or Beckett — is that we continue to make sacrifices to gods we know are not there, because we don't know what else to do.

These five phases of civilization are cycles that run within the larger cycle of Western Civilization itself. They can be applied with profit to the ancient era, the Middle Ages, and civilization since the Renaissance.

Previous to World War Two, irony had been mostly the property of comedians, gay people, and to a lesser degree the educated in general. But after Dachau and Hiroshima, irony became the property of the masses. Art turned decisively against a culture that could produce these horrors: to celebrations of rebellion and Whitmanesque embraces of behavior the cultural mainstream regarded as degeneracy (the Beats), to the destruction of representation in painting (abstract expressionists), and to music which was atonal, random, or raucous. The search for meaning in modern life took refuge in popular music and fueled a tremendous growth in self-help movements and synthetic religious cults. High art fell into the hands of writers, painters, musicians, and others who, influenced directly by European intellectuals, deconstructed literature and the arts by interpreting every poem, novel, or painting as an ironic commentary on how it had been constructed.

Perhaps the most courageous philosophic attempt to confront meaninglessness in the wake of World War Two was existentialism, which received wide currency in the fifties and sixties, largely due to the popularity of writers including Jean-Paul Sartre and Albert Camus. Paul Tillich, analyzing existentialism from the position of a man of faith in *The Courage to Be*, offers a rather tortured view of its appeal:

> Existentialism, that is the great art, literature, and philosophy of the 20th century, reveals the courage to face things as they are and express the anxiety of meaninglessness. It is creative courage which appears in the creative expression of despair.... If life is as meaningless as death, if

guilt is as questionable as perfection, if being is no more meaningful than non-being, on what can one base the courage to be? ... There is only one possible answer, if one does not try to escape the question: namely that that the acceptance of despair is itself faith and on the boundary line of the courage to be. In this situation the meaning of life is reduced to despair about the meaning of life. But as long as this despair is an act of life it is positive in its negativity. Cynically speaking, one could say that it is true to life to be cynical about it.... No actual negation can be without an implicit affirmation. The hidden pleasure produced by despair witnesses to the paradoxical character of self-negation. The negative lives from the positive it negates (New Haven, Yale University Press, 174–76).

This is rather cold comfort, although the best works of existential literature do suggest some comfort can be found by cultivating firmness of character in an unsponsored world. Tillich is onto something here, perhaps best expressed by Susan Sontag's comments on Camus:

Being a contemporary, he had to traffic in the madman's themes: suicide, affectlessness, guilt, absolute terror. But he does so with such an air of reasonableness, measure, effortlessness, gracious impersonality, as to place him apart.... Starting from the premise of a popular nihilism, he moves the reader — solely by the power of his own tranquil voice and tone — to humanist and humanitarian conclusions in no way entailed by his premises. This illogical leaping of the abyss of nihilism is the gift for which readers are grateful to Camus (*Against Interpretation*, New York, Farrar, Strauss and Giroux, 1966, 53).

Here Tillich's view of an absolute negative producing a positive is realized; the best existential writers find that meaningless itself can spur our efforts to find new and productive ways to be human, which often turn out to be the same old ways. Sontag points out (*Against Interpretation*, 95) that freedom is the keynote of existentialism. The good of it comes in the challenge — almost the game — of being free responsibly; that creates a work of art.

The terrible events of the twentieth century in some ways had devalued both Eros and Agape: in Auerbach's terms, the background didn't have anything meaningful to say to us while the foreground, far from being the illuminated world of Homer, bleak and ugly, saw nature and heroism retreating on every front by late in the century. And yet the human world burgeoned during this period, in population, in material wealth, in better health care and longer lives. Two ideologically opposed superpowers fought a deadly struggle for preeminence over fifty years without producing an apocalypse. This itself provided some grounds for optimism, both in the capitalist West and among the newly liberated Russian satellites. It's telling that the population of Western Europe stabilized in the second half of the century while the less developed countries doubled their populations and then doubled them again. The United States fell somewhere between the two, always bolstered by immigration.

The increasing ability to improve oneself, both materially and culturally, was sufficient reason to live and hope for increasing billions of people who had never heard of existentialism. This raises the question of whether the pessimism of twentieth century literature and philosophy produced and consumed by the affluent and educated, mostly Western elites, was more out of touch than usual with the temper of the general population. In fact intellectuals and artists for the most part retreated from their roles as cultural arbiters, largely into the academy, while the populous found reasons to believe in everything from movie stars and rock and roll to sexual liberation and Wall Street.

In this atmosphere, Camp offered a measure of relief from meaningless irony — the wisdom of Silenus. Still a form of irony, Camp encouraged a sense of play, in contrast to the humorless semiotics of the academy or the ruined fragments that were the best of twentieth century literature. Structuralist criticism preached, ironically and with a certain weariness, the totally self-referential artifact. Camp, by contrast, preserved the possibility that works of art, including personalities, could have at least an "as if" relationship to truth. Susan Sontag first recorded the upsurge of Camp in the middle of the century in "Notes on Camp" included in *Against Interpretation*. It's endearing to revisit this prophetic essay fifty years later because it has become a Camp object, written as a series of "notes to self." One can't help imagining Sontag took Wittgenstein's gnomic philosophical tracts as her model. In her spirit, I summarize her interpretation in a series of quotes from her notes:

> To start very generally: Camp is a certain mode of aestheticism. It is one of the ways of seeing the world as an aesthetic phenomenon (277).

> Sometimes whole art forms become saturated with Camp. Classical ballet, opera, movies have seemed so for a long time (279).

> The best example is in Art Nouveau, the most typically and fully developed Camp style (279).

> Camp taste draws on a mostly unacknowledged truth of taste.... What is most beautiful in virile men is something feminine, what is most beautiful in feminine women is something masculine (279).

> To perceive Camp in objects and persons is to understand Being-playing-a-role (280).

> Today's Camp taste effaces nature, or else contradicts it outright. And the relation of Camp taste to the past is extremely sentimental (280).

> Camp is the triumph of the epicene style (The convertibility of "man" and "woman," "person" and "thing") (280).

> Behind the "straight" public sense in which something can be taken, one has found a private zany experience of the thing (280).

One must distinguish between naïve and deliberate Camp. Pure camp is always naïve. Camp which knows itself to be Camp is usually less satisfying (282).

"Life is too important a thing ever to talk seriously about it." — *Vera, or The Nihilists* (286)

[T]hird among the great creative sensibilities [after high culture and extreme states of feeling] is Camp: the sensibility of failed seriousness, of the theatricalization of experience. Camp refuses both the harmonies of traditional seriousness, and the risks of fully identifying with extreme states of feeling (287).

Camp and tragedy are antitheses. There is a seriousness to Camp (serious in the degree of the artist's involvement) and, often, pathos. The excruciating is also one of the tonalities of Camp; it is the quality of excruciation in much of Henry James, for instance ... that is responsible for the large element in Camp in his writings (287).

The whole point of Camp is to dethrone the serious (288).

The connoisseur of Camp has found more ingenious pleasures ... the coarsest commonest pleasures, in the art of the masses (289).

Camp taste is by its nature possible only in affluent societies, in societies or circles capable of experiencing the psychopathology of affluence (289).

"One must have a heart of stone to read the death of Little Nell without laughing," — in conversation (291).

The experiences of Camp are based on the great discovery that the sensibility of high culture has no monopoly on refinement. Camp insists that good taste is not simply good taste; that there exists, indeed, a good taste of bad taste (291).

Camp is a kind of love for human nature (291).

The ultimate Camp statement: It's good because it's so awful (292).

It's almost quaint to note that while Sontag hints here that Camp is in its origins, as Paglia observes, a male homosexual sensibility, she never says so outright. Sontag's definition of Camp took on wider reference and interpretation as the century developed. Christopher Isherwood originally defined Camp as mocking something you take seriously, and herein lies its genius: Camp allows the thoroughly disabused and ironized individual to in fact take something painful or absurd seriously by engaging it in serious play, rather along the lines of the Sumerians. No one who has ever attended a movie by Marilyn Monroe, or a concert by Judy Garland or David Bowie, could doubt that the mass of the audience found serious meaning contained in a Camp presentation.

In the second half of the twentieth century, workable international institutions such as the U. N., NATO, and even the Soviet block and the organization of Non-Aligned Nations gathered most of the world, including remote countries untouched by modernity, into awareness of, and involvement in, debates on world affairs. The Cold War, for all the sense of apocalyptic doom it generated, had its advantages. US–Soviet competition, because it froze the international situation, guaranteed that since world war was impossible, the serious and vicious smaller wars that broke out either between surrogates of the superpowers (Korea, Vietnam) or in indigenous regional nationalist conflicts (the wars in the Middle East, the wars between India and Pakistan) would be contained and, ultimately, optional rather than matters of national survival.

For the first time, the battle between Eros and Agape was being fought out globally and along clear ideological lines: liberal capitalism, with its respect for individual rights and freedom of discourse represented a nearly perfect Socratic construction, while Soviet Communism, with its deep background emitting oracular commands and promising to bring about heaven on earth, offered a perfect secular parody of revealed religion. Despite the spread of independence and self-government among countries freed from colonialism and the grim contest of the two superpowers along the predictable fault lines, the world map probably changed less during the second half of the twentieth century than in any comparable period in history, importantly due to the international forum created by the United Nations.

For the United States, an additional advantage of the Cold War is that it turned out it could be won. A struggle between radically different visions of human society, its outcome could be foreseen well before the Berlin wall fell. Appropriately, in the end, one side triumphed in this cultural war by cultural means: from the ground up, people in non-aligned societies voted with their lifestyles and purchases for American values and goods over Soviet tanks and thought control.

After World War Two, wrenched from its traditional isolationism, the United States, especially in the wake of the Marshall Plan and the reconstruction of Japan, for the first time and decisively stood forth as the greatest power on earth. American politics and popular culture increasingly set the style in music, clothes, and lifestyle, especially among the young, first in the industrialized countries, and then gradually in the urban centers of the communist and developing countries. America held a key advantage here because its open society gave free reign to rational science which produced tremendous benefits for the world as a whole, from the green revolution that radically reduced starvation in developing countries and dramatic advances in health care that ended age-old diseases to the proliferation of cheap, useful technologies that transformed the lives of billions of people world-wide who had been living in medieval or even Neolithic conditions.

Eros cares about things and styles, the sensible world rather than a mythical apocalyptic future. And American style, in the serious sense that Auerbach uses the word, was about to take the world on a long pop-cultural ride that unfolded largely under the radar of the philosophers.

One of the greatest legacies of World War Two for America was the desegregation of the military under Truman. The process of black liberation had a profound effect on society for the rest of the century. A great number of trained and educated black men and women flowed back into society from military service, helped energize their communities, and pumped new blood into the civil rights movement. Many soldiers had been treated equally in the military, earned the opportunity to go to college through the G.I. program, and refused to return to serf status. A sense of guilt for passively conspiring in injustice spread among the moderate white population and led to an acquiescence on reforms: Brown vrs. Board of Education, the refusals to sit in the back of the bus, the sit-ins, the thuggish reaction of local officials in the south to peaceful marches, the collaboration of many churches and white young people, and the march on Washington led relative rapidly to the Civil Rights Act, the Voting Rights act, and both public and private affirmative action programs. The late sixties witnessed the inevitable white backlash in the form of street battles against school desegregation and black backlash in the form of urban riots, but the social composition of America had changed for good and generated a revolution of rising expectations among other disenfranchised oppressed groups, first women, then Hispanics, and, towards the end of the century, gays.

After the war, society attempted to slip women back into their traditional homemaker roles but that didn't stick, although the rebellion took some time to gather steam. The broad availability of the Pill by the sixties gave woman far more control over their sex lives, posing increasingly complex challenges to the Patriarchy in all its ages and forms. Radical feminism such as it was, abetted by more mainstream efforts like Betty Friedan's *Female Mystique* and Gloria Steinem's writing and magazine, put the subject of female equality on the coffee table, although progress in achieving vital practical goals like equal pay progressed slowly, and the Equal Rights Amendment failed by one vote. Nevertheless, the progress of woman towards equality has been inexorable; advances in the workplace have proceeded steadily, incomes have risen, they increasingly populate executive offices and high positions in government, and recently one was very nearly elected President.

Meanwhile, the vast baby boom generation discovered its demographic weight and financial clout, or perhaps moviemakers and advertising executives discovered it for them. Their soundtrack, in fact their religion, was rock and roll, a synthesis made possible by an improbable three way collaboration among folksingers, black rhythm and blues singers who could finally get on the radio, and a British invasion by artists who had already made these materials their own. Here was another side effect of gradual black liberation. Lifestyles previously confined to smoky jazz bars became the property of millions of baby boomers; young people learned to dance with their whole bodies, explored artificially expanded consciousness by use of (for the most part) recreational drugs like marijuana and LSD, and inherited sexuality without consequence in ways and numbers that fast-forwarded the bending of Eros towards its Dionysiac pole. The Beat writers like Ginsberg, Kerouac, and Burroughs had provided the template for transgression: defiance of authority, celebration of the repressed (homosexuality, black music, the underclass, contempt for possessions), constant motion, the drug-fueled search for the ecstatic moment. Woodstock convinced a critical mass of American youth that they had found their own culture.

The baby boomer generation began to self-identify politically too as opposition grew to the Vietnam War. This mixture of sexual liberation, tribal music, and politics proved very combustible. After Nixon invaded Cambodia, several protesting students died at the hands of the National Guard. For a year or two in the early seventies many young people, and a significant number of adults in authority too, thought revolution a real possibility.

As the structure of adult authority collapsed, young people turned to prophets nearer their own age, deeply serious artists such as Bob Dylan and John Lennon, heroes who, characteristically of the increasingly egalitarian and ironic age, disclaimed the mantle of leadership. The baby boomers would grow up, of course, but they, and more especially their children, would largely dismiss the inequities of the past based on racial or sexual bigotry as benighted archaisms. It is a well-kept secret, obscured by years of vigorous rear-guard action by conservative forces who often governed during these years, that what we call the "sixties generation" won the cultural wars. The state gradually retreated from its interference in private lives. Barely into the next century, we have elected a black President. The other day gay marriage was approved in Iowa.

Contributing to this revolution was the increasing democratization of communications technology. In the sixties, for the first time, most students had a record player in their dorm rooms. By the end of the century, they had a cell phone stuck to their ear and access to all the information on the internet, including opportunities for dating, virtual sex, and making friends. These trends will transform person-to-person contact; the early rushes already suggest that the plethora of cell phones, text messages, and twitters may reduce the capacity for one-on-one contact and encourage persona-invention, the self once removed and therefore less examined.

Never has the gap between serious philosophy and popular culture been greater than it was in the late twentieth century. But one theorist during his evolution from Marxism through semioticism, has evolved some productive ways of viewing the great challenges forced on epistemology by the triumph of popular culture. Jean Baudrillard (b. 1929), in *Simulacra and Simulations* (1981), argued that late twentieth century culture has become a self-referential system of signs in which it is no longer possible to distinguish image from reality. Writing in *Philosophies of History: From Enlightenment to Postmodernity* (Oxford, Blackwell Publishers Ltd., 2000) Robert M Burns and Hugh Rayment-Pickard observe:

> It is this condition, which Baudrillard calls "hyperreality" that forms the basis for his thinking about the post-historical condition. Hyperreality comes about because of the development of modern technologies of communication. The modern pervasiveness of news, television, advertising, computers, video cameras has expanded and empowered the realm of images within our culture. Moreover we now depend upon these images for our individual, cultural and historical self-understanding. This dependence comes at the price of the disappearance of "real life" as it was once understood and the emergence of hyperreality: a simulation that substitutes for what we thought of as "reality." In this process, argues Baudrillard, we are transformed from being spectators of the media into being its products. We are "objects transposed to the other side of the screen, mediumatized" (Baudrillard, 1977, p.22). Although the world around looks and feels real enough to us, the appearance of the world has been conditioned for us in advance, and we have no access to this world apart from this conditioning (*Philosophies of History*, 2000).

There is no need to dismiss Baudrillard's insights because he feels compelled to use academically fashionable terms like "posthistorical" (history hasn't ended). The last statement, that we have no access to the world apart from this conditioning, is simply untrue; although venturing into nature by taking a hike in the Rockies or spending a week working on grandfather's ranch has become a somewhat concocted escape from hyperreality itself, it's still possible to live in the mountains, by a lake, or near the beach, cultivate a garden, and encounter nature every day. And while its true that analyzing a movie as a phenomenon is different from analyzing nature as a phenomenon, it's not that different from an ancient Greek pondering a statue by Phidias. We can most usefully interpret Baudrillard as commenting on the vast dominance of concocted aesthetic experience over encounters with "reality," by which he must mean unmediated nature.

Baudrillard is absolutely right to suggest that living primarily in a world of concocted images must be changing human perception and information gathering in important ways. We can turn to a historical example for some frame of reference to interpret what hyperreality's future impact may be on Western — and world — culture. Hyperreality has happened before, in the image-intense and information-saturated world of late Hellenism and the early Roman Empire. Its effect then, as we have suggested earlier in this essay, included the gradual infantilization of the whole population. We will see if our culture, facing the same challenges, can keep its balance between setting long-term goals and the immediate gratifications of electronic access.

Baudrillard, consciously or not, echoes an insight of Marshall McLuhan's here that provided the central thesis in *Understanding Media*:

> After three thousand years of specialist explosion and of increasing specialism and alienation in the technological extensions of our bodies, our world has been compressed by dramatic reversal. As electronically contracted, the globe is no more than a village. Electric speed in bringing all social and political functions together in a sudden implosion has heightened human awareness of responsibility to an intense degree.... This is the Age of Anxiety for the reason of the electric implosion that compels commitment and participation, quite regardless of any "point of view." The partial and specialized character of the viewpoint, however noble, will not serve at all in the electronic age (20).

Thus the bequest of the twentieth to the twenty first century: globalization with its inevitable cultural clashes, vast population growth, intellectual and spiritual despair, increasing prosperity though very unevenly distributed, the onslaught of a virtual community of computers, cell phones and their successors, the prospect of ecological meltdown, relative world peace, irony, camp, and hyperreality.

14. Conclusion

The twentieth century was simultaneously the most enlightened in history and capable of the most efficient evil. What light can the dialogue between Socrates and Jesus shed on this apparent contradiction? As a result of the last century, six billion people currently experience generally rising standards of living, increasing experience of self-government, and the anxiety of individual choice. At the same time, the explosion of population, industry, and technology has begun to wreak grave and irreversible damage on the biosphere. Are these recurring wounds — the cold and hot wars, the gulags, the concentration camps, the nuclear nightmares, the environmental destruction, the social and religious hatreds, the hyperreality — the necessary consequence of Apollonian progress in a Dionysiac world? Are they analogous to the cathartic release from selfhood of the Greek tragedies, or indeed the ancient Greek propensity for perpetual war? Did the alienation attendant upon individuation result inevitably in a longing to subsume personality into a mass led by a human God, if no other was available?

Traditional non-Western civilizations — Babylonia, Egypt, Persia, China, India, the Aztecs, the Incas — have generally managed evil by making power and belief a state monopoly, controlled by a god-king and administered by a mandarin class. Evil and death have been propitiated by literal sacrifice or the more sophisticated sacrifice of spiritual exercises. Such strategies have worked, often well, but at the cost of repressing individual initiative, free thought, and the participation of the governed in the governing.

How has Western Civilization defined and managed evil differently? Can we bridge the gap between Socrates' view that evil is ignorance and the Judeo-Christian position that evil is inherent in human nature? Part of the answer is that the vast majority of humanity isn't gifted with the intellect, education, or sheer time to be philosophers. Western history provides ample evidence that human beings can arrive at the highest reaches of moral wisdom by reason or by faith. It simultaneously demonstrates that seriously held convictions derived from reason or religion can lead to dreadful atrocities. Most of these, if not all, have been rooted in the noble conviction that humanity can be perfected, either here on earth (fascism, communism) or in a transfigured afterlife (most contemporary Western religions).

Perfecting humanity on earth — eliminating evil — has been a specialty of the West, as has the related option of separating Church and State. But the greatest Western philosophical or religious thinking has always been tempered by the awareness that, while a high standard of conduct is approachable, all human knowledge is partial. Evil may be error but it is also inevitable in any human being, who can possess at best provisional knowledge of ultimate truth. Western history has achieved what it has because Agape and Eros have fundamental disagreements. But people in grave doubt about the purpose of human life, forced to choose among belief-systems, and reaching desperately for something to have faith in, are the most likely to commit great evils in the name of an ideal, and this has always been a graver danger from the acolytes of Agape than the devotes of Eros. As Socrates said, Heavenly Eros first teaches us to know what we don't know. The flaw in this wisdom: most of humankind cannot persevere in a state of perpetual uncertainty, and reason cannot provide them certainty about the purpose of their lives.

Western history suggests that neither Eros nor Agape alone has provided a sustained meaning to human life in the aggregate. Eros can veer too easily towards hedonism and decadence and Agape too eagerly (because only Agape can be certain it's right) into bigotry and persecution. Are Eros and Agape, then, both carrots dangled in front of donkeys, games? If so, and if the success of a philosophy or theology is to be measured by its capacity to provide people — and cultures — a reason to live with pleasure and a sense of purpose — the answer is yes. Like Apollo and Dionysius, they must be yoked to generate meaning and ways to live. We can conclude, then, that the unique evils of Western civilization, whether they be religious persecutions, Robespierre's tyranny of Reason, or the totalitarian horrors of the twentieth century occur when either Eros or Agape tries to enforce a complete victory over the other.

The existence of evil poses the central challenge to any religion or philosophy because it is a metonymy for the larger question: how does life "mean"? Another way to put it: Why go on living if our portion consists largely in loss, betrayal, disillusion, decay, suffering, and death? Because they seem to be the only creatures that know they are going to die, humans demand meaning over and above mere being. Schopenhauer locates this impulse in "the blind will to live." The search for meaning is clearly inherent in human nature: Piaget chronicles many children between two and nine who spontaneously generate their own myths about birth, death, and the afterlife. Most human cultures have provided meaning by creating a collective mythology into which the child is integrated by rights of passage that transfer loves and fears to higher and socially crucial things: the community, the family, internalized values, life goals.

Unsurprisingly, reflecting on coming-of-age rites in *The Masks of God*, Campbell finds that the mythological rites of passage in primitive and archaic cultures have a much higher rate of success at generating meaning than those of advanced civilizations such as our own:

> It is possible that the failure of mythology and ritual to function effectively in our civilization may account for the high incidence among us of the malaise that has led to the characterization of our time as "The Age of Anxiety".... [W]hen an essentially cerebral emphasis preponderates in the schooling of the young, as it does in our highly literate society, an alarming instance of serious failure is to be expected in the difficult passage of the critical threshold from the system of sentiments proper to infancy to that of the responsibilities of the hour.... (92).

Of course a tribe possessing a unitary mythology has an easier job of converting a child into a socially useful adult than does a complex culture where many myths and philosophies compete. Commenting on the Neolithic triumph of agricultural over hunter-gatherer cultures from 6,000-3,000 BCE, Campbell continues:

> A world vision derived from the lesson of plants, representing the individual as a mere cell or moment in a larger process — that of the sib, the race, or, in larger terms, the species — so devaluates even the first sign of personal spontaneity that every impulse of self-discovery is purged away. "Truly, truly, I say to you, unless a grain of wheat falls into the earth and dies, it remains alone; but if it dies it bears much fruit." This noble maxim represents the binding sentiment of the holy society — that is to say, the church militant, suffering, and triumphant — of those who do not want to remain alone (240).

Agape, religious or political, governs the "holy society." However, the Erotic component in Western civilization, for better and worse, drives individuals to be more than a cell.

But the West's pursuit of the *principium individuationis* has its costs, as we have seen. Induction into tribal adulthood — or even into the mythology of a great static culture — can encourage social functioning while preserving many youthful and magical ways of thinking. A child's love will animate a doll, and ascribe higher thought to an animal, awareness to plants, or sensation to a stone. Such sentiments can provide a wonderful source of life-long spiritual sustenance if it leads the adult — through "intimations of immortality" — to conceive of the universe as a living thing. But it is not a substitute for the level of mature thinking or mythmaking that can produce a successful life in a complex community.

An Erotic civilization that encourages individual seeking and striving is far more likely to generate alienation than a community with a shared, revealed myth. Alienation spawns neurotics, adults who retain childlike thinking. Such people — and they constitute a large and growing proportion of our current "hyperreal" culture — believe what they read in the tabloids, consider sit com characters their friends, feel they deserve lives like stars in the movies, gorge at McDonalds, look to ersatz religions to relieve their frustrations, or have their relationships chronicled in country Western songs. So triumphs the infant who demands to be parented forever and resents the real world for withholding perpetual indulgence. Or another way to say this: hyperreality can provide enough synthetic substitutes for experience that an adult can easily avoid forging his maturity on the anvil of reality. We can hope that if clearly presented with this choice, enough individuals will choose the hard Socratic path of Heavenly Eros — "Know Thyself" — as in their self-interest and the interest of their civilization. Immediate gratification and mutual vilification between the proponents of Eros and Agape increasingly pervades American life and politics in an age where there are no noble causes, but the American social system has produced noble causes before.

All people are born needing an explanation, and Mircea Eliade (*Myth and Reality*, New York, Harper & Row, 1963) typically finds it in ritual return to the "dream" or "strong" times when the tribe or culture received its purpose and belief-system directly from the gods. *But the children of Socrates and Jesus also demand in addition a progressive narrative.* Both Heavenly Eros and orthodox Christianity portray our current life not as an end in itself, or a static reenactment of enduring myths, but as a way station on the road to a better place. This distinguishes the West from civilizations that portray the individual afterlife as dreary or non-existent: most primitive mythologies, pre-Socratic Greece, the main tradition of pre-Christian Judaism, Gnostic religions that describe an unending battle between Good and Evil, the ancestor-worship of Confucianism. Even the Buddhist escape from Maya involves erasing the ego rather than immortalizing it.

Functional societies must operate on the basis of accepted standards of behavior, and Socrates was surely right that in the post-Neolithic world, fulfilling lives can best be lived in well-governed states that operate on the basis of tolerance and reason. Jesus was right in his implied assertion that only awe for something incomprehensibly greater than ourselves can cause us to sacrifice short-term self-interest for the greater good of the whole — in other words, to grow up. Heavenly Eros validates at least a partial faith in the instinctive conviction we are born with that the sensual world is endowed with a beauty we can approach, incorporate, enjoy, or be motivated by, including sex. Agape, sterner and closer to the wisdom of Silenus, insists on a remote and arbitrary divine communion, but it still suggests this life is a route to somewhere.

However, it's worth noting that most of Western literature — always torn between Eros and Agape — ends up suggesting that the quest is more important than the goal. It's the adventure and the agony on the way to and from conquering Troy, Romeo and Juliet achieving rapture on the brink of death, Hamlet revenging his father, even waiting for Godot or the Trial that will finally produce justice in Kafka or on TV — that keeps us engaged, interacting with the sensory intimations of immortality. When we arrive at the end of the quest, the history of Western imagination suggests, Troy wasn't worth the effort, home is boring, the second coming is infinitely postponed, bliss is fleeting, revenge consumes everything in its path, neither Godot nor divine justice ever arrive in a human lifetime. But the stories, and the values great art embodies, whether in the *Iliad*, Plato, the *Bible*, or Shakespeare provide great exempla of right conduct, ways to construct meaning and purpose in life. Post-structuralist social critics, like the minor writers of the Roman Empire, may be right in their implicit agreement with the wisdom of Silenus, but they have yet to find a way to be useful outside of the academy.

Campbell offers another angle on this issue:

> Kant, in his *Prolegomena to Every Future System of Metaphysics*, states very carefully that all our thinking about final things can only be made by way of *analogy*. "The proper expression for our fallible mode of conception," he declares, "would be: that we imagine the world *as if* its being and inner character were derived from a supreme mind" [italics mine].

> Such a highly played game of "as if" frees our mind and spirit, on the one hand, from the presumption of theology, which pretends to know the laws of God, and, on the other, from the bondage of reason, whose laws do not apply beyond the bounds of human experience.

> I am willing to accept the word of Kant, as representing the view of a considerable metaphysician. And applying it to the range of festival games and attitudes just reviewed — from the mask to the consecrated host and temple image, transubstantiated worshiper and transubstantiated world — I can see, or believe I can see, that a principle of release operates throughout the series by way of the alchemy of an "as if"; and that, through this, the impact of all so-called reality upon the psyche is transubstantiated. The play state and the rapturous seizures sometimes deriving from it represent, therefore, a step rather toward than away from the ineluctable truth; and belief — acquiescence in a belief that is not quite belief — is a first step towards the deepened participation that the festival affords in that general will to life which, in its metaphysical aspect, is antecedent to, and the creator of, all life's laws (*The Masks of God*, 28–29).

Human culture then, as Huizinga observed, is serious play, play designed to ally with Good and ward off Evil. Insofar as they create a functional community, games are as true as useful can be. All great civilizations have their sacred games, but Western games, unlike repetitive ritual play, are quests into the future rather than the past; they have winners and losers, and the excitement derives from the fact that the result is not yet known.

   It would be only a small exaggeration to say that, over the last century, the dialectic between Socrates and Jesus has been globalized. Modern European and American systems of economics, politics, culture, philosophy, science, technology, and religion have been exported, transforming ancient and emerging nations and provoking both enormous imitation and reaction. As recently as the beginning of the previous century, there was no need for a global debate between Christianity and Islam, the world's two great militant faiths, because they encountered each other only casually and on the margins. Recently, global tensions have turned importantly on U. S. attempts to impose Socratic values — rational secular government and democracy — on an Arab Muslim culture so imbued with Agape that hundreds of its youth are happy to blow themselves up, believing they will enter directly into a voluptuous heaven. India, China, and what was once known as the Third World have spent the period since their achievement of independence debating the proper mix of capitalism and socialism, democracy and dictatorship, science and faith, all Western constructs.

   This international clash of Eros and Agape has coincided with a fundamental struggle about core values within the United States itself. Founded as a secular, tolerant nation, a child of Socrates and the Enlightenment, the U.S., for all its undercurrents of divine mission, has generally — sometimes in concert with Europe, often interrupted by realpolitic alliances of interest, and always with the prodding of its vigorous interest groups — expanded the national and international reach of secular government, religious freedom, human rights, science, and democracy. Recently, that has changed in ways that raise again the question of whether Heavenly Eros can provide sufficient spiritual sustenance to a mass national or global population. Crude as it is, the image of Blue and Red states crystalizes the ancient Western debate between Socrates and Jesus and that same struggle is being carried out in dizzyingly complex ways throughout the world.

   Temporarily the globe's only superpower, the United States has been thrust into the role of arbiter. Having intervened decisively in two world wars and outlasted Leninist and Maoist Communism (themselves transplanted European ideas), the U.S. has inherited world leadership for the moment. One might expect that its traditional values would be globally triumphant as well, and a case could be made for this view. For the first time in history, the majority of Earth's population is governed by what could at least loosely be called democracy. Even a modified totalitarian system such as China's (importantly modified, it must be said, by Confucianism) has succeeded in lifting hundreds of millions of people out of poverty in a generation, largely by means adopted from the West. American culture and its imitators reign from the movie industry of India to the phenomenal popularity of musical and other Western styles among young people worldwide. Now literate, much of the Earth's population has access to twenty-four-hour-a-day cable news and to all the information and misinformation on the Internet.

This triumph of the pagan Eye and its quarreling twins, Orphic music and Apollonian reason, is particularly ironic at a time when Agape is resurgent in the United States in the form of politicized fundamentalist Christianity that until recently exerted a decisive influence over a supposedly secular American administration. On the firm ground of Agape, many American Christians and the Papacy find themselves in agreement with much of Muslim teaching — on the same side of the Eros/Agape moral divide — while the U.S. is "at war" with militant Islam. Many more Americans currently believe in Jesus' Virgin Birth than in evolution or the demonstrable antiquity of the universe. From these statistics alone, we may conclude that even in the most sophisticated, well-informed, and well-wired civilization in the history of the globe, the staggering achievements of Erotic Reason may not be able to retain the allegiance of an increasingly infantalized mass population. The resurgence of Agape in the United States and the Muslim world is occurring not despite the achievements of Erotic reason and science, but because of them.

What are the future prospects for a global civilization drawn into the debate between Agape and Eros? We've already suggested that in a mass culture, a religion will always beat a philosophy, because a religion offers not only eventual release from the miseries of this world in a future paradise, but also a sense of community in the here and now. This is why a hundred people today could offer a plausible interpretation of Jesus' message for every one who could do the same for Socrates. As Barzun suggests: "[T]he question of whether any government can subsist without a common religion — by which I do not mean a common theology — remains an open one." (*Classic, Romantic, and Modern*, 34) While a philosophy may drive cultural development, the salvation — or consolation — it promises can be achieved only individually, temporarily, and as the product of a lifetime of effort.

Does philosophy, and its children reason, science, and ethics, provide hard truth while religion provides false hope, opium for the masses? Unless one is sure that a particular faith guarantees bliss in the afterlife the answer must be, partly, yes. Thinkers and artists who are part of that small percentage of the population initiated into the philosophy of Heavenly Eros generally make the cultural and intellectual advances; Pound called artists "the antennae of the race." These new ways of thinking — or coping with what is to come — invariably challenge the received assumptions of the majority of the population until they are incorporated into the culture or rejected.

Socratic Heavenly Eros has been the driving force behind Western civilization, but the truths provided by pure reason alone don't give us a reason to live,

as Socrates himself knew. So how can a mass, self-governing population generate meaning and reward the mature behavior necessary to sustain a progressive
civilization? Recently, Western cultural criticism has often suggested that nothing Means — not philosophy, not history, not religion, not art, not literature.
This acceptance of the wisdom of Silenus is wrong on its face because each of
these disciplines in all their forms Intend to Mean, and the disputes between
and among them provide us with strategies to endure what we must and enjoy
what we can. That reason cannot prove an absolute meaning for human existence
doesn't, at least according to Heavenly Eros, prevent us from discovering or creating meaningfulness where we can without resort to claims of revelation. But
it does appear that a majority of the population, whether in the Roman Empire
or in our own day, if forced to choose, will opt for a comforting mythology over
the facts. Results aren't in; perhaps we face a future in which religion matures
(as it has in the past) to the point where it concentrates on creating supportive
communities and ministering to needs in the larger society while tamping back
its insistence on controlling the personal moral behavior of the entire population.
Trends among even very religious young people seem to be pointing that way, at
least for the moment.

This essay has constantly circled around dualities: Socrates and Jesus, Reason and Faith, female and male, Eros and Agape, God and Man — and dualities
within dualities: Apollonian and Dionysiac, Classic and Romantic, Church and
State, Catholic and Protestant, Thesis and Antithesis, Eye and Ear, Shame and
Guilt (see Agape and Eros chart, pp. 69–70). Hegel may have defined the dialectic
in which a thesis generates an antithesis and they interact to produce a synthesis,
that becomes a new thesis, but he didn't invent it: Western thought had been
dualistic and progressive from its origins in both Hebrew faith and Greek reason
even before these two complex strands began to interact with and against each
other. We've already seen that both the Socratic and the Judeo–Christian traditions contain suggestions of a contest between humanity and the divine.

This ongoing clash of opposites accounts for Western Civilization's restless
inquisitiveness over the last 3,000 years, its impulse to build, discover, see, and
know things for a fact. It shares its religious dimension with other great civilizations such as China, India, and pre-Columbian America in the sense that communal faiths provide a sense of purpose and standards of conduct. But uniquely,
Christianity had to argue persistently with the Erotic philosophical tradition
personified by Socrates. We find the only convincing historical comparison in
the first Moslem millennium, and its glory days were permeated with a fusion of
the biblical tradition and Greek thought too.

History suggests that neither individuals nor civilizations can thrive without belief in some higher purpose than science can — or will ever be able to —

provide. The greatest scientists, including the brilliant atheists who rejected the idea that the world could have been produced by an omniscient, omnipotent and omni-benevolent Deity, still tend to reject the Silenic vision of an entirely blind, mechanistic, and materialist universe. In general, following Plato, they portray it as a conscious being, unified in ways that we have not fully grasped, struggling to become. From the other side, Christian theologians since the Roman Empire have accommodated facts, accepting a form of "as if" by interpreting the *Bible* as a series of metaphors and allegories propounding moral truths. Both reason and faith, in other words, can, and indeed must, provide visions of value that cannot be objectively proved.

The question for our age, typified by the worldwide rise of fundamentalism and the pseudo "debate" about Intelligent Design in the United States is: In this most globally Socratic of all periods in human history, can faiths survive and grow in open defiance of established facts? Does the need for certainty in the face of growing relativism positively favor religions that defy reality? Can we resist St. Bernard's injunction that it's "blameable to know" and still preserve "the blind will to live"? A rational view would argue that one can accept all the findings of science from Darwinism to an ancient, expanding universe and still legitimately speculate about — or believe in — a higher purpose to life than that offered by the wisdom of Silenus. Fundamentalists argue that only a literal reading of the Bible can generate elevated ethics, but this is demonstrably untrue. Time will tell if we are witnessing a collective "failure of nerve" in Western civilization's restless and productive quest to have a quest.

The genius of the systems of Socrates and Jesus is that both, in their antipodal ways, encompass vital elements of the other. Socratic reason was under girded from the start by a lively awareness of the Dionysian which is in the strictest sense Agape — being seized from without: the Orphic surrender to death and rebirth; speaking in tongues. Meanwhile, primitive Christianity acquired, from Augustine to Aquinas, a vast superstructure of Hellenistic reason. Their struggles create the framework for discussing what meaning and standards for right conduct we can find. The interacting dualities within each and between them are the moving parts of Western Civilization and explain its uniquely propulsive character.

The two-thousand-year dialogue between Socrates and Jesus has given the Western world its moral compass. Although they approached them by very different methods, Socrates and Jesus agree on many attributes of the ethical life: respect all human beings as equals in the eye of the Divine, love thy neighbor, help those in need, don't confuse wealth, social distinction, or ethnicity with personal value, subordinate selfish interests to the good of the larger community, always try to tell the truth if it can be determined and heard, and teach the paths to self-awareness. It is this coincidence of Socrates' and Jesus' values that, throughout the debate about whether to get there through Agape or Eros, has created the fixed star of Western philosophy, religion, and the cultures they have generated or influenced.

Afterword

Much of this book has focused on epistemology, that is, how individuals perceive the sensible world. It has also stressed how much of the Western struggle for meaning has been pursued through literature, that is, style. This Afterword explores the challenges of writing poetry in the twentieth century by examining the work of four key American poets: Ezra Pound, William Carlos Williams, Wallace Stevens, and especially John Ashbery, who is all foreground in the Homeric tradition. It suggests the difficulty of a positive erotic epistemology in an ironic age. It may also suggest why modern poetry has ceased to be a part of the mainstream discourse about how life means, a fairly recent development.

The task of creating a popular "language to think in" about contemporary civilization has passed to singer–songwriters and more than anyone else, to our greatest living American artist, Bob Dylan. In his work, in contrast to Ashbery, who demonstrates Eros *in extremis*, he demonstrates Agape *in extremis*, a background ever pressing in on us, but uninterpretable, perhaps empty:

All Along the Watchtower

"There must be some way out of here," said the joker to the thief
"There's too much confusion, I can't get no relief
Businessmen they drink my wine, ploughmen dig my earth
None of them along the line know what any of it is worth."

"No reason to get excited," the thief he kindly spoke,
"There are many here among us who feel that life is but a joke

But you and I have been through that, and this is not our fate
So let us not talk falsely now, the hour is getting late."

All along the watchtower, princes kept the view
While all the women came and went, barefoot servants too
Outside in the cold distance, a wild cat did growl,
Two riders were approaching, the wind began to howl.

Dylan has to be not read but listened to, very carefully.

JOHN ASHBERY'S LAST STAND FOR EROTIC EPISTEMOLOGY

In the opening lines of *Houseboat Days* (New York, Penguin Books, 1977), John Ashbery offers this wry assessment of his relation to his contemporaries:

So I cradle this average violin that knows
Only forgotten showtunes, but argues
The possibility of free declamation anchored
To a dull refrain ... ("Street Musicians")

Usually, the more extreme Ashbery's irony, the more radical the claim for his art. The "aw shucks" pose pivots into "the possibility of free declamation." This self-deprecating stance has been a conventional piety for American poets at least since William Carlos Williams compared himself to a lame dog in the "Preface" to *Paterson*. In Ashbery, it protects and validates an inheritance from America's master of high rhetoric, Wallace Stevens. The obscure but human family in "Street Musicians" being evicted into "the way it was, and is" has left behind the vanishing home in Stevens' "The Auroras of Autumn." Ashbery's work, especially in the 1970s, revises the actions of Stevens' meditations, achieving an advance in twentieth-century poetics. Ashbery weds Stevens' self-revising rhetoric to Williams' rejection of transcendence and linear action. The result is a poetry that can acknowledge the relative or conditional status of the poet himself without lapsing into solipsism or appealing to transcendence. Ashbery is attempting to save the beautiful ruins of Eros, its pretty pieces, by regarding them with a strictly Apollonian eye that admits of no transcendence.

The relative form dominated major American poetry in the last century. Its characteristic action is the inventive mind's possession of a relative world. Pound insisted, "Relations are more important than the things which they relate" (Ernest Fenollosa, *The Chinese Written Character as a Medium for Poetry*, Ed. and Trans. Ezra Pound, New York, Arrow Editions, 1936, 26–7). Pound and Williams created a juxtapositional, non-linear structure that emphasized the relation of each element in the poem to every other. In both poets, however, one absolute remained unquestioned: the selecting, sovereign status of the poet himself. The danger of such an approach, as Williams was more aware than Pound, is solipsism.

After early experiments with similar imagist strategies, Stevens developed a rhetoric that acknowledges the dynamic quality of the poet's imagination. Williams asserted, "coining similes is a pastime of very low order ... Much more keen is the power which discovers in things those inimitable particles of dissimilarity to all other things which are the particular perfection of the thing in question" (William Carlos Williams, *Imaginations*, New York, New Directions, 1970, 18). Williams was concerned to preserve the integrity of "the thing itself"; this explains his juxtapositional structure that places things in relation in order to throw them into relief. Stevens' concern, by contrast, was the version of the thing. For Stevens, the making and unmaking of metaphors provided the intrinsic principle of the imagination's operation. The poem is not a sequence of juxtaposed images or, as Pound called them, "luminous details," but a record of the mind's approach to and retreat from such apprehensions. Stevens' later poems develop a form based on positing, then deconstructing, successive absolutes or fixed points of reference.

In "The Auroras of Autumn," for example, Stevens recapitulates Western man's successive figurations of divinity: the Babylonian world-serpent, the archaic Great Mother, the Judeo–Christian Father, and the Romantic "grim and benevolent imagination." In each case the absolute that guarantees an ordered world is first posited, then dismissed by a shift in perspective. Any absolute must necessarily remain fictive or at best indicative in a relative world. As it approaches identification with each divine sponsor in "The Auroras of Autumn," the imagination discovers an evasive strategy to preserve its autonomy and the variety of the world upon which its authority is based. The eternal and omnipresent cosmological serpent of Canto I is reduced to the mortal, and therefore accessible, garden snake. The action of the poem proceeds through a series of such falls, metaphor collapsing into simile, reducing each absolute to its source or analogue in ordinary human experience. This in turn clears the ground for a *new* "idea of order."

John Ashbery adopts Stevens' approach but makes a significant revision of his own. In Stevens' later poems, successively dismissed fictions of absolute perspective culminate in a moment of apocalyptic insight: the "innocence of earth" in "The Auroras of Autumn," or the assertion "as I am, I am" of "Notes Towards a Supreme Fiction." These poems, like "Sunday Morning," preserve the linear action of a Keats ode: successive failed approaches to value culminate in a moment of triumphant vision that is then questioned or qualified. Where Stevens employs the relative form to rescue, by ultimate qualification, the Romantic lyric approach to value, Ashbery poems take the absence of any absolute as their point of departure.

Ashbery thereby achieves a pure poetry of the foreground heralded by Stevens. Bloom has observed that Ashbery rejects "the privileged moment of vision" (Robert B. Shaw, Ed., *American Poetry Since 1960*, Chatham, England, W. J. MacKay Ltd, 1974, 97), as Stevens does not. Here, Ashbery remains faithful to Williams' despair of transcendence "which made everything a unit and therefore part of myself" (William Carlos Williams, *Letters of William Carlos Williams*, New York, McDowell, Obolensky, 1957, 147). The observation emphasizes equally Williams' rejection of any absolute, transcendent realm, and the solipsism his solution invites. For Williams and Ashbery, all elements of the poem exist on the same level of reality, including the imagination of the poet himself. The opportunity for valid vision is distributed equally over the whole surface of the poem, unlike Eliot with his anti-romantic romances or Pound, frozen in his battle to stuff fragments of culture into a jar, make them cohere, or relate them by embalming them. We can see here the democratic illumination of Homer, sacrificing suspense to consider each event or object in the immediate present. This is pagan and Socratic but with the strictest Apollonian limitations; no moment of Orphic insight can intrude, or at least be taken seriously.

Ashbery's *Houseboat Days* catalogues his revision of the typical Stevensian action, and his acceptance of Williams' unitary world. In "The Auroras of Autumn" the theater, festival home — metaphors for a divinely sponsored world — erode and collapse as successive absolute perspectives are dismissed. In Ashbery these shelters of the mind persist only as random wreckage. The restoration of the cancelled gala in "The Explanation" (*Houseboat Days*, 14) proves to be an "unsuccessful stage adaption." In *Three Poems* Ashbery writes: "... in place of the panorama that used to be our customary setting, and which we never made much use of, a limited but infinitely free space has established itself" (John Ashbery, *Three Poems*, New York, Penguin Books, 1972, 3). In "On the Towpath" (HD, 22) a "barrier of fact" shields the sky from the earth. The gods are no longer capable of even the evaporating gesture of Stevens' "The Comedian as the letter "C"" although they persist in "Business Personals" (HD, 20) as "pink and blue handkerchiefs." The disintegrating absolutes have been replaced by the at least apparently random shuttlings of reality. Frequently, as in "Unctuous Platitudes" (HD, 12) "out of nothing/something will come." Just as often each particular "Goes over Niagara Falls in a beer barrel" (HD, 51).

Stevens' poems assert by their action that the randomness of reality must be countered by the intrinsic ordering impulse of the human imagination. This strategy commits Stevens to a linear poetic action in which order masters randomness, at least for an instant, approaching a "victory," however qualified, for the imagination. But in *Houseboat Days*, Ashbery asserts that meaningfulness depends on randomness. "Syringa" (HD, 69-71) meditates on the stance of Emerson's Orphic

American poet and his avatar, Stevens' "major man" in a relative, unitary world. It acknowledges Ashbery's reliance on Stevens' method and documents his revision of Stevens' linear, apocalyptic action. "Syringa" reflects on the implications of Stevens' "It Must Change" for poet, world, and poem. The opening lines record an immediate fall from an absolute sponsored world — "everything changed" — and assert: "The seasons are no longer what they once were, /But it is in the nature of things to be seen only once." "Syringa" evokes with appropriate whimsy figures such as General du Puy and other monoliths in Stevens' poetry who refuse to acknowledge the perpetual transience of reality:

> No use standing there like a gray stone toga
> > As the whole wheel
> Of recorded history flashes past, struck dumb,
> > Unable to utter an intelligent
> Comment on the most thought provoking element
> > In its train.

Comment such as the poem "encapsulizes" — packages and fixes — "the different weights of the things." But scarcely can Ashbery deliver such a formulation before he must let it be rejected by events: "one cannot guard, treasure/That stalled moment." The "stalled moment" is the moment of transcendent vision that is the pivot of every great lyric from Wordsworth to Stevens. In a random world, each moment is at least potentially of equal weight.

This implies a poem whose subject or goal must self-destruct, leaving the trace of the poem's content, relations, action, as "Syringa" confirms:

> And no matter how all this disappeared
> Or got where it was going, it is no longer
> > Material for a poem. Its subject
> Matters too much, and not enough, standing there helpless
> While the poem streaked by, its tail afire, a bad
> Comet screaming hate and disaster, but so turned inward
> That the meaning, good or other, can never
> Become known.

In a world where all things have been revealed as symptoms of transient processes, the streaking evidence flourishes itself but leads nowhere. At the point in the poem where Stevens would approach an absolute, an idea of order that could provide temporary shelter for the imagination, Ashbery turns away:

> The singer thinks
> Constructively, builds up his chant in progressive stages
> Like a skyscraper, but at the last minute turns away....

Such constant deconstructions of particular poetic strategies allow for fresh combinations and renewed sight "like the clear dark blue/Eyes of Harold in Italy, beyond amazement, astonished/Apparently not tampered with" (HD, 40). In "Credences of Summer," Stevens wrote "The singers had to avert themselves/Or else avert the object"; Ashbery injects this tangential relation between poet and poem. A given system can produce only permutations of the original set. The newly seen emerges from a rhetorical strategy that makes random combinations possible. Most often what surprises us in such cases is the familiar in a new aspect.

Ashbery insists on the provisional nature of objects and experiences by rhetorical devices that include tentative or negative analogies, conditional constructions, and hypothetical propositions. This is part of the explanation for his famously wandering pronouns; the other is his approach to a public voice. The content of these poems subsists in autobiographical fragments, but the second and third person pronouns claim a more general validity for the patterns of awareness enacted. "We are all," Ashbery says, "aspects of a consciousness giving rise to the poem" (William Packard, *The Craft of Poetry*, New York, Penguin Books, 1974, 172). Such evasive strategies allow Ashbery to avoid the radical distrust of words common in so many of his contemporaries and reflected in his own earlier work on the grounds that every word is provisional, revised by the poem's action. Harold Bloom writes: "Use the rotted names, Ashbery urges, but cleanse them by seeing you can't be apart from them, and are partially redeemed by consciously suffering with them" (*American Poetry Since 1960*, 97). Ashbery matches Stevens' mocking lists of Romantic paraphernalia with his own more affectionate catalogues of words and phrases abused by a commercial culture. What is so often described as Stevens' "gaudiness" is transformed by Ashbery into a camp humor and romance of the trivial.

Ashbery's *Self Portrait in a Convex Mirror* (New York, Penguin Books, 1975) represents his most successful exploration of the poet's stance in a relative world. We are now in a post-Stevensian landscape where the proscenium has collapsed and "the event arrives/flush with its edges" (SP, 79); "long ago the evidence meant something" when, in Emerson's terms, words were signs of natural facts and natural facts were signs of spiritual facts. Unsponsored by any absolute order, however, the most obvious aspect of things is their transience: "the sands are hissing/As they approach the beginning of the big slide/Into what happened" (SP, 81). In such a world, the poet must find some strategy other than elegy, that is, perpetual mourning.

"Self Portrait in a Convex Mirror" opens with the suggestion, couched in evasive analogical phrases, that the poem, like Parmagianino's painting seeks "to protect what it advertises." The painting advertises the painter's triumph over time. Far from being caught up in the big slide into what happened, Parmagianino's image is "Living and intact in a recurring wave/Of arrival" (SP, 69). A work of art holds this power over us because all other aspects of experience can express their being only in the process of self-annihilation, "Like a wave breaking on a rock, giving up/Its shape in a gesture that expresses that shape" (SP, 72). The portrait achieves its exclusive order by subordinating all other elements to the central self. It invites the poet to take refuge in the final fictive absolute: the art object. This is the Stevensian temptation to inhabit the "supreme fiction" in which the order of the mind becomes the order of the world. Ashbery refuses this relief: the Dionysiac urge to *be* a work of art.

The danger of this strategy represents the poem's, and the self's, central problem:

> The soul establishes itself
> But how far can it swim out through its eyes
> And still return safely to its nest? ...
> The soul has to stay where it is...
> This is what the portrait says (SP, 69).

Parmagianino's protective portrait brilliantly anticipates the threat to twentieth century self and poet in a relative world:

> One would like to stick one's hand
> Out of the globe, but its dimension,
> What carries it, will not allow it (SP, 69).

The poet has slipped within the mirror as Parmigianino has sealed himself within the protecting globe of the self.

Like the divine figurations in "The Auroras of Autumn," the portrait "organizes everything" (SP, 71) at the cost of solipsism. Accepting the order of the work of art appeals very strongly to the poet, for "Today is uncharted, /Desolate, reluctant as any landscape/To yield what are the laws of perspective" (SP, 72). The very self-sufficiency of the portrait provides an antidote in its "strict otherness" (SP, 74) to the solipsism threatening the poet. Moreover, it achieves its ideal order without appealing to any dream of transcendence, proclaiming, "Everything is surface." (SP, 70). But accepting the portrait's "ideal beauty" leaves us "To awake and begin living in what/Has now become a slum" (SP, 73). The problem with the portrait is the problem with any "stalled moment': by comparison it devalues our daily experience.

"Our landscape is alive with filiations, shuttlings" (SP, 75), but Parmagianino's strategy cannot confront the metamorphic variety of "today':

> ... something new is on the way, a new preciosity
> In the wind. Can you stand it,
> Francesco? Are you strong enough for it?
> The wind brings what it knows not, is
> Self-propelled, blind, has no notions
> Of itself. It is inertia that once
> Acknowledged saps all activity, secret or public ...
> This is the negative side. Its positive side
> Making you notice life and the stresses
> That only seemed to go away ... (SP, 75)

"Today" is a voracious subject, threatening "to siphon off the life of the studio, deflate/Its mapped space to enactments, island it" (SP, 75). But only if the poem refuses the painting's "ideal order" can it prevent the "locking into place" (SP, 76) of the literal, the uninterpreted contemporary experience that encroaches on the studio, the painter's and the poet's.

"Our time gets to be veiled, compromised/By the portrait's will to endure" (SP, 78) and this provokes a distancing of the Master:

> Your argument, Francesco
> Has begun to grow stale as no answer
> Or answers were forthcoming (SP, 76).

"You can't live there" (SP, 79) in Parmagianino's solipsistic order. Ashbery has transposed Stevens' strategy of approaching, then deconstructing absolutes onto a work of art. The falling away characteristic of Ashbery's poetry is a fall into metalepsis, the revision of previous tropes, that is the basis of Western figura-tive — that is, poetic — discourse. Only this refusal of solipsistic stasis, and the concurrent figurative revision, permits the poem to examine and deconstruct the grounds of its own rightness. Paul DeMan comments, "the imagination takes its flight only after the void, the inauthenticity of the existential project has been revealed" (*Blindness and Insight*, New York, Oxford University Press, 1971).

The rejection of Parmigianino permits the contemporary cityscape to emerge into the poem, which the poet's imagination had projected to be a "slum':

> The city falling with its beautiful suburbs
> Into space always less clear, less defined
> Should read as the support of [light's] progress

The easel upon which the drama unfolded...
Today has that special, lapidary
Todayness that the sunlight reproduces
Faithfully in casting twig-shadows on blithe
Sidewalks. No previous day would have been like this (SP, 78).

The poet has achieved a "cresting into one's present" analogous to Parmagianino's "recurring wave of arrival." "This nondescript, never-to-be-defined daytime is/The secret of where love takes place" (SP, 78). We can neither adopt nor reject completely the "waking dreams" of our past, such as the portrait or a Keats Ode, where aspects of ourselves confront us as a new experience. But the poet can transform the portrait's self-protectiveness:

Therefore I beseech you, withdraw that hand,
Offer it no longer as shield or greeting
The shield of a greeting, Francesco (SP, 82).

Even in the last lines of the poem, the discontinuity that permits the new to emerge asserts itself through a change in perspective. We watch Parmigianino shrink back in time as through the wrong end of a telescope. Francesco's retreat signifies that Ashbery has abandoned the solipsistic creation of his own self-portrait to mirror "the present we are always escaping from" (SP, 78). What is reflected, however, has not been tamed, and still preserves its potential wildness:

We have seen the city: it is the gibbous
Mirrored eye of an insect. All things happen
On its balcony and are resumed within ... (SP, 81–82)

The city of God has become the city of man. It is a landscape without transcendence in which surface "is not/Superficial but a visible core" (SP, 70).

In Ashbery's mature poetry, Stevens' relative rhetoric is placed in service of Williams' anti-Romanticism. In this last vestige of what could still be called romantic poetry, Ashbery preserves his connection to Eros only by the most stringent enforcement of the rational Apollonian Eye. He adopts Williams' unitary world without courting the solipsism of *Paterson*'s King-self. He adopts Stevens' form while refusing his ultimate endorsement of the apocalyptic imagination. Ashbery has transformed Stevens' Blue Guitar into an "average violin" on which he can play the constant dialectic of past and present, literal and interpreted, natural and made that salvages a stark Apollonian epistemology or at least the fugitive pieces of it flashing by.

BIBLIOGRAPHY

This book has benefited from the wisdom of innumerable writers who are not directly cited in the text; I thank them all. I would especially like to express my gratitude to authors who are cited frequently and helped shape the book: Plato, the writers of the *Old* and *New Testaments*, Erich Auerbach, Camille Paglia, Peter Gay, Andres Nygren, Friedrich Nietzsche, G. F. W. Hegel, Norman Cantor, and W. W. Tarn.

Abelard, Peter, *The Confessions, Sic et Non*

Aristophanes, *The Clouds*

Aristotle, Collected Works

Arnold, Matthew, Culture and Anarchy, Chapter IV, 1868

Ashbery, John, *Houseboat Days*, New York, Penguin Books, 1977

Ashbery, John, *Self Portrait in a Convex Mirror*, New York, Penguin Books, 1975

Ashbery, John *Three Poems*, New York, Penguin Books, 1972

Auerbach, Erich, *Mimesis: The Presentation of Reality in Western Literature*, Princeton, New Jersey, Princeton

University Press, 1976

Augustine, *The Confessions, The City of God*

Aurelius, Marcus, *The Meditations*

Barzun, Jacques, *Classic, Romantic, and Modern*, Chicago, University of Chicago Press, 1961

Berlin, Isaiah, *Karl Marx*, New York, Oxford University Press, 1963

Bloom, Harold, *Visionary Company*, New York, Cornell University Press, 1971

Brown, Norman O., *Life Against Death*, Middletown Connecticut, Wesleyan University Press

Burns, Robert M. and Hugh Rayment-Pickard, *Philosophies of History*, Oxford, Blackwell Publishers Ltd., 2000

Bury, J. B., *A History of Greece*, New York, Modern Library

Campbell, Joseph, *The Masks of God*, New York, Viking Press, 1970

Cantor, Norman, *Medieval History*, New York, the Macmillan Company, 1963

Cleugh, James, *The Medicis*, New York, Dorset Press, 1975

Cohn, Haim, *The Trial and Death of Jesus*, New York, Harper and Row, 1959

DeMan, Paul, *Blindness and Insight*, New York, Oxford University Press, 1971

Dante, *The Divine Comedy, On Monarchy*

Darwin, Charles, *The Origin of the Species*

Davies, J. D., *The Early Christian Church*, Garden City, New York, Anchor Books 1967

Descartes, Rene, *Collected Works*

Diamond, Jared, *Guns, Germs and Steel*, New York, Vintage Press, 2005

Dimont, Max, *Appointment in Jerusalem*, New York, St. Martin's Press, 1991

Eliade, Mircea, *Myth and Reality*, New York, Harper and Row, 1963

Eliot, T. S., *Collected Works*

Fenollosa, Ernest, *The Chinese Written Character as a Medium for Poetry*, Ed. And Trans. Ezra Pound, New York,

Arrow Editions, 1936

Freud, Sigmund, *Civilization and its Discontents*

Frost, Frank J., Lexington, Massachusetts, D. C. Heath and Company, 1992

Frye, Northrup, *The Anatomy of Criticism*, Princeton, New Jersey, Princeton University Press, 2000

Garraty, John A. and Peter Gay, *The Columbia History of the World*, New York, Harper and Rowe, 1972

Gay, Peter, *Freud*, New York, Doubleday, 1988

Gay, Peter, *The Enlightenment*, New York, Knopf, 1966

Gibbon, Edward, *The Decline and Fall of the Roman Empire*

Herodotus, *The Histories*

Hesiod, *Works and Days*

Hibbert, Christopher, *The House of Medici*, New York, William Morrow and Company, 1975

Hobbes, Thomas, *The Leviathan*

Homer, *The Iliad, The Oddysey*

Hume, David, An Inquiry Concerning Human Understanding

Grimm, Howard, *The Reformation Era*, New York, the MacMillan Company, 1967

Isaacson, Walter, *Einstein: His Life and Universe*, New York, Simon and Schuster, 2007

Kant, Immanuel, *Critique of Pure Reason*

Locke, John, *An Essay Concerning Human Understanding*

Lucretius, *On the Nature of Things*

Machiavelli, Nicolo, *The Prince*

Marx, Karl, *The Communist Manifesto, Das Kapital*

McLuhan, Marshall, *Understanding Media*, New York, McGraw-Hill, 1964

Newton, Isaac, *Principia Mathematica*

Nietzsche, Friedrich, *The Birth of Tragedy from the Spirit of Music*

Nygren, Andres, *Agape and Eros*, New York, Harper and Row, 1969

Packard, William, *the Craft of Poetry*, New York, Penguin Books, 1974

Paglia, Camille, *Sexual Personae*, New York, Random House, 1991

Plato, *The Republic, The Symposium, The Phaedrus, The Apology*

Roberts, J. M., *Twentieth Century*, New York, Penguin Books, 2000

Rousseau, Jean-Jacques, *The Confessions, The Social Contract, Nouvelle Heloise, Emile*

Schopenhauer, Arthur, *The World as Will and the Idea*

Shakespeare, William, *The Tempest*

Shaw, Robert B., Ed., *American Poetry since 1960*, Chatham, England, W. J. McKay Ltd., 1974

Smith, Adam, *The Wealth of Nations*

Sontag, Susan, *Against Interpretation*, New York, Farrar, Strauss and Giroux, 1966

Tacitus, *The Histories*

Tarn, W. W., *Hellenistic Civilization*, Cleveland and New York, Meridian Books, 1968

Taylor, C. C. W., *Socrates*, Oxford, Oxford University Press, 1998

Thucydides, *The Peloponnesian Wars*, New York, Modern Library, 1951

Tillich, Paul, *The Courage to Be*, New Haven, Yale University Press

Voltaire, *Collected Works*

Williams, William Carlos, *Imaginations*, New York, New Directions, 1970

Williams, William Carlos, *The Letters of William Carlos Williams*, New York, McDowell, Oblonsky, 1957

INDEX